CON MAN

CON MAN

THE MAKING OF A MONSTER

A NOVEL

J. W. BENNETT

Printed in the United States of America

ISBN Paperback: 978-0-9861879-0-2
ISBN eBook: 978-0-9861879-1-9

Interior and Cover Design: www.creativepublishingdesign.com

ACKNOWLEDGEMENTS

This book has been such a journey. I wrote the entire book long hand, one copy, no back up. Once written, there were still the jobs of developing a website, finding the right places to advertise and the right consultants and designers. This project has cost lots of money and time. I owe a huge hug and thank you to you, Steve. For years, you have not only believed in me, but, more importantly, you haven't run from all the crazy stuff that prison has thrown in our path. You're the most patient, kindest and caring person. You have been my rock, without you I wouldn't have been able to realize this dream. Your faith in me is a true miracle, one I probably don't deserve. Nonetheless, thank you for your suggestions and editing, all done while you work 12-hour days. This is such a gift you have given me Steve, your loyalty amazes me.

And a very loud thank you to Ashley. Ashley somehow deciphers all my hand written notes and does all the typing. I know my handwriting isn't the easiest to read. Ashley you are one of the strongest women I've ever met. You allow nothing to stop you and you go your own way in life. I know they made the saying *let me hear you roar* all because of women like you. Keep your chin up, if everybody saw life the way you do, then the world would be a better place.

INTRODUCTION

My name is Rick Smith. I am your average white man who grew up white trash and out of control. I've lived in the gutters my whole life. I can remember all the way back to 5 years old, and even then life was a struggle. Food was little and far between, clothes and shoes' cost money we didn't have, so we did what we could to get by. I learned real quick how to survive; I learned how to steal and how to bat my eyes the right way to the church people—they gave the best free food ever.

My mother's name is Amy. I don't have a clue where she was born, but she gave birth to me in Lexington, Kentucky. My dad's name is Bruce. He was a guy who could work all day. He would work hard as hell, but he loved his beer. He would spend almost all his check on getting drunk every night. Outside of work and beer, my dad's other love was beating my mom every day. I used to think back then she didn't deserve it. Nowadays, my mother is a piece of shit. However, I'm getting a little ahead of myself.

My mother only had me as her child. When she got tired of getting beat up, she just up and left dad. Mom took me to Akron, Ohio where she found this woman's shelter. I watched her play her cards so well, that she was the abused-mom-on-her-own. Even at five, I had to admire the con in my mother. She would bilk people for anything she could get by playing the victim. It seemed that things were starting to look up. Even so, it didn't take long for mom to jump into smoking crack. It was even harder to watch her bring in 20 different men a day than it had been to watch her get beat.

At my age, I was smart, plus my mom didn't feel the need to lie to me. By seven, I knew that life's a bitch, and it's all about getting money. I felt like I had life figured out, but that didn't last long before my world crashed in on me then everything changed. The Children's Service Board stepped in to take me away. I hadn't seen dad since we left Kentucky but the way I got it, he was a drunk and mom was a crack head, so I couldn't go to either one. It was a hard thing for a seven-year-old to hear, that I would have to go to a new family. They tell me I can't see my own anymore. But I was not the normal seven-year-old, so I learned from this too.

Life already reared its ugly head. It made me tough to the core. I was also obsessed with making money. Day one, I already knew these idiots in the Children Service Board didn't have a clue about kids like me. After all, I learned from my mom two years ago how to work the system. It was 1988 when they took me. They looked at me as a cute, seven-year-old victim of his parents. I looked at them and thought "suckers." All through the 1990's they sent me to dozens of children's homes, group homes, and detention centers all throughout Ohio. I didn't care plus I didn't make any friends my heart didn't love anymore. I never saw my mother again or my dad. I didn't care because in my mind, they taught me what I needed to know; or at least all they could teach me.

At eighteen years old, the Children's Service Board threw me out. I got on a bus then headed back to Kentucky. I was broke, hungry and homeless. I needed to get my feet into a hustle. I needed money, and fast, but I hadn't yet learned how to be a con. I was hoping to find Dad, but that was a lost cause. So I did what any honest, poor white trash does; I started kicking in doors mainly taking food, money or whatever seemed valuable. Now don't get me wrong here, I'm a small guy—140 pounds of wiry muscle packed into a 5' 8" frame with green eyes and black hair (and not bad looking). But I've been short for all my life, and it gave me a small man complex. Kicking in doors made me feel like a grown man.

Five months into eighteen years old, I kicked down a door, and I'll be damned if there wasn't a big black guy standing there in the living room looking at me like, "I know you just didn't kick that door in you little shit." Fortunately, I carry a metal bat with me because, I guess the look he gave me sent my little man complex into a rage. I ended up beating that black guy with a bat for so long that I didn't even realize the noise around me when people came out from other houses, then called the cops.

It turned out that the black guy was robbing the place also. He came through a window in the back, where's the luck in that? He survived, he just spent a long time in the hospital. Mainly he had to get a lot of staples in his head. I was charged with assault with a deadly weapon along with breaking and entering. It worked in my favor that I was young, plus the black guy didn't live there either, so the judge gave me 10 years in prison.

While waiting on the bus to take me to prison I lay in that dirty, cold jail cell and thought to myself "this is my life now." I am going to tell you my journey of prison, then the other things that turned me into the con man, a great lover and how a piece of white trash finally made a comeback.

Chapter 1

THE BIG GREY GOOSE

All that is necessary for evil to triumph is for good men to do nothing. —Edmund Burke 1729-1797

On May 13, 1999, I turned 18 years old. I was born on Mother's Day. A fine mother's day present I am sure, but she is and was a worthless mother also—so I guess we're even. On October 16 of 1999, I am arrested on felony charges. I go to court for five months. Then on the 20th of March 2000, I plead out to a 10-year sentence. I have next to no education, didn't know shit about the law plus, they know I was broke. The whole system has a plan for all of us broke motherfuckers.

It didn't matter any ways because I had too much hate. I cannot seem to even see the world or nothing in it as it is. All I can see, or feel, is my anger. The judge said 10 years then asked did I have any comments after he went through his spiel about did I fully understand everything that he said. I tell the judge, "Yeah I got something to say, you can suck my white honky dick!"—You should have seen the look on his face. They pushed me out of that courtroom fast. The rats (guards you'd call them) like to man-handle you when they get mad. They roughed me up pretty well, really not much I could do about it being in shackles and handcuffs, but it was worth it just to see that old judge's face. Plus, all the rats did was drag me at a speed I can't walk cause the shackles. That makes the shackles peel my skin.

They push me back to a room the size of a bathroom. It is packed with 30 other people in it going to court. They've got us boxed in so tight I can't smell nothing but piss and bad breath. My dude, Eric Jacobs, sees me and nods. He's all the way in the back of this packed little room. I push my way back to him, there is no being polite in jail or prison. People prey on weakness. Only the strong survive in this world so you don't say *sorry*, or for sure, you don't say *excuse me*. I just mow my way to the back. Being polite or kind is a weakness that will get you raped or badly prayed on in here.

On the way, some dude calls me a bitch or something because I bumped into him too hard. You get tested like this a lot, words like "bitch" and "rat," you can't let any of it go at all. You learn that very fast. So I turn around to look for this guy who just called me a bitch, and since I can't punch him (being in handcuffs) I spit in his face. That's not the thing to do either, because he spits back on me this really nasty stuff, I can't even get off. It's stuck now on my face until I get back to the jail. I never even would see that guy again. I try to rub it off a little by rubbing my shoulder on my face; it helped some.

Eric is a big country boy. He has got to be 240 pounds, mostly muscle. He gets a lot of respect just because of his size. Well that and his bald head, then on top of it all he's got a broken nose which makes him look pretty disturbed. It always pisses me off a little how big guys just get respect on account of their size. Then you got us small guys who have to always show out on a motherfucker. Eric is in for robbery in the 1ˢᵗ degree; he got drunk and tried to rob a bank. Which holds 10-20 years in prison.

I made it to Eric and said, "What's up honky?!"

Eric looks mad and tells me "Nothin's up."

I try from a different angle, "They gave me 10 years today honky. Now I guess I'm gonna see what prison is all about. Hey man, are you listening to me?"

Eric just gives me a faraway look and says, "Yeah I hear you. They sentenced me today too. They gave me 20 years. My mom is going to probably disown my stupid ass. First time I ever caught a felon then not only do they give me the max time; they also refuse probation.

I don't know what to say to that because I don't have a family. So I just say, "Hey honky, this is our life now, you got to let that shit go. Plus you know if you had a simple $2,000 lawyer you wouldn't have got that."

"Yeah that's easy for you to say Crazy, 'cause you got nobody in here or out there. I still love my mama." They nicknamed me Crazy at the county jail. The other inmates always thought I was up to no good, or crazy shit, so the nickname Crazy stuck with me. I say, "Either way, we're headed back to the jail then soon we'll be headed to the big house. So whatever is going to happen will happen, no way we can stop it honky."

Eric replies, "Yeah I feel you on that Crazy!" Then like a light bulb popping on, Eric seems to lighten up. "I hope the bus comes really fast to get us 'cause at least in prison we can go outside. "

"Everybody Out!" The rat is yelling at us.

"It's time to head back honky, at least this court shit is over."

On my way back to the jail, I got to wonder whether I will even make it out of prison. Will I be killed or will I have to kill to protect myself? You try to stay away from thoughts like this but Eric had spooked me a little, also I got to admit to myself 10 years sounds like a long time. Eric is 21 years old, which is young like me, but he is bigger. I am 18 with a small frame that doesn't seem like a good combo for a prison. I am thinking that it means I'm going to have to prove myself more.

We made it back to the jail in time for chow. To say Fayette County Jail served nasty food would be an understatement. They had these sack lunches waiting on us. The meat is so thin that I don't have a clue what it is. It's slimy, smells, and has a green tint to it. I still eat it, I have no choice. You either eat it or buy food off the canteen, and I got no money to buy food. Eric gives me his sack 'cause he has noodles in his locker. His mama sends money to him.

We eat then get sent back up to the pods where we all live. Eric lives in my pod and sleeps four bunks down. I'm too wired to sleep, there is way too much on my mind. I want to play spades and gamble.

Eric has a lot of heart, and he don't like to fuck people around. When I gamble, Eric knows I got no way to pay it. That if I lose, people can accept that, or we fight. Eric doesn't have an issue with fighting, but he likes to be in the right. I know all this but I want to still play spades anyway, so I tell Eric I need him to be my spade partner.

Eric protests, "Why don't I just give you the noodles' Crazy?"

"You know you're my honky, but I don't want no handout. I want to pave my own way, besides if shit hits the fan, you step to the side, then I'll handle it, I'll claim you didn't know."

Eric just gives me a look like I am an idiot, "Come on now Crazy, you know I can't let nobody jump you. All we got is each other in here."

I nod and say, "So you're going to play or not? I need a couple of hours plus these guys are easy any ways. " I'm probably no doubt being an ass hole but hell I want to gamble.

He gives in with a shrug, "Okay Crazy; I'll play for a couple of hours, not like there's anything else to do." We find the guys then strike up a game. We don't play for money. We mostly play for things we can use like Ramen noodles in a cup, or stamps are the most-used items. I hope to win a lot, but if I lose, then I got to show out some.

I realized all the way back in the group homes and foster care that I got the gift of gab. At first, I thought everybody could do it, then I realized my talent is beyond what lots of people could do. I could even talk the smartest kids, and adults, into stuff I wanted them to do for me. Its like words have always come to me on whatever subject. I just knew what to say to win people over.

The card game has gone south. I have lost 26 noodles! I don't know how it got that bad. It got a lot worse when I told the two I played against that I'm not going to pay anything. On top of that, it turns out these two were brothers, actual brothers. Who the hell would have guessed that? I should have known that or at least asked around but like every lesson, I had to learn it the hard way. They also happen to have a cousin in the pod. Suddenly, it's like a fucking family reunion up in here, and I am such an idiot that I didn't have a clue.

No one takes bad news well but in prison, giving someone bad news might cost you a trip to the hospital or worse. That's why you got to be on your guard when you have something to say that you know isn't going to be received well. Don't just stare at the guy you are talking to, look around you for any threats. I tell the guy to my left, he is beat, and I am not paying shit then the guy on the right sucker punches me so hard I fly out of my metal chair. Before I can get up, the cousin joins both brothers, they're kicking and punching the shit out of me. If it wasn't 'cause my honky, Eric, I would have went to the hospital that day. It turns out, gambling isn't a good hustle for me. I need to step up my game!

All of us are sent to the hole. If you watch "Locked Up" or some other prison show, you probably hear them call this the Segregated Housing Unit or SHU. But we all call it the "hole" because you sit in a cell all day by yourself with nothing in it. There is nothing to do but jack off or stare off into space. I am cool with it though, because my pride didn't want anybody to see my black eyes. I don't think there is any type of rating system for black eyes but if there was one, then I would be at the top number.

I sit in that cell for one month and 25 days, two days after my 19th birthday before they tell me to pack up (as if I had a lot of stuff or some shit) that the prison bus is here to get me. They walk me down the jail hallways in shackles and cuffs. It is like four in the morning, and for real I just want to go back to sleep. Outside there is a huge bus that is grey. It looks like a grey Greyhound bus. Eric is here too, what is the luck my buddy goes with me? Plus, there have got to be at least 50 other inmates standing around in this basement sally-port.

Eric tells me they call it the Grey Goose. He isn't mad at me over the fight. Hell, for real he doesn't even bring it up. We are both too anxious with thoughts of what prison will be like. So we step onto the Grey Goose and prison, here we come.

Chapter 2

FISH TANK

*We tiptoe through life hoping
to safely make it to death.* —Unknown

The fish tank is exactly what it sounds like. They strip us down, spray us with cold ass water, and then ask us tons of medical questions. This is where they give us our prison number. It's like one big tank, the sorry ass state set up to send people to classify what level of danger you are, so they can figure out where to send you next. They tell us to expect to be here about two months before they ship us off to the penitentiary. For some a camp where they have no fence around the prison, or class D jail.

They shave my head and throw some white powder all over me saying it's for lice or some shit. Then we shower with about 30 other men. It is here, our first day at the fish tank, where my honky Eric gets a new nickname. They're calling him Country now. He does sound real country with his southern accent.

My prison number is 142586. After my haircut, shower and pointless-ass medical questions, I get my picture taken then put my new number under my chin giving my best smile for the camera. I'm dressed in blue scrubs and flip flops. They give me two extra tops and bottoms for the scrubs.

They send Country, me, and the rest of us to a room where we can get our state soap, toothpaste, toothbrush, then tissue, so we can wipe our ass. They call the room the "clothing house," I have no clue why, but really I don't care. I'm ready to get to where our bed areas are and lay down for a few hours. The bus ride, rats, convicts, all of it has been long; I am already sick of all this. Plus, I need to take a piss.

In prison, you learn patience very fast. You learn it because everything takes forever to do. I get my shit paper and hygiene, but it don't matter if I am last or first; we all have to wait on each other regardless before the rats walk us to the next place. We all have to be done together. This is also why no one likes "fish," guys who are new to a penitentiary. Because we slow everyone down asking stupid questions, or at least, some do.

The fish tank is probably the loudest place I have ever been. That says a lot for real because I've been around. Nonetheless this place is set up where it is made into a circle. In the middle of the circle is where two rats hang out trying to bust a motherfucker for shit. Most of these rats are young and think they're tough. Their mouths are really loose. I will for sure have to cuss a few out to show them what's up.

Around the circle is six huge pods that are all open wings, A-F each holds about 300 convicts. In the back of each pod are two commodes plus one stand up. No doors or nothing around it. You just walk up and do your business while everyone can see everything. Two fucking toilets for 300 fucking people. In addition to the toilets, we have two sinks plus a shower with three shower heads. All this is open, no privacy at all. I'm 19 years old and like to jack off 5-10 times a day. Now the only way to jack is to just say fuck it, and fuck who cares, I'm doing it.

The TV is in the front of the wing; it stays blasting something all day long. The phones are built right under the fucking TV, now how fucking stupid is that? You're trying to talk on the phone while you got the fucking TV blasting above your damn head. To the right of the phones is the microwave where everyone lines up to heat their food. They also use pencil lead, tissue and foil; that will spark a flame onto the tissue, so they can smoke.

They line us up in the hallway around this circle with the rats. The rats give us a lock then tell us, people steal so make sure we lock everything up. Seriously? People steal? We're all criminals you dumb-ass rat! I want to laugh but I just bite my tongue because I'm not trying to go back to the hole so soon.

Behind me, a fight breaks out, and I realize it is one of the guys who was on the bus with me. I hear several convicts yelling "Get that fucking ratting-ass inmate!" The guards are trying to break it up, but this black guy is beating the shit out of this white guy. The white guy is bleeding already from several places on the face. Dumb-ass rats can't figure out how to stop it. The inbreeds get frustrated, I guess because they just start to mace the both of them in the face. Then here comes about 10 more ratting-ass cops down the hall to help out.

The black guy is going off even with his eyes swelling up from the mace. "You ratted on my brother you piece of shit! Thought you were going to get away didn't you bitch?"

The white guy is either knocked out or passed out 'cause he isn't responding at all. My eyes are running because the dumb-ass rats used too much mace. They tell all of us to take a bed roll off the table. It has two sheets, blanket, towel, and two razors.

The bed rolls have our names on them plus where we're supposed to go. Two other convicts are stealing from the white dude that just got his ass beat. While they steal his bed roll, I start to think that an extra blanket would've been nice. I wish I thought of that, but I didn't even know dude's name.

"Hey honky, where they got you going to?"

"They got me going to A-wing Country. Where they got you going to?"

"Ah, shit honky, I'm going to D-wing. We'll have to see each other in the chow hall or the yard during our yard time I guess," Country says sounding disappointed. Shit is really weird but Country and I have been doing our time together for almost half a year. So it sucks to be tossed out of your comfort zone.

"Hey Crazy." A guy named Red, at least that is the name we always called him, pops out of E-wing.

"Yeah, what's up Red?"

"I overheard you tell your honky that you're goin' to A-wing. You be careful over there Crazy! They got a lot of young black dudes in there, and they fight a bunch and steal everything!"

"Yeah okay Red, thanks." Red walks back to his wing; he's already been here for about a month. I've not seen him since he left the county jail. Country can't send him at all, for some reason.

"That guy gives me the fucking creeps Crazy." I laugh at Country because look where we are at and *Red* gave him the creeps?

"All these fucking guys give me the creeps, honky! Not just Red, all of them, we need to watch; they think we're new, so they are going to try to take advantage of us in every way they can. Don't worry though I got your back."

"Yeah well a lot of good that is, you're in A-wing, and I'm all the way in D-wing," he says looking down at his state-issued flip flops.

They done put the white dude that got beat up in a wheel chair and are pushing him away. The black guy who beat him up, they hand cuff him and drag him out of the tank. They'll put him in the hole.

The guards start to yell at us, "Everybody to your wing right now! It's lock down! Get your asses moving! NOW!"

"Fucking rats always think they're tough!" I say this more to myself than Country.

"Yeah, they do but we got to go honky! I'll see you at dinner time if they let our wings out together."

"Alright, honky, later." I head to A-wing. The paper on my bed roll says I'm in bunk 265-Top.

I walk into A-wing and there are about 75 bunks going down one side and 75 down the other, all double bunks. I get to my bunk, and my bunkie is laying on the bottom bunk. I put my stuff down on my bunk then pull out my prison time sheet they gave me. I hand it to my bunkie and walk to the back to go to the bathroom. I need to take a piss after that three-hour bus ride!

The reason I gave my time sheet to my bunkie is because it shows my charges. I need the word to spread that I'm not in here for touching little kids. I might be a heartless motherfucker but even I got my standards, and kids are not at all a good thing to fuck with. It takes a sick motherfucker to touch little kids.

It stinks like hell at the toilet. It doesn't help that there are people hiding all around the walls in here smoking. I get ready to walk back out, but some skinny white dude says to me "Hey, I'm called The Rock!"

"Yeah, well they call me Crazy. What you want Rock?" I feel my palms getting sweaty. I get tense in these situations because you never know how it's going to go down. It's not that I'm scared, but I'm so antisocial I don't know what to say. I got some fucked-up social skills, I guess.

"Hey calm down Crazy! I just got a question for you, OK?"

"Yeah, it's cool."

"You see this white dude next to me Crazy? He came down today off the bus with you. You know him?" He asks pointing to a skinny white dude he's holding by the arm. He looks maybe in his late twenties. I can see he looks somewhat feminine with his blond hair and blue eyes.

"Nah, I have never seen him in the jail, but maybe he was in a different pod than me."

"Well, what pod were you in Crazy?"

"I was in B-pod on the 7th floor."

"Well what do you think of that, check in?" Rock asks the young dude tightening his grip on the dude's arm so tight that I see the young dude wince.

"Come on Rock, I just got the pod wrong!" The young dude pleads.

"You see Crazy, my bitch right here said he was in B-pod, 7th floor, but you never saw him before right?"

"Nah, I've never seen him at all." To be honest I'm glad I haven't seen him because I don't want to get involved.

"Well, you see Crazy; I found out my bitch right here is in prison for having sex with his six-year-old son! So not only is he a sick-ass cho-mo faggot, but now I just learned he is a check-in also."

I'm at a loss for what to say here so I just tell Rock, "I hope he don't tell on you, be careful honky."

"Oh I plan to be careful. I'm going to fuck this bitch, and I plan to let all the blacks fuck him too. Crazy, if you want some of this, I'll let you take a turn before I give him to the blacks. You let me know."

"Please don't do this to me Rock. Please!" the boy says and starts to sob.

"Shut up bitch," Rock says and slaps him on the back of the head.

"Ok, Rock, I'm out of here." I say then walk off.

I return to my bunk, but the haunted look that young dude had in his eyes will probably always stick with me. Calling a dude a "check in" is a put down, it means you're weak and will most likely be asking for Protective Custody or PC. That also means, you're going to rat on the dudes that fuck with you. On top of being weak, this dude's a child molester, or *cho-mo*. Things are going to be hard for him.

My bunkie is waiting on me when I get back. I can see he looks like he's ready to talk. He's just standing by the bunk looking at me as I walk up. He's about 20 years old or so.

"Hey what's up bunkie?" I say.

"You gave me your time sheet honky; you didn't need to do that. I already knew this morning all about you. Word travels fast on inmate.com." He says this last part with a sort of smile. "Anyway, my name is J-bird honky. I got 30 years for murder."

"My name is Crazy and I can tell already it's crazy in here."

"Yeah, it can get live at night. I normally try to drink hooch to kill the time. I got 3 gallons in my locker right now. You want to get drunk tonight?"

"Nah, no offense honky but I like to pave my own way and pay for my own stuff."

"You got money Crazy?"

"Nah, but I plan to get me a hustle. I just need to figure it all out. You got any ideas J-bird?"

"Well I know dudes that will pay you 30 or 40 dollars to hold and make hooch in your locker."

"Man, 30 or 40 dollars is what the fuck I'm talkin' about. That would get me all my hygiene and some noodles. I need that deal J-bird!"

"Well Crazy lots of these guys try to fuck you around. I'm going to do you right and take you to my dude Tiny. Tiny will give you 40 dollars he will also give you like a half-gallon of it for yourself."

"Cool, that's what I'm talkin' about! Let me just make my bed then we will go see Tiny." Probably 40 bucks don't sound like a lot to nobody else, but it's the difference between eating the crap in chow hall and eating a good hot ramen noodle. That also means I can buy stuff to drink and have extra hygiene. So hopefully this dude is going to hook me up right.

Chapter 3

DRUGS + HOOCH = FUN

*The big question is whether you are going to be able
to say a hearty yes to your adventure.* —Joseph Campbell

It turns out Tiny is a 260-pound black guy that is all muscle. I don't really have an issue with black people, but jail and prison teaches you to stick with your own kind. That is just how it is in here. I have no issue with trying to get my hustle on though. I'm just not going to be looking for a friend in Tiny. Hell I'm really not looking for any friends from anyone.

"Hey Tiny, what's up with you?" J-bird asks as we walk over to Tiny's bed area. He sleeps towards the middle, on a bottom bunk.

"Nothin' up J-bird. Who is the new dude you got with you?"

"This here is Crazy, my new bunkie, he's cool. He wants to get his feet wet."

"You want a shot of coffee Crazy?" Tiny asks me.

"Nah, I'm good; I don't drink that shit. Besides I like to pave my own way." I say while keeping my face straight so he don't see how nervous I am.

"We all like to do that Crazy but not everybody knows how. J-bird here is a good hustler, at least you got a solid bunkie. Let's get down to business Crazy. J-bird told you the basics, right?"

"Yeah he told me what I need to hold."

"Here," Tiny pulls out his locker box out from under his bed. "Why don't you have a seat Crazy, let's talk."

J-Bird just sits down on the end of Tiny's bunk. Tiny pushes the box up against the wall so all three of us can sit close to each other. I thought about telling him I don't want to sit down. That last ass kicking I got while sitting at the jail still played on my pride. I figured if I take another ass kicking, I'd rather do it standing up, but I knew if I refused to sit down the trust level would be rocked. If he don't trust me with his supply to make the hooch, then I got no hustle, and I'm back to being broke. I just hold my tongue and sit down.

"So here's the deal Crazy, I'm going to put 10 gallons in your locker box. That's a lot of hooch and I'll have one of my dudes come over and make it all. The only thing you need to do is keep your locker box locked. Then after about two days I'll need you to start letting the air out the bag. The bag will swell up and if the air isn't let out it will blow. It will smell really bad when you let the air out so you need to do it after the rat does a round. On top of that I'll give you some smell good stuff to spray. I'll have it all put in your box tonight. I'll give you forty dollars tonight. I will also give you a half- gallon of the hooch so you can get your drink on!"

"Okay Tiny, it all sounds good to me I am down for whatever. I need the forty to be mostly in hygiene though. Is that an issue?"

"Not at all Crazy, I got you."

"Okay I'll see you tonight player."

"Okay"

J-bird hadn't really said much at all, but he really didn't need to. We walked back to our bed area. I sat down on my locker box, and J-bird sits on his bed. It's loud as fuck, feels like an oven in here as well. It's so loud I don't have a clue how a person sleeps or thinks. But thinking is exactly what I was doing. "Hey Bird you said the stuff in your locker is yours right?"

"Yeah why? What's up?"

"Well, you drink and sell, or you just do one or the other?"

"I do both honky, although I normally try to make enough back to make a bigger load every time so I can make more money. That way I have more to drink," he says with a big old grin.

"So Bird, how much does a gallon sell for in here?"

"Shit sells fast around here. You've got all the other wings too, and we can move it all around. I just have to be careful around the rats. A gallon sells for 30 dollars all day in here," J-bird says, looking around to make sure no one is listening.

"That's damn good for real. So he puts 10 gallons in my locker, and he makes 300 dollars? Wow!"

"Well not really 'cause he gives you a half gallon so that's 15 dollars then the 40 dollars he gives you to hold. So that is 55 dollars plus it costs about 50-60 dollars for all the stuff to get 10 gallons going. So about 185-200 dollar profit seems like."

"Man, that's what the fuck I'm talking about Bird! I'll make this first one and get my hygiene but the second one I make I'll hold the whole 40. If you help me get the stuff together, I'll put that whole 40 on a third batch with you. Shit honkey it will be all our own money to make."

"I like the way you think Crazy. I know you like to pave your own way, but we should celebrate our new hustle. I'll give you a half gallon tonight then when you get your half-gallon you can give it back if you want. But we're getting drunk tonight honky! "

"That's what's up then J-bird."

"You going to love this pineapple hooch I made."

"CHOW TIME A-WING," I look up toward the door. There are two rats screaming for us to get to chow.

"You going to eat, Bird?"

"Hell yeah I'm going to eat that slop. It's supposed to be beans, meat and rice—although I don't have a clue what type of meat it is. You going Crazy?"

"I'm hungry as hell, so I'm for sure going and my honky Eric is going to meet me there. They call him Country. I'll introduce the two of you."

When we go to dinner, Country, Bird and I sit together to eat. I have got to admit the food may be crap, but it is fucking heaven compared to the jail food. Plus they give more on these trays than in the jail. Country was so jealous that we're getting drunk tonight, and he can't come. Country is a whole different person when he's drunk. In fact, that's why he robbed the bank. He's a bipolar red neck so when he's drunk, look out. I'm not really ever trying to get drunk with him. Truth is, I have a small man complex, and I know it. Drunk or not it wouldn't take a lot for my rage to kick in and Country and I would get into it. Not that would necessarily end our friendship. I'm not like a lot of people; I believe in giving my friends complete loyalty. Fight or no fight, but the only thing that breaks my trust is if you rat on me. I can't hang out with no rat. So if I fought Country, I could shake hands with him afterwards and carry on as if not a thing happened as long as it stayed between us. But not a lot of people are like that, most tend to hold a grudge if you kick their ass. That is why there's no drinking with Country.

When I come back from dinner, I head back to take a piss. Rock is back here, and some black guy has a knife to that boy's throat over in the corner. He is fucking that white kid in the ass. The kid is crying and making an awful noise while Rock is watching out for rats.

I don't have anything against gays, in boys' homes, I grew up around it, but it just isn't for me.

As I'm leaving the bathroom, the kid turns and looks at me with tears rolling down his face, little cuts are on his throat where he squirmed too much then the knife cut him. That stupid kid says to me "Help me please." I tell the kid that men help themselves then I walk back to my bunk. It's really sad to be honest. I don't feel sad for the kid; I feel sad the kid is so much of a coward that he would allow men to do that to him. If it were me, I would've gotten a weapon, then one of us would have had to die. I get up in my bunk to rest, but I fall asleep.

"Hey Crazy wake your ass up honky!" Bird yells. "It's time to have some fun. You been sleeping like a baby up there." J-bird is in a very good mood and is full of himself.

"What time is it, Bird?"

"It's about 8 PM honky. It's time to have some fun."

"I got to take a piss Bird. I'll be back to get that hooch. Do you have a cup, I can put it in honky?" I don't even have a fucking cup.

"No big deal honky, I got you."

When I get to the bathroom, I see it's been turned into a kitchen/party/smoking/drug room. People at the sinks' cleaning jack mach and it stinks like hell. I take a piss then go to the sink to splash water on my face and rinse my mouth out. A Mexican and a white dude are at the sinks. I roll up on the white dude. "Hey man, what's your name?"

"Rooster, why? What's up?"

"Well Rooster I need to use that sink for just a second then I'll be out your way. "

"Nah, youngen, I got my fish all on the spots I cleaned down. I'm not going to move everything to let you splash water all over it. I'll be done in about 30 minutes."

"30 minutes?! Look Rooster, first off, my name's Crazy I'm not youngen or nothing else. Second, I'm not trying to cause trouble but there are only two sinks, and I'm not waiting no 30 minutes."

"Well Crazy you got no choice but to wait 30 minutes, 'cause I'm not movin', *Youngen!*"

Rooster is about 200 pounds, but it's all fat. Not sure why he has the name Rooster, but I know he is insulting me by calling me youngen, after I told him not too. Maybe they call him Rooster because he can crow like one. Let's check it out.

I sucker punch Rooster dead in the head then he falls back into the sink yelling, and I'm on his ass. I sucker punch him again in the side of the head, and he falls over. I grab him by the foot and drag his punk ass over to the corner then I football kick him in the head. Blood splashes on the wall from his mouth. I yell at him and tell him, "I only wanted the fucking sink for 30 fuckin' seconds you fucking asshole." I feel arms wrap around me and pull me back, and I am ready to swing on whoever grabbed me. He says in my ear to calm down, and I realize it's my dude Bird that is holding me, and I stop. I look down and see dude is bleeding pretty good in the mouth. Shure didn't sound like no rooster I've ever heard before.

"Damn Crazy, what you trying to do? You trying to kill the fat fuck?"

"Nah I just sort of lost it, Bird."

"Yeah I can see that." Bird bends down and lightly smacks the dude on the face to get his attention. "Hey, this is over dude. Next time just share the fucking sink. Got it?"

"Yeah. Yeah I got it."

"Alright, get your fish and get out of here so Crazy can calm down." Dude gets up then grabs his fish and takes off. "Well Crazy, it seems you kicked the party off early. You ready to go get drunk?"

"Yeah, I'm ready now just let me wash my face off real quick."

"Okay I'll see you at the bunk."

I wash my face off and rinse my mouth out then turn to walk back to the bunk. Rooster is standing next to my bunk talking to Bird, and I can see he has a bad cut on his lip.

"Hey, what's up Crazy?"

"Nothing is up ass hole!! What you do want to be up, Rooster?"

"Hey man, calm down honky, I just want to say sorry man, I hear you are good people, and I should have just moved for a second. I just got caught up. I don't want no beef with you or Bird."

"Look Rooster, I really am not in the mood to deal with you. I just wanted to wash my face. I didn't want to go through all this drama just to wash my damn face. So you go back to wherever you live and stay away from me. Just don't talk to me, okay?"

"Yeah I get it, Crazy. Bird, thanks for breaking it up."

"Hell Rooster I didn't do it for you. I did it for my dude so he didn't go to the hole. Now get the fuck out of here."

I go ahead and sit on my locker that is up against the wall. Bird hands me a cup of hooch. "Man honky, that dude is a bitch," I say. "Who the fuck says sorry after they get their ass kicked?" Bird just looks over his shoulder and sees Rooster in his bed area talking to a couple of guys.

"Yeah, he's a bitch, but just watch your back 'cause if he puts a hit on you, you won't see it coming. Motherfucker'll just walk up to you then blast you in the face."

"This fucking hooch is some good ass shit. Tastes like pineapple juice and vodka or something. I already feel a buzz after just three swallows of it."

"Ha ha ha, you one of them light weights. Don't be trying to go to bed early, we got all night and don't be throwing up neither."

"You laugh all you want Bird, but I'm nothing but 19 and I've never drunk that much before." I down the rest and hold out my cup.

"Alright," Bird says and pours me another.

"Hey, what's up Bird?"

"Not a lot Pistol, what's up with you?"

"I got a deal for you or your dude here."

"Alright Pistol, have a seat on my bunk and let's hear it." Bird says.

"What's your dude's name Bird?"

"Shit Pistol, he's sittin' right there, ask him."

"My name is Pistol honky, what they call you?"

"I'm Crazy or at least people call me Crazy; I may be crazy also."

"Ha ha, I like that, I heard about you beating dude up in the bathroom." Pistol says. Pistol looks like one of those old cons that has been in prison for a long ass time. He has tattoos everywhere and just looks like a convict with his grey beard and solid grey hair. Not to mention eyes that look like a killer. I get the vibe without anything needing to be said; Pistol is dangerous. Besides, he's cut up like hell for an old guy.

"Why they call you Pistol?" I ask him. Pistol pulls his shirt up to show me a tattoo of a .38 revolver around his stomach. The gun looks like it's inside a holster, ready to be pulled out in a draw. "Nice ink work."

"Yeah I got these done back in the early 80s at Eddyville State Prison."

I ask, "So what's the deal, Pistol?"

Pistol looks over his shoulder toward a bunk area stating to Bird and I, "I live on the top bunk over there. My bunkie is some fucking wino that is in prison for his sixth DUI. He has got a ton of fucking money. You see him over there sitting on the table on the far end drinking a cup of coffee, the older guy with glasses on?"

"Yeah, we see him honky."

Pistol goes on, "well, my bunkie has a locker box full of nothing but food. He just spent 100 dollars out the window today. Plus he has more than the 100 dollars he put in there. I want to rob him for all of it. I could easily rob the old fuck but he's got a lock on the box. I don't want him to check in and go to protective custody before I can get the lock off so what I need is one of you two to help me scare him and smack him around a little and make him give me the combination to his lock."

I am slowly finishing my second cup of this pineapple hooch stuff. It is so good, and I'm for sure feeling a strong buzz. I don't answer Pistol for a moment because I see Bird is thinking. I also need a moment to think. To Bird, I say, "Honky let me get another cup of this." Bird reaches into his locker and dips my cup into the bag.

"Here you go."

"How many do I got left Bird?"

"I'm not sure but we'll figure that out later." Bird looks at Pistol with an evil smile and says, "Honky, let us think about it a moment. We won't be long at all to come and talk to you. We just trying to get our buzz on first."

"Yeah, okay. I'll tell you what, for just listening to me, I'll give you something to help your buzz. I have these pills that are called '93's. Their real name is Effexor, but this is some shit honky. It might be dummy dope, but shit will juice you all the way up. Here's three and here's three for you Crazy. I'd suggest you just take one and put the rest up 'cause they are fucking powerful." He hands us both pills then, "I'm out of here, talk to you honkies later."

As Pistol goes, I look down at the pill in my hand. Bird pops one, so I say fuck it also then pop one of mine.

Chapter 4

24 HOURS IN THE TANK

Man is the only animal whose desires increase as they are fed; the only animal that is never satisfied. —Henry George

The thing about hooch is you either know how to make it, or you don't. Lots of people have their own personal touch to make it taste good or make it strong. If you make a bad batch, you drink it and not only will you have the shits all day, but you will hardly get a buzz at all. My dude likes to make it with potatoes, sugar, pineapples and pineapple juice mixed with the yeast we get from the kitchen. He believes the potatoes and pineapples turn into vodka, or at least as strong as you can get it in here. It tastes very good but you got to strain it, and since we don't have a strainer. We have to strain it with a sock. Of course, we use a new sock, but you got to get all that yeast out and chunks of pineapples because it could make you sick if you don't. However, I do have a couple of buddies who are serious about getting their buzz, and they'll eat those pineapple chunks that are left in their cook. They say they don't get sick, so I guess it varies from person to person.

The hardest part and most risky is during the cooking. You can't just leave it in the bag in your locker. You got to take it out and take it to the shower. Then let the hot-water heat it up because it cooks better when hot. Plus you can finish a whole 10 gallons in five or six days tops as long as you keep it warm. Otherwise, it cooks slow or not at all. It is best to take a shower three times a day and keep it warmed up so the sugar and yeast will cook. Bird explains all this to me as we get drunk.

It is a risk packing it to the shower and just standing in the shower with it. Bird tells me he will buzz for me and watch for rats. So when he tells me, a rat is doing a round, I will have time to sit the hooch down in the corner and lay a towel on it.

I'm on my third cup of hooch, between that and the "93"pills Pistol gave me; I'm rocking! The 93 pills are mixing with the hooch or something, and I feel like I have a thousand watts of energy and also feel completely buzzed.

That's when Tiny's dude shows up. "What's your name homey?" I think I said this with a slur, but I'm pretty sure he understood me.

"They call me J.R. little homey. I was sent over here by Tiny to start this hooch up in your locker."

"Yeah, that's cool. But don't call me little, I'm not feeling that shit at all."

"Oh, well my bad homey! I don't mean no disrespect or none of that. So you don't need to feel that way homey. Everything's cool!"

"Yeah, everything's cool, it's all good. I just hate being called little. So what do we need to do to get this started?"

"Tiny said they call you Crazy, right?"

"Yeah, that's what they call me."

"Well Crazy, all you need to do is open your box. I'll do all the work and will tell you what you need to do for it every day. You for sure got to release the air out the bag, at least a few times. Do you know you got to take this to the shower a couple of times a day and heat it up?"

"Yeah, my dude Bird, right here, told me all about it."

"Okay Crazy, I need you to go buzz the door and watch for rats. Just rub your head if they're moving this way. It will take me about 30 minutes to get all set up."

"Okay that's cool J. R." I turn to J-bird to see what he thinks of all this. "What you going to do Bird?"

"I'm going to chill here and enjoy my buzz. Don't go up to that door starting no shit Crazy. You drunk and feeling good but with this in your locker, you can't get in no trouble okay?"

"Yeah, that's cool. I'll finish this cup, and that's it. I'm not even gonna take this up there with me."

While I finish my cup, J.R. goes to his bed area, grabs a whole net bag full of stuff and comes back to our bed area.

"Crazy, this here is the whole kit to make it all."

"Okay, cool, I'll go buzz at the door. Bird I'm leaving this cup in the corner up against the wall 'cause, I don't want the guards to get it and smell it. I'll clean it out, after I'm done buzzing."

"Okay cool Crazy."

"Alright, I'm out. Oh yeah and J.R., my stuff that's in my locker, just lay it on my bed. It's nothing but a change of clothes and some hygiene."

"Nah Crazy, you can sit it in my box," J-bird tells me.

"Yeah, that's even better Bird and good thinking honky."

As I am walking to the door to buzz, Pistol and Rock see me then try to wave me over to the bed area where they are talking.

"I can't talk now honky, I got to go up here for a minute. I'll be at the door for a little while.

"Oh okay. Well, shit honky we not doing nothing we'll go with you. Nothing else to do, is there Pistol?"

"Nah, Rock there isn't. So let's go Crazy. What you doing anyway?"

"I'm buzzing for something Pistol."

"Well let me help you 'cause, I see you're doing it all wrong. It's no big deal, Crazy you just new at this shit, pull a chair up. Grab one of them plastic chairs and get as close as you can to the door, act like you watching TV or talk to us but don't let the rat see you looking at them at all. If they see you watching them, it will hip them and they may think something is going down. They're not stupid as they look, they have been doing this a while, they know what a buzz man is. They see you looking at them; they'll come over just to be the rats they are and try to check out what's up."

"Okay I feel that Pistol, I appreciate you teaching me. I need to learn all this, and I realize I'm a fish at it. I might've looked at the guard but I got it now. So good-looking Pistol, hold on while I grab a chair."

"Grab us one also honky!" Rock yells to me.

"Yeah I got you two." As we all sit down in a spot by the door, I got to thinking, *why doesn't Pistol use Rock for his little scheme and why is he trying to use me?* "Hey Pistol, you know what we was talking about earlier?"

"Yeah, I remember but keep it down, I don't want one of these guys near us to hear and tell him."

"Yeah okay, I feel that," so I lean over and say in his ear, "why you want me Pistol? Why can't you use Rock?"

Pistol kind of gives me this weird look, "Look Crazy, I'm not trying to use you nor do I got any type of hidden agenda. I just seen you had nothing honky, on top of that I heard you are good people. I figured this is easy come up and gives you and me a chance to get some canteen and hygiene. Rock already has stuff from the hustles he's into."

"Hmm, yeah, I can feel that, and I'm sorry I came at you like that, but you know I'm new at this. I'm just trying to watch out for myself."

"Yeah, I know all that, and you should be *very* watchful of people in here. You're young so they'll think you're gullible honky but I'm old school. I'm a proud honky and got pride in my race. I don't get into using my own race, unless they're weak like my bunkie."

"Have you been to other prisons before Pistol?"

"Yeah, Rock and I both have. I've been to the Castle. It's a maximum-security place, but that's the nickname of course. The real name is Kentucky State Penitentiary."

"Where all you been to Rock?"

"Shit honky, I've been to the Pink Palace. It's a medium-security prison. It's full of fags, rats, and lifers all scared to do shit about it. It's a fucked-up place, for real, can be very dangerous."

"Okay Pistol I'm game. I'm in honky! When you want this to go down?" I don't want to think about it anymore so I hurry up and agree because I know I won't break my word.

"Well we can do it in a couple of hours after you done doing what you doing now. My bunkie said he is going to take a shower in a couple hours. We'll roll up on him while he's in the shower naked. And that will scare him more because he's not going to know what level, we'll take it to. Make him feel like we're going to rape him if he don't come off the combination."

"Okay that's all good. When I get done with this. I'll go back to my bed area and chill with Bird where we will enjoy our buzz. But, I'll watch for him to walk by to the shower. When he does we'll go in on him."

"That's what I am *talking* about Crazy."

As I sit there and wait on J.R. to get done. I'm thinking to myself, *this is one fucked-up place*. I'm not at all dumb enough to believe Pistol or Rock are friends. If he'll rob his Bunkie, then he'd rob me too if I let my guard down. These fucking people prey on weakness. I don't give a fuck who you are, you come in here on some soft ass shit that you going to do good, join some programs or church or both. Then sharks like these two will make sure you have a hard time.

I don't think of myself as a shark. I'm just a young guy, who's trying to make it. Young or not, I have been doing this long enough to know I can't show that I'm scared. I fully realize that in this world; I got to act as a shark to blend in, or they will be on me next. Pistol just said as much when he's talking about his bunkie being weak. To survive in here, you got to be strong or find someone to protect you. No one does anything in here for free so protection has a cost. These fucking people love young guys like me. The blacks especially love white dudes and love to try to turn a young dude out but I'll be damned if I get turned into a fag or a check in.

J.R. comes up behind me, "I'm done Crazy and everything is good."

"Good timing for real, here comes the guard to do his round or do something. Who knows what the rat is doing."

"I'm out of here; I'll talk to you guys later." J.R. walks off, I turn to Pistol and Rock.

"I'm so fucked up, I need to go to my bed area." Bird looks fucked up laying in his bunk, "Honky, you look high as hell!"

"That's 'cause I am high as hell hokey! Ha ha ha" and I can't help but to laugh with him.

"What you laughing at honky?"

"You look like you're going to throw up," I say.

"You don't look no different than me!" J-bird says with a big shit-eating grin on his face.

"That's what I find funny honky. I ain't been here 24 hours I've done got tore, the fuck up," I say returning his grin.

"You want another cup of this hooch?"

"Nah, I can't stand another cup Bird. That fucking pill we took is tearing my ass up too. Besides that three cups have already got me past drunk. That's some strong shit honky." We're sitting here cutting up, and I see dude's bunkie head to the shower. "Oh shit I'm out of here Bird, I agreed to that deal with Pistol. I get half of everything in his locker. That is over $50 worth of stuff. We will eat good honky. Oh, I guess I'll need to put that stuff in your locker, cool?"

"That's all good but where you going now?" J-bird asks.

"Dude just went to the bathroom to take a shower. We going to roll up on him in there."

"Shit honky, I'm going with you. Somebody needs to watch your crazy ass. If dude tries to buck and not come off that combination you so crazy you may fucking go ahead and kill him just to make a point!"

"Nah, honky fuck that, I ain't trying to do life but who knows what'll happen when I get mad."

"Let's go honky," J-bird says and starts to head to the shower.

In the bathroom nobody's here, only Pistol who's taking a piss at the stand-up toilet."

"What's up Pistol?"

"Shit honky, I done ran everybody out of here."

"That's all good and I see dude's in the shower. Pistol you buzz at the door, make sure we good then Bird and I will go in there, okay?"

"All-good honky."

As I enter the shower dude turns around with soap all over him, he notices Bird and I. "Hey man, I'm in here. I don't want nobody taking a shower with me. Get out of here! Now!"

I react by moving really quickly to him and smack him so hard he falls to the floor. He comes back up and swings on me, but I move to come up behind him and put him in a head lock.

"Let me go motherfucker! I'm not a fucking fag, what the hell are you two doing?!"

"Listen up, my name is Bird, my dude Crazy right there is going to rape you unless you want to make this easy and give us your combination to your locker." I pull him into a tighter hold to show him what bird says is real.

"Fuck you! I'm not letting you rob me or rape me, you fucking bitches" I slam him to the ground and with my other hand that's not around his neck, I grab his ass cheek. He makes a grunt sound either from the impact from hitting the floor or me grabbing his ass cheek hard.

"See honky, I'm no bitch. Your mouth is going to get you in trouble in here. My dude will rape you, and it don't matter if you think it won't happen, you can't stop it. This is happening so you got a decision to make honky, material stuff took from you or we take your manhood. So unless you want to get a dick rammed up in you, I suggest you give me your combination, *bitch*!"

"Man, I'll give you my combination, but you give me your word you're not gonna let your dude do this. I can't get raped! Please don't let him do it! I'm begging you not to let this shit happen."

"Shut up honky and stop your fucking crying. A minute ago, you were a tough guy. I promise you that if you give me the combination me and Crazy will roll out together, that nothing will happen to you. Once we're gone, you are gonna wait in here then let us have the time to empty your locker. I'll come back and tell you when you can come out now after that it's all done. We won't bother you no more, got it? Now give me the fucking numbers!" Bitch!

"25-16-5 Now will you let me go? My shoulder hurts man," he says while his nose starting to run.

"Fucking weak ass honky. Come on Crazy let's go do this!"

I slap the fucker on the face lightly and tell him, "You stay in here till we come get you! You disobey and our deal is off the table, and I'm going to drag you back in here and get some of these fat fucking cheeks you got! Got it?"

"I promise I'll wait here and won't move. Just please leave me alone. I don't want any problems I swear I'll do as I'm told! Just please don't hurt me."

"Weak ass motherfucker," Bird says again as we roll out and tell Pistol we got it, and we're good to go to get everything out of his locker and pack it all to J-bird's bed.

"Make sure he don't leave the shower until we're done Pistol, then we'll split everything and be done."

"I got the door Crazy, you two go do you. I won't let the bitch come out or none of that!"

In the end, I got $66 worth of stuff, shampoo, soap, deodorant, toothpaste, lots of Ramen noodles and a few cans of Armour chili. The bunkie's name turns out to be Jordan. A wino with a name Jordan, rare huh?

Jordan didn't go to the guard or none of that. He stayed in the pod, but he stopped going to canteen altogether. He might have been out of money, but I'm pretty sure he had money on his account. I just think that whole scene shook him up really bad so in the end, he said *fuck canteen* and just ate the state food.

I don't feel bad about it at all. That probably sounds fucked up, but I look at it this way. If he wasn't a bitch, he wouldn't have given it to me. Why should I sit here and do without when I'm strong enough to get what I need? Life isn't fair, right? I'm sure if you're a bitch or a punk you'll for sure disagree but real men do what is necessary to survive in this fucked-up place. With that 66 dollars, I'm going to add it to the 40 I get from Tiny. Start my own batch of hooch up maybe sooner than I thought.

The days went by pretty fast after that. J.R. came back for the first batch and starts up the second. From time-to-time he comes to check on the hooch. J.R. is a real dark black guy. He is short but built pretty big. I get the vibe, he doesn't like white guys, but I'm cool with that. I went ahead with the plan to make two batches. Just stack my bread up some.

"This stuff, will be ready in two more days. It smells good as hell when it is done. After that are you going to be ready to make another batch, Crazy?"

"Nah, I'm going out on my own after this and start my own shit and make enough to hopefully get me a TV."

"Oh shit, you can't do that Crazy. Tiny runs the hooch in this pod. You can't just go and step on his toes, Crazy."

"What you mean step on his toes? He don't own this wing, and he sure as shit don't own me."

"Crazy you don't know what you're talking about. Here in prison, you can't step in a then take somebody else's hustle, that's being disrespectful. The money he's making, you would end up taking instead. That's just not good business at all, you can't do that Crazy."

"Well J.R. I respect you and Tiny, so I'll try to sell mine in a different pod if I can, but I got to do what I can to survive. I need a TV, radio, and sweat pants. If every hustle really is took like you are saying, then I'm fucked, and I'm not feeling that. I'm not trying to disrespect anyone, but I'm making this hooch J.R."

"Well, alright Crazy but I'm telling you Tiny isn't going to be feeling that."

"Well I'll talk to Tiny later when I get around to it, but I done got my mind made up. So it is what it is." As J.R. walks off I wonder what that was all supposed to mean. I don't want to have to fight Tiny, but if he tries to tell me what to do I'll have to do what I got to do I guess. I can't let nobody tell me what to do. That's just not cool.

A couple more days go by, and I don't have any type of talk with Tiny. Not because I was scared, but I figured J.R. done told him. So I feel like me going to him is a bitch move. I don't need his permission at all. I feel that me going to him is kind of like asking for his approval or some shit. Fuck all that shit. I'm just going to do me. I'm going to make my stuff then if he don't like it. We can have a talk, but he will have to come to me. We can take it to whatever level he wants.

I spoke to Bird about it because he also makes hooch. I was curious if they said something to him. Bird said he drinks mostly all of his, that he only makes a few dollars from white guys who would only buy from a white guy. So they haven't said anything about it.

On the fifth day, the hooch is ready. To be honest I feel like it isn't worth the 40 dollars and the hooch I got. I mean, I had to take this stuff to the shower two to three times a day. Packing 10 gallons in a plastic bag is no easy task. Just so the bag wouldn't bust. I always had to put it in a mop bucket and wheel it to the shower. Shit is crazy not to mention a lot of fucking work. I'm ready to set out and do my own thing.

In the five days that past, that Jordan guy and like ten other people transferred to other prisons. I heard Jordan went to a prison called the Castle where Pistol came from, but I'm not sure. I heard it's a pretty rough place. That he will have a hard time if he went there. With him only having D.U.I charges, I can't see him going to a max prison.

"So here's the deal Crazy. This stuff is done but we'll leave it over here for now. It's all sold, but the people won't really come get it until tonight. We'll get all this out of here by tonight."

"That's cool J.R., I'll be in the pod all day. I'll go to lunch and dinner but other than that, I'm here, so just come get me when you ready for it."

As J.R. was leaving Bird started to laugh. "What you laughing at honky?"

"Man, Crazy, that dude can't stand you! You can tell he dislikes you a lot. What did you do to that guy?"

"I don't give a fuck what he thinks, Bird. His black ass is mad I'm not going to make hooch for his people no more. Plus I think he is on some kill whitey shit or something."

"Yeah well, Crazy you making a ton of enemies. You just watch your back, okay."

"I always watch my back Bird. I've always known it's not easy for a honky to make a come up. I'm just trying to survive but people always hating on me."

I wound up not going to lunch. I wish I'd missed dinner; it was some fucking Sloppy Joe but made of nasty ass soy patty shit. By then it was like 8 PM, and I was just hanging out with Bird when Rock pulled up. "What you honkys up to?"

"We not doing nothing Rock. Just sitting here reminiscing about the streets, me and Bird both white trash, so we can relate."

"Yeah, I don't even like those talks for real," Rock says with a sour look on his face. Lots of people hate to talk about the streets, they say it just makes their time harder.

"Well let's talk about that guy you had, that bitch, what happen to him?" I ask.

"Man, we had so much fun with him that night. You would've noticed if you wasn't so high," Rock laughs, either remembering his own good time or maybe remembering how high we were.

"Yeah, well that shit they call 93 had me and Bird tore *all* up."

"Well I had him back in the bathroom. I fucked his cute little ass out for like 30 minutes or so. Hell, I came twice. Then I turned around and started to sell him out. Dude's so cute and young that I had 22 people get on that deal. I charged ten dollars, and I got to say bitch was crying like a real girl, by the time he got to number nine or ten. I had to give that bitch a couple of breaks and made him shower about 10 times that night. You guys not going to believe this though."

"Why what?" Bird asks.

"Some fucking snitch in here dropped a rat letter on it, but bitch tells the rats nothing happened. They still move him over to C wing. Anyways, bitch comes to me and wants me to be his fucking man! I'm still making a lot of money off him. He seems to like it, fucking weirdo!"

"You give him any of the money, Rock?"

"Nah Bird, I don't because he's in prison for touching that little kid, and I'm not feeling that. If it wasn't for that I might've gave him some, but with his charge, I'm going to treat him like a bitch. Keep it like that!"

"Yeah, I for sure feel you on that all the way," Bird says. "So Crazy, where's your dude Country?"

"That honky done caught the flu or some kind of bug. He has been laying in a lot just not coming out. He gets money and just eats a lot out his locker. That honky goes to canteen almost every week."

"Yeah, well I hope he feels better real soon. It really does suck to be sick in here. Medical in this place will kill a motherfucker before they help you. Any ways I'm out of here, going to play some chess with Pistol. That honky has done got re-classed to the Pink

Palace, and the bus will come get him any morning. I'll sure miss him for real, but I'm sure he'll be glad to get out of here. I hear you get lots more yard time over there."

"Well, alright Rock, you take it easy don't forget to tell old-ass Pistol, Bird, and I said 'what's up' okay?"

"Yeah, I'll tell him for you, I'm out of here."

"Bird you know soon as J.R. gets this hooch out of here or the rest of it. I'm gonna start my own shit. He already come got a lot of it, plus I have all the stuff to make my whole batch. I can probably start eight gallons or a little more."

"Yea, I know Crazy; you got the shit in my locker. Did you talk to Tiny or what?"

"Nah, I'm not going to. I feel like going to him is a bitch move. I don't need his fucking permission. I just don't feel that I need to tell him my business or explain myself."

"Crazy, you got so much shit to learn for real! It's not a bitch move or asking him any kind of permission to do what you want. It's all about respect in here and your word being good. Since he was making hooch first in here, it's just respectful to talk to him. Not to talk to him is like you saying he is some kind of yap and fuck him!"

"Yeah, I feel all that Bird but call it pride, ego or small man complex, but I'm not talking to him about nothing. I'm going to do me."

"Yeah, okay, that's cool. You know I got your back honky. I'm not seeing him or none of his friends, Crazy. You're not the only crazy white trash up in here."

"Yeah, well I'm super gutter white trash, and I'm not going to let no black guy stop me from getting out the gutter. Fuck that shit,

I'm starting my hooch tonight." I look over my shoulder. I see J.R. heading our way, "Speak of the devil, here he comes."

"What's up Crazy...Bird?"

"Nothing up J.R., we just sitting here talking. You here to get the rest?"

"Yeah, I'll get it out your way. I'm just going to grab the bag then take it to dude."

"That's what's up J.R."

"Also Tiny asked me to ask you if you want to start another batch tonight. He said he's got your 40 dollars right now. He said he's got several locker boxes full of different stuff, and he will let you pick whatever you want."

"Well, all that is very nice J.R., but I'm good for now. That shit was hell packing back and forth to the shower. So I'll step back for now. I will let Tiny know if I change my mind. I'll come talk to him okay?" I say while giving him a look to let him know I'm done talking about it.

"Yeah I'll tell him all that Crazy." J.R. pulled the leftover four gallons out of my locker, doesn't say another word and rolls out.

"Well that is that Bird, I can start my own thing now. Time to make some real money. All the work in this hustle, I feel like I need to make a lot more than forty dollars and some hooch to drink."

"All right Crazy let's get all this shit out. I'll teach you how all this goes." Me and Bird sit there and make the eight gallons up. He tells me after we strain it that it will look like a lot less. J.R never asked me to strain his and Tiny's stuff. The way I got it, they sold it not strained. I just left it up to the customers to do it or not.

As we work, and I think about all the trips I'm going to have to make to the shower with this shit, I am thinking that there has got to be a better hustle than hooch or this silly small stuff. Something that brings in a couple hundred dollars a week at least. I feel in my soul there had to be a hustle that I could find that could do that. I just need a path to get there.

Chapter 5

HERE I COME K.S.R.

Success is a series of glorious defeats!
—Mahatma Gandhi

The next couple of days go by pretty fast. I'm at lunch with Country and Bird. The hooch is cooking real well. In the last couple days, Bird and I added some more sugar to it.

Lunch is like any other day. We come and stand in a line that is wrapped around the chow hall's wall, all the way outside. It takes about 30 minutes or more just to get through this fucking line. Then they scan my ID to make sure I don't come back a second time. The state loves to starve us. They got this 50,000 dollar system just to make sure we convicts can't come back a second time in line.

They push my tray out of a slot that's built into the wall. I can't see any kitchen workers or anything back there. They got the juice we get in huge five-gallon coolers. The rats tell us we can only have two cups. The salt and pepper shakers are on this same table. The

Kool aid always sucks. The punk-ass inmates will have enough to make three gallons but will make five gallons out of it. You got these punk ass inmates who would rather help the kitchen then help their own convicts.

The chow hall is huge. In the movies, you see long metal tables. That's how it was back in the 1970's and 80's I'm told, but they got square wooden tables here that only four people can sit at. Plastic hard chairs to sit in, and it's loud as fuck in here. Over a hundred people having different conversations and there is no air conditioning. So on top of being loud, it's hot as fuck. That is prison for ya. Everybody has some story to tell about their glory days or something.

Pistol was going to come to lunch with us, but the rats told him to pack up. He thinks he's going to the Castle instead of the Palace. He says that Eddyville is a five-hour drive. Five hours in chains and shackles, fuck that shit.

"Hey Crazy, they packing Pistol up right now right?"

"Yeah Country, he's headed to the Castle he says; He is a good honky. I'll miss him for real."

"Well, I hope he likes it better at the new place. I don't know him very well. I was sick for a week but now that I'm better and coming out. He's rolling out of here."

"Well you two, I'm headed back to the pod to take a shower and a nap."

"Alright Crazy, I'll be back there in a little while," Bird says.

"Alright Bird. Country, you better start coming out more and talking to us!"

When I get back to the pod. I see three guards standing by my bunk. I walk up to them then ask, "What's up CO?"

"We want you to open your locker up right now."

"Why is that CO?"

"Because we told you to."

Fuck it, I open it, so they see the hooch. What else can I do? Not like I can run with it to the bathroom. The C.O. tells me to turn around so he can put cuffs on me. That we're headed to his office.

As I am walking up the pod, I am worried the rats would guess I had no property in my locker box. That they would put two and two together then figure out I'm using my bunkie's locker box. If they think that, they may shake him down and J-bird's hot with hooch in his locker also. I am hoping I could run into somebody I know, then just tell them, but everybody was at chow. Tiny and J.R. were standing up at the door. I figured I could tell Tiny. He knew Bird, but soon as I thought of this. I see J.R. go one way towards the chow hall, and Tiny goes the other way.

The rats take me out in the hall and into their office. Tiny is sitting in here with some dick head guard. I found this kind of fishy, but I figured the rats would tell him to get out. Instead, after I enter the room, the two rats that Tiny was talking to, stand up and walk to the door. Right before they leave, one of the rats looks at me.

"You sit in that chair there, Crazy." The rat says pointing at a chair that's kind of off in the corner. I am thinking to myself; I'm *in handcuffs, and they're walking out.* I've heard some fucked-up stories, even before I made it to prison and these rats think I am just going to sit down and let Tiny beat me up in hand cuffs or hell, maybe worse? *I'll kill this motherfucker if he tries to rape me.*

You never know what the rats will do. We're supposed to call them by their last name to keep our relationship as professional as possible. It don't matter though 'cause, there is a ton of dirty fucking guards trying to make a come up. I am too, but they are in a better position to do it. Anyway, this rat's name is, I believe, Jefferson. He's a sergeant I think but since they all wear the same black uniform and same badge on their chest. I can't tell the difference between them, except the rookies. The rookies have no kind of bars or nothing on their shoulders. They only have an ID badge clipped up on their shoulder. Their shirts are kind of like military shirts. They have that extra piece of cloth going across their shoulder so they can clip their ID badges on it. That's where their rank bars go too. For the deaf-ass rats they get a small speaker that connects on their shoulder. Then the cord runs down their back, and they connect it to their radio. That way whatever's said on the radio, the deaf-ass rat can hear it.

This rat has sergeant stripes up on each of his bony ass shoulders. He looks at me with his beady-ass rat eyes, or I think of them like that.

"Nah, I'm cool rat. I'm not sitting down for you dick sucker. There ain't a thing you or your porch monkey can do about it! I'll take whatever this is standing." I understand this is a crazy way to talk, but they don't call me Crazy for no reason. Besides, I'm a fan of destiny and faith. I fully believe what will be, will be. There is no way I can change it; all I can do is go with it.

"Well Smith, I don't give a shit if you sit or stand. I am just trying to be nice. Tiny, you got one minute, and we'll be back."

"Yes, Sergeant Jefferson I understand and thank you." Tiny responded

They all walk out, and I figure one minute isn't shit. I can handle whatever for one minute. Fuck them rats anyway, I hate how they call me Smith. They refuse to call us by our nicknames, but that's cool because majority of convicts have one. Most had theirs from the streets or got it in jail or soon after. It's a way to keep our names from the rats when an inmate rat drops a letter. That's the convict's theory, but it's a stupid ass theory since the inmate rats tell on whatever. So they'll figure out your real name and tell on that. It's a stupid theory but there's a lot of stupid ass theories in prison you got to go by, or it'll lead to problems. If I've learned anything already. All convicts are a bunch of, "full of shit" motherfuckers, almost all the time.

"I don't much like that you just called me a porch monkey Crazy. You being racist now or did the white boys turn you into a Nazi?"

"I'm from the trailer parks, porch monkey, and I don't let nobody make me what I am or ain't. I just call shit as I see it, right here you are all up on the porch being a yes man for the rats. "

"We don't got a lot of time Crazy, so I'm not gonna argue with you. I don't give a shit what you think of me anyways. You young white boys that come up in here all fresh from the streets act like you know everything but don't know shit. The trailer parks isn't shit compared to the hood I came from white boy.

"Now I had no issue of you wantin' to stop making hooch. I wouldn't have said another word to you at all about that. But for you to think you could come up in here just in the short time you have, thinking you gonna to make hooch on your own while making money that is my money to make? Nah, white boy, you got the whole game fucked up.

"My people, J.R., told you I had the hooch game locked in. You still said fuck me and fuck it. It looks like it's really fuck you white boy!"

I am so taken aback by that, I didn't know what to say. I had thought not being a rat is the number one golden rule all convicts knew. The ones that were rats I had always thought went to protective custody or stayed in the hole. However, if I am hearing him right, he's telling me he told on me because he wasn't going to let me sell hooch and take some of his profit.

"So you telling me you ratted on me, all so you can make all the money for yourself?"

"I'm not sure Crazy, but maybe they make us in the hood a lot smarter than you in the trailer parks. I'm trying to tell you I'm a businessman. I learned as a teen selling dope on the corner that it's easier to feed the rats a morsel of information for them to look the other way. Then it came to me as I got older, why shouldn't I use this blessing to get rid of my competition?"

"That' right, that's why I called you a porch monkey. You see, us from the trailer park may not be as smart as you from the hood, or maybe it's that we are but one thing; we don't sell out our own kind. You all up on that corner rapping and smiling with your homeys and the whole time you looking and listening for something to stab your homeys in the back with. I got to say I'd rather be dumb than be all up on that porch being a piece of shit like you!"

"Well as I said, Crazy I don't give a shit what you think because you never gonna understand the game like I do. All I brought you up in here for is to give you the respect to let you know what I did, but you a naive white boy. You in a world full of sharks and nobody gives a shit about you or what you want. They only care how they can use you in some way, if you're no use, they don't fuck with you. This is the world you are stepping into white boy. I see the hustler in you, but you won't never go anywhere with it unless you harden your heart and grow a set of nuts. A real hustler don't give a shit about anything but the game. The result is we marry the game and not some prison fucking code or nothing else. We learn to blend in, but always stay true to the game always be married to it only. That's my advice to you white boy."

"Is that what you tell yourself, porch monkey, to help yourself feel better about being a fucking rat?" Just then the door opens, and the rats come back in the room.

"Times up. We gave you three minutes so you owe us for this Maynard. Don't you forget shit like this can get us all in trouble if Smith here gets to running his damn mouth."

"Yeah, well, white boy ain't gonna talk. You got nothing to worry about," Tiny says.

"Well get your ass back to your pod, you better also get us some good information for all this, or we'll bust your little hooch business. Then *you'll* be the next one on the way to the hole."

As three guards came in behind Jefferson, Tiny is going out the door. I know his last name now, *Maynard;* I'll remember it for life. Ratting motherfucker will get what's coming to him. Sellouts only blend in for so long. That fucking porch monkey will get his.

I knew I would stay mad for life at Tiny, but I had to keep it real with my own self. I am new at all this, I just got my ass served to me, and I haven't even left the fucking fish tank. I thought that at the worst, I would have to do is fight Tiny or a friend of his. I never imagined this could happen. If I did, or even if I understood the game better. I could have had another person hold my hooch. Come to think of it, I'd say that's why Tiny don't hold his. I'm not sure if I'm naive or not, but I see I got to learn this shit around me a lot fucking faster. My entire fucking hustle was just given to the fucking ratting ass guards. All because of one fucking mistake. If I had known to let somebody else hold it, I would still be in there and the worst case, it would've been that guy going to the hole while I start over. Well, if I could've re-hustled the money.

I got this system of my own called The Scale of Life. I have used The Scale of Life since I was about thirteen years old. My scale is simple to use, it just takes some balls. I put everything in life into two categories. The first category is called the *upside*, and the second category is called the *downside*. I don't give a fuck who it is or what it is, if The Scale of Life tips to the downside, I drop it and walk the fuck away. I'm done with it completely. There's been nothing in my life I couldn't walk away from. That's where balls and courage is needed. If The Scale of Life tips toward the upside, I fully embrace it and go with it. Making hooch tips to the downside.

I know people say the best things in life are the things you fight for. I'm here to tell you an idiot said that, or some spoiled-ass kid that had everything. For those who come from trailer-park poor, we've been fighting all our lives for something or another. A fucking meal or school supplies or hot water to take a fucking shower. Where's the fucking good in that? I've been fighting all my life, not one good fucking thing has come out of it. The only good I've got are the things I've learned to take or have the balls to earn. If I ever could, I would tell the idiot that said that, that he should learn The Scale of Life. When shit tips to the upside then you fucking fight for it! But run like hell when it tips to the downside.

I hear Sergeant Jefferson talking on the phone, but I can't make out what he's saying, he doesn't talk long though. He hangs up then comes over to me.

"Follow me to intake. You'll be put in a holding cell until transportation comes gets you. You're going to the hole over at Kentucky State Reformatory."

"Why can't I go to the hole here?" I ask him.

"We don't have a hole here smart mouth. Now get your ass moving, or I will drag you all the way to intake and I promise you Smith. You won't like it if I have to drag you there."

For real, I want to fight with this rat, but I see it for what it is. There's several of them, they'll probably try to write me up for assaulting them, and I've heard an assault on a guard is a year flat in the hole. For each assault you get more prison time. It would feel good, but I put all this on The Scale of Life making it tip all the way to the downside in every way for me, so I get to walking up the hallway.

"Lead the way rats," I say loudly to them.

"You got a smart mouth Smith. You'll learn really fast how to shut it in here. "

"Yeah, sure thing. I'm sure I'll be reformed real fast Sergeant Fucking Jefferson."

As I follow him, I realize we're headed in the same direction that we came into this prison from. After walking up several long hallways, sure enough, it's where I took my shower and got all processed into this dumbass place. There are three cells lined down the wall. I saw these cells when I came in, but I didn't have a clue what they were used for, now I do. The rat opens the last cell with a key on his belt.

"In here Smith. Now! You will not beat on the door, or we'll give you more write-ups and you will not yell or destroy this room. We'll be back to get you when transportation gets here."

"What the hell is a write-up rat?"

"It's a form that I write up every rule you break, then you go to something called 'court call'. At court call, they will decide what to do about it. They'll give you more hole time for each write-up. Different write-ups hold different amounts of hole time. They will explain it to you when you get to K.S.R., now get your fish ass in that room."

"Yeah, yeah, I may be a fish, I can be all that. I'm not a fucking rat though you fat motherfucker." Before I fully get into the cell, the rat tells me to let him take the cuffs off first.

I walk in the cell then he slams the door and looks into the window. "You know Smith, every time you call me rat, I could write you up for disrespecting a staff member. That holds fifteen days in the hole. Or I could just go to medical and get some pills and throw them in your cell and write you up for having them. Then you'd get more prison time. You are in our world Smith, so I suggest you learn how to shut your fucking mouth, you young fucking punk!"

"I'm not in your world rat. You give me more hole time that's cool. Then you give me more prison time, but I promise you I will meet you again. There's no need for me to make no threats. I know what I can do and can't do. I promise you that if you lie on me and get me more prison time, I'll find you some day. That day you won't like at all."

They just walk off, don't comment on anything I've said. The room they got me in is cold as hell. They got the air conditioner rolling in here, and the room smells like shit. There's a small wooden bench going down the back wall, on one side, there is a stainless steel toilet with a sink attached together. The room has gang names written all over the walls. The toilet-sink looks like it hasn't been cleaned in forever. That's where the shit smell is coming from. The door's have a slot in the middle of it, I've heard them call it a "tray slot." There is a square long window in the middle of the door. There is no window to look outside. It's just cold and fucking depressing, not a damn thing to do. If I lay on the wooden bench I would only be able to lay on my side, but it's so fucking cold. I doubt I could just lay there and not freeze to death and shake like hell with my thin blues on.

Besides, the guard for real has got me worried by what he said. I figure I'll just walk back and forth so if the rat tries to throw something in my cell, I can grab it and flush it real fast. So I'll walk and watch the door. Hopefully, they'll come get me out of here soon.

I am probably only in that cold-ass cell with my fucking toes freezing for about a half an hour until they came to my door. I got to be honest though, it felt like five fucking hours or more. People have no idea the things we take for granted on the streets. I would've sold my soul for something to pass the time. To be able to wrap something warm around my feet? Wow. I would have killed for that. All you got in this cell is your mind to play with you.

"Hey Smith what size do you wear?" I've never seen this rat before.

"I wear a large top and large bottom. Why you askin'? Where is Sergeant Jefferson and his pack of rats?"

"I need to get you an orange jump suit, so I can get you all changed out for being transported. I'm going to ignore what you said about Sergeant Jefferson and the staff with him, but they all work in general population area. I run intake; you can call me Officer Thompson. You give me no shit and I'll give you no shit, understand?"

"Yeah, I got you Officer Thompson. For real, I just want the fuck out this cell. I'm froze half to death so if it gets me out this cell faster by shutting my mouth or being respectful to you, then I can pull that off, Officer Thompson."

"Okay I will be right back with your orange jump suit." About two minutes later, the tray slot opens up and Officer Thompson pushes a rolled-up orange suit through it. "You need to remove all your clothes Smith. Hand me your blue, top and blue bottoms. You'll keep your socks and boxers, but I need to check them first for contraband, then I'll give them back. Oh and I only have extra-large jump suits so that will have to do."

"Yeah, yeah, I got it Officer Thompson." I take everything off and hand my clothes through the tray slot. I'm really fucking cold now. Even so, I can't put on this orange suit until he gives me my boxers back. Just standing here naked as hell.

"Lift your arms up Smith, let me see under your arms. Okay good, now take two steps back from the door. Now turn around and spread your ass cheeks, bend down and squat three times while coughing on each squat as you bend."

I've been through all this silly shit before. I got to tell you though, the feeling of being violated never goes away, no matter how many times I do it. They make you go through that same process every time they move you in or out of a prison. Hell, they may do it while in the pods if they feel you got something on you. I'm not sure what they expect. Do they expect you to squat and cough, and a key just falls out of your ass or something else? Trying not to think of all the weird, gay shit these guards do. I squat and cough three times.

"That's good Smith, now just let me see the bottom of your feet... okay...good. Now turn around and lift your dick and ball sack. I gotta make sure you got nothing under your balls or tied to your dick. Okay good, here are your boxers and socks. Get changed into your orange suit. I'll be right back to get you when K.S.R. is here to pick you up."

He walks away. I've never understood this though. The dumb-ass rats do this all the time. He stripped me out, checks me for any type of contraband, then they up and leave. But hell, I know we going to go through this every move, so why would I fucking hold something on me? I'd just sit it in the cell or lay it in the dirty ass sink and grab it when they walk away. I think they're so fucking lazy. They fuck this up all the time. I think they supposed to handcuff me, then come in this cell and check it or search it but they are too stupid.

Most of them are just good at being a fucking ass hole or just being paid to bring drugs in, they too dumb for anything else. It's like most of these rats have been bullied their entire high school years or further back. They get just a little power over us with that badge. It's like us criminals remind them of their bully, so they take that weak-ass shit out on us.

I was raised in Ohio, so I was raised mostly city, but I still have a country side too. I come from complete white trash, and I'm very, very proud of what I am and my lifestyle. I have faith and pride in white people only. I think every race should have pride in themselves. Every race should love who they are. I say all that to say this, these guards here in Kentucky, they're not trailer-park or country. They are not at all like the white people I love and respect.

These guards are mostly inbred hillbillies who have very little education. They don't even need a G.E.D or high school diploma to work here. Most of them are full of hate and resentment. I can only figure their hate is on account of, they're the weak ones that got picked on growing up. They couldn't do a damn thing about it then so they get a job as a fucking correctional officer and realize they have all of us criminals over a barrel. They got guns, but most of us aren't scared of dying. It's not the guns that stop us. It's getting tons more prison time that stops us from beating them up. We know these rats got sharp mouths and there are still lifers that will try them. For the rest of us that have an out-date, we let most this shit go. We know these rats won't miss a court date. They'll press charges on us so fast. Hell, more than half these inbreed motherfuckers would tell on their own mothers. There is no loyalty in any correctional guard. They will tell on each other or their family, and have no values or loyalty. They have a fucked-up way of thinking. To say we convicts have a love and hate relationship with them is to put it mildly. They lost the power to be a man as a kid, a bully took it from them, now they try to get the power back from us.

"You ready to go Smith? I'm here to cuff you up."

"Yeah, I'm ready to get the hell out of here. I'm sick of being cold. Sick of smelling piss. This is for the birds."

It takes around twenty minutes to get me cuffed. They tell me to come up to the tray slot and put my hands through it. They cuff my hands, open the door and pull me out into the hall. Then they put a black box on the chain between the cuffs to hold my hands apart and run another, long heavy chain through a hole on the black box. Then pull pull it through the loops on my scrubs, locking it in the back. This way, my hands are held to my waist. After that they put shackles around my ankles, tight as hell.

The walk to the car only takes about five minutes. I am seated in the back seat. Two guards in front, both had guns on their hips. After I sit down, they shut the door and off we go to my new home. I couldn't wait to get there to get the shackles off. The dumb-ass rat put them so tight they are rubbing the skin off my ankles. Plus I got a fucking itch on my nose that I can't even reach with my fucking hands stuck to my waist and to this dumb-ass chain. Hurry up K.S.R. PLEASE!

Chapter 6

THE CON IS SHOWN TO ME

If not you, who? If not now, when? —Hillel the Elder

That was my first time at R.C.C., or Roederer Correctional Complex, whatever you call it. For real, I like to call it a cesspool. Nonetheless, the first time I got here a few weeks ago I was so built up in so many feelings, and I was talking to everybody around me, so I missed what the building looked like. Now I got nobody to talk to besides I'm wide awake, and the cars' heat is bringing my limbs back to life, so I get to see the building from the side as we drive away. It looks huge to be honest. All the fucking fences and razor wire going up and down the fence makes it look like a fucking Nazi camp or something. Hell, they even got razor wire going across the ground. It got not just one fucking fence going around it. They put a second one around it that's about eight feet from the first one. Guess they thought if you get past the first one, then you will sure-as-shit not get past the second. That's not even counting the guard towers on every corner with guards walking around up there with huge guns. Between the fences, razor wire lays in circles across the ground.

From what I can see of the buildings, it looks like several huge circles. These circles each have huge pods that are as long as football fields all about five feet from each. Each pod has a skinny long hallway that go from one pod to the next. It all looks depressing. The pods are the wings, and right now I wish I was back in one.

I sit and wonder what Country is up to, or if I'll ever see him or J-bird ever again. I've not had a lot of friends my whole life. I got a weird personality also I feel uncomfortable around crowds or just around people in general. Seems like most people in boys' homes and prison love to hang out with groups or around gangs. They say there's comfort in numbers. I feel no comfort in numbers at all. I'm a loner and feel uneasy around most people. It was really good to not only have one person I considered a friend, but two friends, a huge change in my life. I hope they are doing okay and will remain that way.

Believe it or not it only took ten minutes to ride to K.S.R. Turns out both prisons are in La Grange. Both are out in the fucking country but just right up the road from each other.

The rats pull into an almost underground garage, then the huge door shuts behind us. There is a huge door in front of us also, and after we're inside, they use the second door to drive out of so they don't have to back up. In the middle of this garage is a set of steps that lead-up to a door that looks like a basement door to the building. The whole garage is no longer then a huge yellow school bus. (Not the fucking short bus some of these rats probably took to school).

They stop the car and turn it off. They both leave the car then go up the stairs, and into the building. Shit makes me mad how they just leave me here. I hate how cocky rats are, to be honest. They would shit their pants if they came out here and saw I done kicked the fucking car window out, that I was hanging out the window or whatever.

Didn't have time to laugh at my own thoughts cause here's the in-breed hillbillies coming back. They don't have their guns anymore, so that's what they were doing. They took their guns in there and locked them up somewhere in something. They come right to my door, open it up, and just stare at me. I know they want me to get out, but as I said, they're always acting cocky. I'm not a trained pet or none of that shit. Just because they open a door don't mean I just act on it. I always wait and make them tell me what to do. Probably immature of me but I don't care. I got to pick my battles these small battles I can win.

"Come on Smith, get out the car, right now."

"Yeah, here I come rat. I don't know what the hell you was all up and staring at me for."

"Well it sure as hell isn't because you are cute or handsome Smith. Get your smart ass out this car and out this sally port. Now Smith."

"Here I come right now. I thought this was a garage. What the fuck does sally port mean any ways? Stupid ass prison names." As I walk up the steps and into the door at the top, I realize I am right; we are in a basement. They walk me down a short hallway, then we stop in front of a door that says property room. This whole building looks like at least 70 years old or older. This basement looks like something out of a medieval dungeon movie.

When we drove in here, before we drove into the garage, all I could see was a huge front building that looked as old as this basement. (I refuse to use the rats' words. Sally port, my white ass.) There is a wooden bench against the wall, right next to the property room's door. The bench looks old and looks like a convict made it 60 years ago or more. Sitting on the bench is one of the most feminine looking guys I've ever seen in my life.

"You sit on the bench inmate Smith. Don't move until the property room calls for you to come in. Before you sit though, come over here and let me take the cuffs and shackles off you."

"Yeah, I need these things off me real bad but I'm not an inmate rat; I'm a convict. Where the hell do you think, I'll go to down here? Through a fucking wall or something?"

"Yeah, you are a real convict inmate Smith, all but a few weeks in the system and done got caught with hooch. You got no clue how to use your mouth but for being a smart ass. Now get your inmate ass over here." As he takes the cuffs and black box off me, this feminine-ass guy on the bench keeps staring at me. After the cuffs and black box come the shackles. I am so glad to get them off of me.

I sit on the bench, the two rats then up and leave down the hallway we came from. Now all there is in this lonely-ass basement is the feminine-ass man and me. He's still staring at me and making me feel uncomfortable but only because I'm not sure if I should beat him up for looking at me like I'm a piece of candy or something or should I just let it go. All this prison code shit, I don't fully understand, but I do realize if I do something wrong it'll follow me, and it will make my time harder. One bad decision, that I didn't even fully understand, and I could lose respect in prison, and that puts all the wolves on me. I don't have any money for them. I'm young; I'm not trying to get raped or get killed in here. Worse is I'm not wanting to kill someone, then do my whole life in here.

"Hey, why the fuck you staring at me like I'm a damn gummy bear or something?" I ask, trying to sound tough.

"I don't mean to offend you at all, I'm no threat to you in any way. They call me Tammy in here. I'm gay, as you can guess by my name. Here in prison, youngin, I'm called a sissy."

"Hum, well my name is Crazy, not at all youngin. I don't got a clue what the hell a sissy is though. I'm not offended you're gay at all Tammy. I am a little offended you keep staring at me though. Just 'cause you gay doesn't mean I am or does it mean you get to eye fuck me. I'm not at all cool with you over there having eye sex on me. Do I look like your own personal eye candy or something?"

"Okay, Crazy, I get what you saying, I'm no threat at all. I was just looking at you 'cause a girl can hope can't she? That's what a sissy is Crazy. I'm all girl in here. I may have a dick, but I'm a girl in every other way. I was looking at you 'cause you fine as hell, but I get it if you not gay. Sorry baby." Tammy says, pitching his voice high to sound more like a girl.

"I grew up all my life in some shit hole or the next. I've ran into my share of fags. I don't got no complex what you are at all. Long as you can respect that then me, and you can be cool Tammy, you understand that? What is your real name Tammy? I don't normally ask, but I'm curious what it was."

"I promise I'll respect you and not ever ask or do something you don't want to hear or do. I might be gay and all, but I am a solid ass person. Do me a favor, Crazy? Don't call me a fag no more, that is a really disrespectful thing to call a person that is gay okay?"

"Yeah, I don't got an issue about that. I'll call you gay or Sissy or Tammy. You still not told me your real name."

"My real name was Tom, people in here just took Tom and changed it to Tammy. Don't call me Tom though, I hate it real bad."

"Well, what's going on right now Tammy? Why they got me sitting out here, do you know why? Why you down here?"

"They got to change you out to seg. clothes. I'm guessing you did something, so now you going to the seg. unit and I got to tell you Crazy, the hole is fucked up here. I'm the property room runner. I live out on the yard. I got this prison job because it's a good hustle, I can get all types of stuff to steal in the property room, take it back to the yard and sell it. All I got to do is help carry other convict's property that gets locked up on the yard. Once they get you processed for here and get you all changed out for the hole, they take you upstairs."

"Why you say the hole is fucked up for?" I ask.

"Well it's like this Crazy, the seg. unit is like 80 years old. It is really nasty and has bugs everywhere. They don't never do any type of bug killing or bug spraying. There is no heat or air conditioner at all. Since we are in June, it is hot as a furnace in there. It can be 100 degrees outside, inside the hole it would be 115 degrees. All the concrete walls just hold the heat in.

"If all that isn't bad enough, you get one hour of rec every day only five days of the week. The other two days you don't come out your cell at all. The rooms are extremely small, you got about ten steps from back to front. You can hold your hands out and touch each side of the wall. You got one nasty toilet/sink and one bed with a mat on it that is as thin as a 200 page book. No table, mirror or anything else."

"You got a huge window in the back of your cell Crazy, that looks out at the yard but this window was made 80 years ago so it's one of them old long and wide windows. Built into a 100 different small square windows. Each cell has about 70-90 percent of these small windows just knocked the hell out. They won't fix'em at all, so birds and bugs just come right in from outside. You can just stick your arm out one of these windows, but you won't be able to break the metal that each of these square windows was built from. Many have tried, but they knew how to build stuff 80 years ago. Even if you could break the metal, if you could slide out the damn window, they built a fence around the hole. It's got razor wire all over it, so you wouldn't get anywhere but in the grass that surrounds the hole. You would just get a lot more hole time." From the look on Tammy's face, it's clear he has done some hole time and sure-as-shit don't want to go back.

"When the hell do I get a shower Tammy? I know these mother-fuckers got to give us a shower."

"Yeah, they give you a shower on Monday, Wednesday, and Friday, three times a week for only ten minutes a shower."

"When do I get to see a caseworker or get my write up and go to court call?"

"A case worker comes by Monday, Thursday, and Friday in the early mornings about 7:30am. You can talk to them anytime that they are doing a round. You got to speak to a caseworker from R.C.C. though not one from here. The sergeant will come get you in about two weeks; he or she will read your write up off to you. They'll ask how you plead and all that. Court call will come about a week after you get your write up. I got to tell you this though, court call was a joke Crazy. They're supposed to have all these policies and stuff to go by and if a policy is broken they're supposed to throw the write-up out. Since it's a cop that wrote you up and it's a cop that runs the court call, I am sure you can put the rest together. Cops stick together, hell why wouldn't they when the whole world hates them. All they got is themselves."

"What are the policies Tammy? What could help me do you think? I got caught with hooch in my locker box."

"Well if dates or times or both are messed up, they're supposed to throw it out. They're supposed to test the hooch to see what it is if it is really hooch or not. They're supposed to send some of it to a lab. Do you know what they did with the hooch?"

"Nah, I don't have a clue. I was walked out in handcuffs. The hooch was in my box still. They did something with it I'm sure, but I don't know what."

"Well if I was you I would tell the sergeant when he gives you the write-up. Ask for the chain of custody, tell him you want to see if it was tested or not. Get it on the write-up what he or she says about if it was tested or not, if it's not tested that's chain of custody violation. Mainly because if it wasn't tested, if court call finds you guilty, you can appeal court call's decision to the warden. You need to tell them it was a bag of water that you was going to use it to wash your clothes. They can't know any different if they didn't test it. You see what I am saying?"

"Yeah, I really needed to hear all this, I got to say you cool people Tammy, or seem to be."

"Oh you wouldn't even talk to me on the yard Crazy."

"I probably wouldn't but it's not 'cause you gay. It's mainly 'cause I'm on other stuff. I don't mess with gays in the sexual way. So we would have no need to talk out there unless on some business." We got nothing to say after that, so we just sit there for a while, then I say, "Man I been out here for an hour or so, how long does this take?"

"You don't need to rush it Crazy, once they take you up to your cell and shut the door; you'll wish you was down here talking."

"Where do they do the one hour of rec at? Why all the damn windows knocked out?"

"Well it's like this Crazy, this is called K.S.R.; it stands for Kentucky State Reformatory, and it's a prison hospital. This is the more relaxed prison setting, with a lot of people sick or crazy here. So the damn nuts bust the windows out. They like to scream at people coming across the yard, tell the people on the yard to send coffee or smokes.

"Lots of prisoners are genius crazy. They got a system that where somebody on the yard takes pouches of tobacco or bags of coffee and wraps them up in these net bags. They roll whatever up in the net bag then toss it over the seg. fence. Somebody in seg. will make a fishing line with a hook made of a pen with staples at the end. They'll fish that net bag right through the window. They make the line by ripping sheets, or they use dental floss they get on canteen in the hole. Then they sell the tobacco and stuff over there. You try to stay away from that stuff Crazy. The old timers love to try to put you young guys in debt. They hope you can't pay the debt and try to turn you out or make you their flunky."

"Well Tammy, I'll kill a motherfucker before I let them turn me out. Nonetheless, thank you for telling me all this, I just got gamed at R.C.C. and no; I don't at all want to talk about it. It's just I realize there's a lot I got to learn fast in here. Shit is like a world of its own, full of sharks, con men, and the worst predators ever. I realize I'm a fucking idiot to the game they got up in here. I won't go in debt though 'cause, I've always paid my own way. I don't accept free things from friends or anybody.

"So what about rec though, Tammy?"

"It's right on the walk in front of your cell, you go nowhere for it. All you do is walk up and down the hallway."

"Come on in here inmate Smith!" Now? Hell I didn't even hear the door to the property room open.

I look around and standing in the door is the cutest blond I've seen all year. She has got to be about twenty-four years old. She looks like she weighs no more than 110 pounds, has a wonderful body on her, great smile—I'm in trouble here.

"Well you going to just sit there and stare at me, or you going to get your ass in here?" she asks looking angry and cute all at the same time.

I get up and walk into the property room. As I walk through the door, I hear Tammy say, "I'll talk to you later Crazy."

I don't even answer him at all I just follow the blond. The property room is not that big. I figured it would have to be huge to hold everybody's stuff. The only thing in this room is a desk and two long wooden tables in front of the desk. Another door is behind her desk. "Kinda smaller than I'd thought to be honest," I say out loud to myself, not expecting her to answer me.

"Well that's just because this is the room. We check the property and get you guys changed out. This door behind me is where all the property goes, it's a lot bigger back there. My name is Officer Webb, you can call me Webb if you want. I already know your name is Rick Smith, Prison number 142586 right?"

"That's correct but why I got to call you Webb? What's your first name? Can't I call you by that?" I ask, smiling my thousand watt smile, hoping she'll relax a bit.

"Already flirting inmate Smith, huh?"

"I'm not trying to flirt at all. I would just like to know your name is all? Is that too much to ask? I'm not Inmate Smith, they call me Crazy or Rick, okay beautiful?"

"Well Rick I'll tell you what, we go by last names because that's how they train us. If you tell me your size for your top and bottoms, and your boxer size, then I'll get you changed out to your seg clothes. Give me no problems at all and at the end I'll tell you my real name. Well, provided you don't tell anyone else I told you, okay?"

"Shit, I'd say that's the best day I've ever had or at least in a long time. Now I feel like coming to the hole is worth it. Wasn't nothin' as beautiful as you over there." When I see she sort of smiles at that, I add, "I got to say, you got the cutest eyes ever. If I'm overstepping any boundaries, I'm sorry, but I just wanted to state the truth."

She smiles at me again, and I give her my best smile back. It feels good to flirt like this. "I wear a large bottom and large top, size 36 boxers will do. Your smile is wonderful on you Webb."

"Tammy come in here right now!" Even when she yells, she sounds sexy as hell to me. Shit goes right to my balls. She can ignore my comments, but I know she hears me.

"Tammy comes into the room!"

"Yes officer Webb, what can I do for you?"

"Go get me a large top and bottom R.C.C. scrub's outfit and get me a size 36 boxers with a pair of socks."

"Okay officer Webb, I'll be right back." Tammy leaves the room.

I lean up against the wooden table in front of her desk. "I got to say that you are one very sexy officer. If that gets me in trouble, I'm cool with that. It's just I've never seen anyone wear that uniform as good as you. Your eyes are so blue, you light up the whole room."

"I'm supposed to write you up for saying that Rick. I'm not going to though. I'm not a super cop or anything like that. I understand it's hard for you guys. I simply try to come in here and earn my paycheck. Just don't overstep because I'm nice, got it?"

"Shit girl, you sexy *and* cool as hell. I wish I could've had a chick like you when I was out. I might've tried way, way harder; Tried to stay out there for you and get a job, so I could've supported you and been there for you."

"You're just saying that Rick. You wouldn't even probably talk to me out in the world. I have no delusion that I'm beautiful. I'm a pretty woman maybe, but I have no tits or ass and my face has acme scars. Besides…"

"Hold up right there! I don't want to hear you say another negative thing about yourself. For you to say, I wouldn't talk to you out in the world. That's the craziest shit I've ever heard. As far as all the other shit you said, I don't at all see what you talkin' about, you're sexy in every way. You need to have more faith in your strength beautiful. Have more self-confidence and better self-esteem. You'll settle for less in life if you don't even believe in yourself."

"Oh you're a sweet talker I see." She says but that cute smile flickers across her face again.

"I'm not sweet talkin' at all. I just call things as I see them. If I would've came up in here, and you was fat or ugly I promise you I would have said not a thing or I would have spoken on it as I seen it. There is no sweet talking when it comes to something as sexy as you. It all comes out real, natural and easy. I can't see how you don't see how cute you are. Regardless if you see it or not, I see it real clearly."

Before she could say anything else Tammy walks in with some clothes in his hands. I could see how she shut a light out in her as soon as Tammy walked in. She went all professional, her cute face went from a radiant smile to a straight face.

"Just set the clothes on the table over there," as Tammy sat the clothes down on the table. I couldn't help but think to myself that if she has me change out in front of her, I'm going to grow fucking hard. I got no doubt about that, and for a white guy, I'm not doing bad at all on the dick size.

"You can wait outside Tammy. If I need you I'll holler for you." As Tammy left, I see him smiling at me. "Seems Tammy likes you Crazy. I've been here a couple years, I know he doesn't smile at anybody. I've had him working with me for over a year, so I should know," she says teasing me.

"I don't care what Tammy likes or don't like, I'm no fag at all beautiful. I don't care how cheesy I sound, but every time you say my name, it not only sends chills through me. It feels like an angel is saying my name." She blushes and starts to say something, but I'm not gonna let her because I feel it's going to be something negative about herself.

"Oh, I knew you were a sweet talker Rick." It's like she fucking made that come out in a purr.

"Just calling it as I see it. You want me to go ahead and change for you?" This orange jump suit is hot." I see the way she's looking at me, so I decide to be bold. "I mean, I'd love to get naked in front of you. A man would be out of his mind if he thought negative about your sexy ass."

"Well Rick I'm supposed to go in the back while you guys change. I've done just that the whole time I've worked here. I've been hit on a lot, but I always paid no mind to it. I understand lots of you must be really horny, being locked up and all. With that said Rick, I'm going to sit right here while you change unless you ask me not to. I don't feel like I need to say this, but I will anyway because it's important; don't go running to your buddies and brag about this. Don't talk about this at all, in fact, I need my paycheck Rick, got it?"

"I'll tell you like this beautiful, I'm not a rat in any way. I'm a gangsta through and through. I'm a very proud piece of white trash. I got no friends to tell this to, plus, I would never want to get your cute ass in trouble. I respect your trust beautiful. You can feel relaxed around me." As I talk, I'm pulling my buttons open on the orange jump suit. I look at her and say, "Hell no I don't want you to go nowhere. I just hope you enjoy this as much I do."

I slide my arms out of the orange jump suit. It's a little baggy on me so after I get my arms out. I just let it drop around my feet. Then I slide my boxers off, fairly fast because I don't want her to change her mind. I see she's nervous, so I figure it's my job to calm her. I step a foot out each boxer leg, and I'm hard as hell as I slowly grab the boxers from the table. I just grab them, but I take no measure at all on putting them on. I look at her, she is looking at me, I stand there naked and give her my best smile. I give her time to check me out and then I ask her, "You like what you see Officer Webb?"

"My name is Megan, I got to tell you Rick, you do have a nice body." Then lower, like she was talking to herself, "That looks like it hurts."

"Yeah, it hurts and could use some loving. You makin' an offer beautiful? I mean, a player can hope, sexy!"

"I'm not trying to go that far Rick, I would like to go that far but wrong place, wrong time." She reaches in the desk drawer then pulls out a bottle of lotion. She sits it on the desk then pushes it towards me.

"This is the best I can offer you Rick. I'm too nervous for more."

"You sound like I should get upset, you sexy as hell. I could look at you all day and jack my dick to your cute face. I feel blessed for this, to be honest. You try to calm down sexy. We're going to have some fun, this is meant to be."

She turns red in the face again, but I give her no more time to say anything. If she changes her mind right now I'd have blue balls for days so I reach for the bottle, squirt lotion on the swollen head of my dick and begin to stoke it as, I lean against the table. As I'm stroking, I stare dead into her blue eyes. After a few minutes, my breath starts to get jagged. She just sits there and smiles so sexy at me. She's trying to play it cool, but her tongue comes out a couple times to lick her lips, damn.

"Is that feeling good Rick? You feel like shooting all over my desk? I bet you want to cum inside of me, don't you Rick?"

"Shit baby, you got such a dirty, sexy mouth. I am going to cum all over your desk. Shit feels so good baby. I could do this forever."

"You gotta hurry up. I'll jack it for you. You can cum on my face. How does that sound to you?" That last part surprised me but what a fucking turn on. I've only been with a few women, and I can usually go for a long time but when Megan tells me she'll jack it, plus I can cum on her face. I almost lose it right then and there. The way she looks at me plus the way she says that like I'm a steak and she hasn't eaten in days, shit tears right threw me.

I walk around the desk, walk right in front of her, she looks up at me and smiles. This woman is sexy as hell for real.

"Go over there and lock the door Rick, if anybody tries to come in, you'll say I went in the back. You didn't want nobody to see you change out so you turned the dead bolt on the door and locked it."

"You damn right that's what I'll say. Anything to protect your cute ass. I don't care what they do to me, I promise I'll protect you."

I walk over and lock the door, but I turn the dead bolt real slow. I don't want Tammy out in the hallway, hearing it moving. After I lock the door, I walk back over to Megan.

I stand in front of her, hands on my hips and my dick bobbing in front of her. I'm waiting for her to wrap her cute fingers around it, but instead she leans forward and takes my dick into her mouth and begins to suck it. Her mouth feels so good that I'm afraid I'll shoot on the spot. I've only been with a few women my whole life and none of them sucked my dick as good as Megan. She slides up and down my dick. It feels sensational. I can see she's enjoying herself, that turns me on more. She's taking over half of me in her mouth. Just when I can't hold it another second, she grabs my cock with her hand, using only her tongue, she starts working the head. The way she works her tongue around my head, then over-the-top working and into my hole, it's working miracles on me.

Oh god, she is so good at this. I can't even believe we're doing this. I'm nervous that we'll get caught, and fucking turned on by it all at the same time. She keeps trying to take all of my dick, I find this so sexy that I start to move my hips, fucking her face. I feel her hands come up behind me, grabbing my ass and pulling me into her, so I start to fuck harder and put my hands on her head. She has such a fine-ass body. Her nails dig into my cheeks, and I keep puling her closer to me. She feels so good. I figure if she went this far why shouldn't she go the rest of the way? Although I don't want to push her too far. I need to go slow with her.

I try to pull back, but she won't let go. "I'm gonna cum" I say in a hoarse whisper, but she doesn't care and it's too late anyway. I thrust my dick one last time then feel my cum shoot into her mouth. I can feel her swallow as my balls pump several more loads into her mouth. It gives me pure male satisfaction to watch her swallow again and again sucking every last drop out of me. Fuck! Coming to the hole has been the best thing ever.

"Wow that felt so good Megan!" I say as she licks the final drop of cum off the head of my dick sending shivers down my spine. This woman is sexy. I'm lucky as hell today.

"I think I'm in love, Megan. That was the best blow job I've ever had in my life. Not only are you sexy as hell, but you got some talent on you beautiful. Damn, you're all that, girl!" I say as she grabs a lipstick and a mirror from her bag then starts fixing her makeup.

She looks up at me and gives me that killer smile of hers. "Well you're pretty good yourself Rick. I got to get you out of here though. Go unlock the door, then get your clothes on fast. I'll call up front and tell them you're ready."

"Okay, I got you Megan. I don't want to see you get in any trouble at all." I say as I walk over to the door, I unlock it slowly again so no one can hear.

As I get dressed it comes to me, my real hustle is my mouth. I realize I'm beyond good with words. I need to find a hustle where I can con people into doing what I ask. I understand now that I've got a way with words, that cutting edge of being blunt, then being real with my words. People are so not used to it, that it gets me hated or loved. There's no grey area with me. I'm starting to see my destiny. Now, I just need to learn what type of con I can get where I can use my sweet talk to make money. The answer to that question is going to be my future (or at least, I think it will).

Chapter 7

THIS HOLE AIN'T SHIT!

Life is what happens while we are busy
making other plans. —John Lennon

As soon as I got my clothes on, Megan looks at me with that wonderful smile of hers. She comments, almost apologetically, "They are on their way to get you Rick. This right here, was great, but I do wish we could've done more, and I hope to see you again. I'll see if I can safely get you sent down here for something maybe. So if a guard comes to your door for any reason to tell you that you're going to the property room just agree, then say you've been waiting forever."

"Shit girl, you know I know what's up, still I feel really blessed you tryin' to school me. You one real-ass chick Megan so I will show you there is real ass dudes too. You're my beautiful blond angel in a dark world. I wouldn't allow nothing to affect that. Even if I never see you again Megan, I will always remember your cute little smile."

"You make me reckless Rick. I feel like I can do things around you that I've only ever thought of doing. Things I have been too scared to ever act on before, you bring it all out in me," she claims.

"Yeah, well I'll tell you like this Megan, it isn't me that really brings it out. It's the real in you that can feel the real in me without any words at all. It creates a connection that wakes a motherfucker up, destiny baby!" She smiles at me again, and I'm grinnin' like a fool.

"Before they get down here, let me get a small kiss to remember you by Megan." I don't wait for her to answer me. I just lean in really fast, kiss her dead on the mouth. As I kiss her, I cup her titty in my hand. Even through her uniform, I could tell she had small, firm titties. Just enough for a hand full. Myself, I prefer small tits over big tits any day.

As my tongue searches her mouth, she runs her fingers over my shaved head and lets out a soft moan. Then, real gently, she puts her hand flat out on my chest and pushes.

"You trying to give me a heart attack Rick? Shit, I'm already horny as hell." She steps back and starts straightening her uniform then checking her hair. "Take your cute ass out in the hallway, before I lose all restraint," she says, returning my smile.

"I got you beautiful. I'll sure miss you, but you should know you'll be in every fantasy of mine. You are one real-ass chick Megan! Plus you're sexy as hell." She gives me that damn killer smile of hers but doesn't say anything, "Take it easy Megan, don't forget me sexy." I walk out the door without another word. I don't want to get her in trouble. If I stand in there, I could stare at her face all day. I mean, would I want to see this prison shit, guards and nasty-ass men all around me, or see her? It's not that hard to answer at all.

As I step out, Tammy is laying on the bench. He sits up when he sees me. "Damn Crazy, I didn't think you were ever going to come out of there, I thought you was clocking out in there or something," he says, frowning and clearly annoyed.

"Yeah well, I didn't want to change out my clothes. I kept thinkin' every time she went in the back, she might pop back out. That I might not be done if she does, and then she'd give me another write up. You know how these rats try to set you up."

"Yeah, I know how they are Crazy, but Miss Webb isn't an ass hole like that, she isn't a super robo-cop."

"How I'm I suppose to know that Tammy? Maybe if you would've told me before I went in. She finally told me if I don't change out clothes, she'll call more rats down here, and they'll make me do it by force. Then I'd get several write ups. So I just changed, but I don't see why they let a woman work here."

"I don't think she would've called back up. I guess I should've have told you she's was cool, it just slipped my mind."

"It's no big..." I say.

"Inmate Smith you ready to go or not?"

I look down the hallway and see two big-ass male guards. It seems guards always have dumb-ass haircuts and are either fat or skinny. These two were fat, overweight rats. It is a very common trait for rats to be overweight.

"Yeah, I'm ready to go wherever. You want me to walk down there to you?" I shout to them but my voice echoes off the walls. It's like a cave down here.

"Well we're not going to walk to you dumb ass!"

As I walk down the hallway to the two rats, I nod a good-bye to Tammy.

Con Man

"I'm no dumb ass at all. I've never been here before. How I'm supposed to know what way to go? Have some respect you fat dumb ass rat."

"Well we're going upstairs, turn around so we can put these shackles on your feet." When they get done with the shackles, they put me in handcuffs, in front. We take a set of stairs up. It got two landings I have got to walk up. Then we go through a door at the top, and we're in a long hallway with offices on both sides. I can see rats in all these offices as I walk down the hallway. I'm just following the two rats in front of me. They have their pants pulled up so tight that they are molded to their asses. It looks uncomfortable for real but I'm not going to say anything. These rats will pull you into a cell and jump you. None of them will fight one on one, or at least, that's what I've seen so far.

At the end of this hall is a huge set of bars from floor to ceiling. I can see a rat sitting behind a desk on the other side of the bars. He gets up, comes over, hits a button then the door in front of us slides open.

I step into seg. Above the door is hung a wooden sign with *Segregation* wrote in white paint. It's got to be getting late. I'm hungry as hell and I want to lay down. Although I'm a little keyed up over Megan, I am still ready for my cell.

The rat at the desk tells the two fat rats that just come and got me that "Inmate Smith goes to seg. three, left-cell four."

It doesn't take long to get there. Its downstairs real close. Just though another door that the rat has to use a key to open. Then we're on the seg. three walk. It looks nasty as hell, also it sounds like at least twenty people are yelling at the top of their lungs. The walk smells like tobacco and body odor. I can see 20 cells down

83

the left side, and 20 cells down the right side. The hallway is about eight feet wide but really long. As I walk to my cell, I see that the doors to the cells are bars. I can see right in. Several inmates are wearing blue scrubs like me, but the rest have red scrubs on. Don't know what red means.

Now that we're on the walk, I can hear several convicts scream, *new fish on the walk! Cute and young, new fish on the walk!* Like it's market day at the fish market. I don't say nothing because these are just tests in prison. They try to break a person, but I can't be broke, so I just ignore them and walk to the cell. I won't miss a rec, we'll see if they talk like that out on the walk. The guard unlocks my door with a key then I walk into the cell and it's every bit as Tammy said. The only thing is, I don't think I got any windows left at all. Not to mention it's got to be 130 degrees in here.

The guard slams my door shut and locks it. "I'll bring you your sheets, shit paper and the hygiene products you're allowed in a minute."

"Okay thank you, for nothing at all rat!" I, myself, hate when a fucking rat thinks I'm supposed to be nice, all because he is going to bring me some sheets. I'll be nice if he brings me a joint or a fucking steak meal. After they get on their fucking knees and suck my dick.

They got this syndrome called Stockholm syndrome. It's where a person falls in love with their kidnapers. I don't have that fucking syndrome at all. I don't want to be in prison. I don't give a shit if I did a crime. If all these fucking rats went home, they would have to let me go or put me down. These rats hold me in here, even Megan is a rat truth be told. Either they can be used for something or don't talk to me at all.

I look out the window of my cell. There's a big fence about 30 feet from my window. It has razor wire on the top. Beyond that is just buildings. Don't know what they're for. I don't see the yard that Tammy was talking about.

As I am looking out the window, the rat came back so I turn to see him pushing sheets in my try slot. The front of the cell is just my door that is all bars, and a tray slot is cut out of the middle. I guess the tray slot is there so I could put my hands out in the hallway so the rats can handcuff me, also its and probably where they push my food tray though.

I pick up my sheets from the floor, and he gives me one roll of shit paper, some state toothpaste, and a state toothbrush. Both are crap, but even worse than all this the toothpaste tastes like shit.

Prison gives you nothing at all but cheap stuff; you sit around with nothing. You watch other convicts eat good food they get out of canteen. You watch them use real Crest toothpaste and real soap. They got all kinds of soaps and body washes on canteen. Plus, floss mouthwash, shampoo and deodorant. Prison gives you no deodorant or mouthwash, floss or shampoo. If you want to clean yourself in prison, the message is very clear and simple. Be a bitch and use state soap that is useless or grow a set of nuts and get out there on the yard and get your grind on. Steal out of the kitchen or property room, extort somebody or something. Just don't be a bitch and do without.

Prison makes you mean like that. Every night you smell this good food being cooked in the wing. You're fucking starving your ass off so you can lay there and let your stomach growl. Or you can go be the white piece of trash you are and do something about it. Normally, with me, the white-trash part will win out. That's why

I'm in the hole really, not the hooch or nothing that I did wrong, I'm in the hole because the fucking state tells me I can have crap in the chow hall or fried chicken in the canteen. You tease a pit bull, and it will bite you sooner or later. That's just how life is.

I don't say anything else to the rat. I get my stuff, made my bed with two regular sheets by taking the one sheet and tying it to the other under each corner of the mat. I got a pillow with no pillow case, go figure.

It is so fucking hot. I'm sweating just sitting here, and I'm already bored out of my mind. I get up out of the bed, walk to the door, I see the cell eight feet across me. There is a white dude in there sitting in the middle of his bed just using a book to write his letter on.

"Hey honky, what's your name over there?"

He gets up and takes two steps to the door. He's in red scrubs. He stops and lights up a smoke. It's so damn loud in here I'm surprised, he heard me at all.

Smoking isn't allowed in the hole. Just about every person in prison don't give a shit about rules though. Nobody feels like they got to obey them.

"My name is Carl, yougin, but people call me C.J."

"Well C.J. my name's Crazy. Why do you have red scrubs on? I got blue ones on, why don't you?"

"Red scrubs is for convicts that are part of this yard. When our hole time is up we go back to the yard. Since you're in blue scrubs, after your court call or hole time, you'll go back to R.C.C."

C.J.'s probably in his late twenties, he is a short white guy. I'd put him at 190 pounds but he' got a pot belly. Normally, we don't ask people what their charges are, we don't ask private questions.

You start getting too much into other peoples' business; they start thinking you're a rat or something. Nonetheless, I figure it's safe to ask C.J. about his hole time. Worst case, he just won't answer me. If he was in for something bad, I would have already heard. Cho-mo's and people with bad cases, that shit follows them from the jail. Everyone knows about them before they even hit prison. So just him at his door and nobody is yelling at him "Go sit down cho-mo" so I'm sure it's all good.

"Hey C.J., what you in the hole for? You got a reading book or something to do over there?"

"Crazy, I'll be in the hole for a long time. I got mad in the dorm when the dorm officer said something to me. I didn't like. I guess I just woke up in a bad mood—I was also high as hell on some pain pills. Anyway, I didn't even think about it, I just punched that rat in the mouth. Hell, I figured after I hit him one time the punishment is the same if I keep going, so I just kept beating him up until other officers arrived. Then they sprayed me with mace and dragged me up here to the hole. I was in an assault cell for 30 days. I got one year in the hole. All the rat got was a fat lip. I wish I would've broken his jaw. He is one of them super Ro-bo piece of shits. They never leave a motherfucker alone."

"What is an assault cell?"

"It's a max security cell where it's got another door that shuts over these bars. Really not much of a difference, but there is no window in an assault cell, and it's even hotter than these cells.

"Also yeah, I got some books over here Crazy. They bring a book cart every week, but never know the day or time. Most of the books are trashed from these idiots around here tearing them up. The books I got, I got from the streets. Some people pee or jack off on the books then let it dry after that they will put it right back on the book cart, nasty!"

"Damn C.J., how you get books from out there? Where from? Plus, that is some nasty shit to do. Lots of fucking weird-os"

"I been in six years Crazy; I got me a good hustle going on. I get put on these ads in the Globe magazine, and I get these gay dudes to write me. They are so easy to hustle, I'm telling ya."

"You were so young, for real Crazy, you could kill the game out. Get you an ad out man. There would be a whole lot that would write you."

"How I get an ad C.J.? I don't get money in, what does it cost?"

"I didn't get no money in either, I just kept up a few hustles out there on the yard until I built the money up. It was the best money I ever spent. It's twenty dollars in one week for a small ad with a picture—the picture is the key. And Crazy, I tell you what, I got twenty four fags that wrote me off that first ad. I took them twenty-four and weeded through them. Turned out only six of them were good, willing to send money. So I turned twenty dollars into 600 dollars a month. All six fags send 100 dollars a month. So to keep it real, as far as I'm concerned, this is the best hustle in here. I've been getting 600 dollars a month for five years. The globe won't let you put a picture in, but some sites will. "

"How'd you get a picture?"

"They take pictures on the yard. It cost a dollar for two pictures. When you get wherever you goin' you can get your own took. They take pictures on every yard you go to. It's the same cost everywhere you go."

"Damn that sounds so good to be real, I need to get me a hustle. They got me over here for hooch. I need to change this shit up, but

I'll have to get me some pictures, then I'll need to get the twenty dollars. So really I don't know when I can get that hustle going. I like the sound of it a lot though. Tell me C.J., what you going to do when you get out? I mean you got an out-date, right? I'm not trying to get in your business, I'm just curious, what do you do on your outdate?"

"Well I do got an outdate in a couple more years. I don't care you ask, you seem pretty cool. The thing is though, I'm not gay at all, so when my outdate gets here, I'll try to pull as much money as I can and get money, clothes or whatever. Then when I get out on the streets, I ain't never going to see them or call them that's just life Crazy. I need them right now because I got needs in here, they need me right now also, because they're lonely. Way I see it, it's an equal partnership. They can get mad all they want when I get out but in the end, we both got something out the deal regardless if the fag don't want to see it like that or not. I'm giving these motherfuckers years of love, calling them, writing. The only thing they don't get is the sex, but I give them the rest. It may seem cold to some, but I promise you the only ones it seems cold to is the weak-minded people."

"Yeah, I feel all that C.J. for real, I myself wouldn't give a fuck about the fags' feelings. I only care if he sends me money or not, I just want to survive. I got no issue with being cold hearted to survive, I can tell you right now I wouldn't lose no sleep over it. I just don't know how I'll get it started but good on you for telling me." We both kind of go silent, but I want to keep talking. Before he sits back down, I ask, "Do you know what these buildings are behind me?"

"Yeah, that's the back of the chow hall, the chow hall for the yard. That new building back there is the nut ward, it's where you go if you cut yourself, or if you're crazy. Hold on for a second, I'll get you some books. I got some books from a dude called Dean Koontz, he's pretty good."

He tosses me the books, and I sit them on my bed. It's so hot in here that I'm sweating from head to toe. I hear a loud noise, so I look out the crack of my door, down the hallway the trays are coming. They're sitting on a metal cart with pitchers of juice. I'm hungry as a motherfucker. Thank goodness the food is here.

The next 30 days go by just like that first one. I just walk back and forth in the cell, read different books that I would've never read any other time—it is beyond boring. I can't even explain what it's like to sit in this cell 23 hours a day. It's hot, and the cell is extremely nasty. It is so small that the idea of walking back and forth is funny, but hell what else is there to do? I feel like one of those pet mice in a small cage, but hell I don't even get the wheel to play or jog on.

When I got put in this stupid-ass hole, it seemed to me my mind wasn't so muddy or depressed. Now it seems like this is caving in on me. I've heard of people killing themselves in here. They couldn't handle this. For me, I'm not feeling like none of that at all. I believe only the weak try to kill themselves. I just feel a little loopy is all. This is making me so mad that I start to realize I'm getting even more violent with sitting in this cell like this. My mind seems to be slipping into a world of just hate.

The hole is making my thoughts more violent and I have felt more hate than ever before. Shit just made me angry with the world, at people in general. I guess some people get depressed, I did the opposite and just hate. No human should be locked down like this.

On my eighteenth day, the rats come to get me and take me out to the desk and read me my write-up. It said it is a category six-four, *promoting dangerous contraband.*

The rat told me it holds 90 days in the hole. 90 fucking days is crazy as hell! That sure the fuck don't match on my scale of life. Shit is for sure all the way on the downside. The shit money I had made doing it, all for the risk of 90 days in hell? The only reason why my scale of life isn't all the way in the fucking red zone on the downside is 'cause of the blond angel in the basement.

The sergeant is not helpful on telling me things. He probably hopes that I get convicted on it. He asks me do I want a legal aid for the write-up. It turns out, they got convicts who get hired as a state job to be a legal aid. They help other convicts, or try to help us, beat our write-ups. Turns out though, the fucking legal aid will help you, but if you can't pay him some stamps or something; he won't help you a whole lot. Everything is always about money.

The sergeant asks also if I plead guilty or not, asks if I want to be notified twenty-four hours before I go to court call.

I don't even get a legal aid. I got no money, and I don't know the person. I plead "not guilty," then say I could care less if they tell me before I go to court call or not.

I remember what Tammy told me, so I ask if what they found has it been tested or not. The faggot-ass sergeant tells me he believes it has been tested, that he is pretty sure it came back positive for alcohol. I am sure he is supposed to check this, I just can't get him to do it. He even refuses to put on the write-up that I had asked about if it was tested or not. I tell him three more times to put it down that I want to know if it was tested or not.

I mean the rat asks me do I have a statement I want to put? He's treating this like a real legal case, but the faggot-ass rat won't put down the statement I said. It's all a set up 'cause it's their world. That's not being paranoid either, this rat is setting the write-up, up as he sees fit. For the most part, he just ignores what I ask to be put down.

I figure I'll have to take this up with court call. I'm know they won't believe me that I asked. If he doesn't record it when he reads the write-up to me, I'm sure court call will believe the Sgt. over me.

A week later, they are handcuffing me again, telling me I am going to court call. By this time, I'm ready to just get it over with. In the back of my mind, I know I can't beat it, but I really wish I could. I would love to get sent back to the property room and see Megan again. More important though, maybe Tiny is still at the Fish Tank. If so, I could get the chance to beat him up, get my lick back for him ratting on me; that would be ideal. I would love to see his ratting ass face when I come walking into the pod.

Court call isn't far away, it's in the office right outside the gate that I came through to get to the hole. They sit me on a bench out in front of the court call door. I sit here about an hour. Everything in prison is a fucking waiting game—you'll learn some fucking patience in prison or go mad inside.

When the court call guy finally calls me, I need to take a piss really bad, they won't do shit about it though. When I went into the court-call room, the court-call officer is sitting behind a desk, so I sit in a chair in front of the desk. He doesn't tell me his name, and I don't ask him at all. He just turns on the tape recorder in front of him and asks my name and number. Then he reads off the write-up asks do I have any comments on it or do I just want to plead guilty.

I ask about the hooch, if it has been tested or not. Turns out it was, so I pretty much have nothing else to say. It was found in my locker and it tested positive for alcohol. I just ask him for a punishment that is easy this being my first time, I ask could he show leniency. He tells me to go wait in the hallway again while he makes his decision what to do, took him about twenty minutes.

He did me a favor to be honest. He could have gave me the ninety-day hole time, but he only gives me sixty days with a 180-day loss of good time. That last part hurts some to be honest. My sentence can be killed at six years and six months with all my good time but it will take close to two years of clear conduct to get the 180 days back. I didn't appeal my write-up to the warden, couldn't see the point in it.

After court call, they take me back to my cell. I got thirty days or so left in seg. I can't wait for it to be over. I did smoke on the streets, but so far I've been able to stay away from it since I've come to R.C.C. and now K.S.R. It's hard to smell it all day though but it also has made me realize how bad people stink that smoke.

Ever since I spoke to C.J. about putting out an ad, I've been doing nothing but thinking about it. I just need to get the resources together before I can do anything.

Five days a week, I come out on the walk for my one hour of rec. They give all R.C.C. convicts rec together, normally around ten in the damn morning. It's good to get out though just to walk up and down the longer walk in front of our cells. It gives me a chance to stretch my legs a little. K.S.R. convicts also take rec. together, normally after we're done with our rec. but never at the same time though. They say that's a security issue for us to come out together. I don't at all know why.

On my 40th day, I am out on the walk standing in front of C.J.'s door just talking to him when two black guys I never spoke to before come up to me.

"Hey kracker, why you're standing out here all in a person's way to get up and down the hallway? Why don't you get out the way?" This from the shorter black guy. He is stocky and probably my age. The other one is taller, looks to be around his mid-thirties. He is not real skinny but fit, you could even say cut up some.

In prison, you get tested like this all the time, people always got a motive for why they do it. In my case, it normally 'cause I'm young. They think maybe they can scare me. After that they would offer to protect me if I submit to being their fag or something. It don't matter because calling me kracker is a disrespectful word for a white guy to be called in prison. Real honkies got a saying; honkies *rumble krackers crumble*. I don't crumble at all. Black guys know what the deal is though. So for him to call me a kracker lets me know this short shit thinks I'm easy prey.

"Well let me tell you something little guy, if you would've just asked me to move I would've did that for you. But seeing you're an idiot who doesn't know how to be polite, let me tell you this in a way even you can understand. *You can suck my honky, cracker dick you short shit!*"

The skinny one looks at the short one then gives him a nod, "Well Kracker, why don't you walk up to the top of the walk? Let's walk into the shower, so we can see if you can fight as good as you talk."

I don't comment at all or respond in any way. I just start walking to the top of the walk. The shower is about big as a cell, so plenty of room to get our fight on. I'm the type of guy who understands violence. I understand the pecking order in life, the strong always rule; the weak are the strong ones' flunkies. There is no in between, you either are weak or you are strong. Everybody has a role in life.

As I walk into the shower area, the short shit follows right behind me. The skinny black guy stands at the door, buzzing for the guards for us.

I'm trailer park trash all the way, so if the trailer parks taught me anything, it was to fight very dirty. As soon as the short fuck steps in the shower area I swing at him and land a very nice three piece across his face. It makes him dizzy I can also tell this threw him all the way off.

Black guys always think white guys are scared of them that can be used against them. A cocky person is always easy to surprise.

After the three piece, I come right in with a good upper cut. I'm hoping to end it fast, but he moves really fast and blocks my upper cut. Then he socks me hard in the eye socket. This makes me mad, so I grab him by his blue scrub shirt and throw him against the wall. I then punch him in the jaw with my hardest punch. It lands so well that he slides down the wall and lands on his ass. I can see I knocked the short shit out, but the animal in me comes out, so I take my knee with all my power, I slam it into his mouth. After that, I put my hand on the wall and lean in so I have even more power to slam my knee into his mouth. As soon as the knee connects, I hear several teeth break out plus I see blood squirt out his mouth. This hit wakes him up where he doubles over and coughs as more blood and teeth fall out. I go to kick him in the face—probably wouldn't hurt much with flip-flops on, but I am going to do it anyway—before I connect, the skinny black dude runs in. I get ready to hit him, but he sees it, so really fast he steps out of my range.

"It's over honky, it's nothing personal at all, okay? You got him down now and rec. is over, and I need to get him back to his cell, so we don't get caught."

I'm out of breath any ways. I don't give a shit if it is personal or not, this is what prison is about. I just walk by the skinny fuck, I walk back down the hallway to go to my cell. My eye hurts like hell though. I bet he didn't think this 'easy prey' would knock his damn teeth out. Whatever his plot was I can say for sure he probably now wishes he didn't try it on me.

Chapter 8

PINK PALACE

In the beginner's mind there are many possibilities,
but in the experts mind there are few. —Shunryu Suzuki

My entire eye turned black and blue. I am glad it is a convict who passes out the food trays. When I went to the shower I just threw my towel over my head so the guard couldn't see my eye.

The good thing is I already got my write up all handled, so I don't need to see a guard for anyone, my eye should heal before they see it. It would be my luck that Megan would pick this time to have me brought to the property room. If that happens at all, every guard from here to there will see it. I'd probably get another write up. Probably a fighting write up. I don't want no write up or any more hole time, but if I do get more time, I really don't give a fuck. It is what it is, shit isn't going to break me one way or the other.

I've been on rec already twice with the two black dudes again. They don't even talk to me at all now. The short black guy's mouth looked real swollen. I hope he is in a lot of pain. I thought about calling him out, go round two in the shower. The only reason I don't is because I got to get out of this damn hole. We got lucky to get away with it the first time.

This hole is so fucking boring, not a thing at all to do. Plus, I got no way to make money in this hole. At least, I can't see a way at all. Making money is really the only reason I want out of here. I'm just doing dead time in this hole. I refuse to bury myself in here with a ton of hole time.

On my 50th day in the hole, my caseworker from R.C.C. woke me up about eight in the morning. It is some old guy, who has a smart ass mouth; they call him Mr. Rens. I don't usually stop him to talk, or ask him any questions. Everything that comes out of his mouth is something slick. I have convinced myself that Mr. Rens won't be happy at all until somebody smacks him in his old-ass mouth, I know he needs it really bad.

"Inmate 142586 come up to your door now!" No one calls me by my prison number. Mr. Rens likes to do it because it's his way of trying to remind you of your status in life. He's a disrespectful old fuck. I realize though, he is just trying to trick my time off. Don't matter, I still bite every time, can't help it.

"My name is Rick or Smith Mr. Rens, not 142586 or none of the other shit you going to say. Understand that old man?"

"Just come to your door, so I can re-class you 142586. This takes like two minutes."

I walk up to the door in my boxers; it's hot as hell in here still. There is no way to sleep or lay down in your seg. pants or shirt on.

I look Mr. Rens dead in the eyes, "My name is Rick or Smith, old man. You want to make this hard? Then you keep calling me out my name, then I promise you this will take longer than two minutes."

I know I got no win. I just enjoy trying to pull their hold card. I like to bluff my way through certain things. If Mr. Rens pushes the issue, I can fight him or for sure cuss him out, possibly even hit him threw the bars. All that though would cost me years in the hole. I'm not trying to do that. So I'll try to make him believe I am willing to do it. Try to bluff my way through it. Try to make him respect me by fearing me.

"Look Inmate, you got over half your hole time in. I'm going to put you in for a new prison. You could come back to R.C.C. at the end of your hole time, or you could be moved to the new prison this week. After this re-class you could leave any day.

"So if you want to stay in here, I can leave then we can do this at another time. So what you want to do Inmate Smith?" The old fuck is doing what I'm doing.

At least calling me inmate is acknowledging I am a person, not a set of numbers or a prison number—it's not the best, but it's some improvement. It's a small win for real, but I'll take whatever win I can get, calling me Smith is a huge win with this old fuck.

"Okay Mr. Rens what would you like me to do?" I'm ready to get myself re-classed, I sure the hell want out of here.

"Well, here's the deal, you could have went to A-Lower custody prison, probably a camp or class D jail. You ruined that with this category, six write up you got. To go behind the fence, you need a score of ten or above. You had a score of a two because your age, then you got four points because your felon charges, that all put your at a custody score at six. The write up you got gave you five points, which put you at a custody score of eleven. If you'll do two years clear you can get the category six write up off your record, then the five points come off also. You understand all that inmate?"

"Yes I get all that, old-ass man," I say in a growl. He's back to "inmate" and he's pissing me off.

"Well since you got to go behind the fence, I'm putting you in for Eastern Kentucky Correctional Complex. You'll probably go real soon, they always need the bed space over here in the hole…inmate."

He does that shit to make a person cuss his old ass out, you got some weird-ass people in here. Some of these fucked-up case workers or guards, it seems they enjoy to be mistreated. It's like anybody can see that you can get along or make shit hard for no reason but you're a fucking weird-o that enjoys to be handled rough.

"So sign this re-class form, then we are all done here inmate, we can get you sent where you need to go."

"Yeah, yeah old man!" I sign the form, he grabs it really fast then he walks off the walk. I'm just glad he is gone to be honest, much more of that I might have lost my cool.

"Man, Crazy, I don't see how you deal with that old ass caseworker!"

"Hell, C.J., I don't have any choice but to deal with him. It's not like they are going to send me somebody all for just me. I bite my tongue, I listen to him, but not really at all paying him any attention. The truth is I can deal with his mouth, I grew up around old white trash that got drunk all day. By night time or late in the afternoon they already halfway drunk or all the way drunk. They are so old with so much hate at the whole world, so they run their mouth at everybody that walks by their porch. They mad 'cause they done got old all by themselves with no one to love them so they turned bitter. It's not his mouth that gets on my nerves, it's how he comes off that not only he feels he is better than us but I also get the feeling he hates me all 'cause we are convicts. I mean who is this old fuck to judge me? Plus, if he hates a person so bad he should go get another job, do us all the favor and die or quit."

"Without a doubt Crazy, you can tell that old fuck don't like us at all. I'm just glad I don't have to deal with him. I feel like I'd probably cuss him out. Then I'd fuck around get more hole time. I'm not going to catch hole time for stupid shit. I get a write up, it'll be for hitting him."

"I don't let them win at all, C.J., I can see that old fuck don't like us. So you don't think it makes his day to see you lose your cool, to see you go off to the point he gets to fuck with your day more? That motherfucker loves that shit, I refuse to let him get me like that. I just smile in his face and ignore his old ass. I feel that kills him inside. That is why I bite a little, but never a big enough bite were it would make his day."

"Yeah, that probably gets under his skin pretty bad Crazy, he's trying to set you off, you over their smiling in his face...ha ha ha!

"So where did they put you in for Crazy?"

"The old fuck said I'll be going to Eastern Kentucky Correctional Complex. You know anything at all about that prison C.J? Have you been there at all?"

"I've never been there. I know that, they nicknamed it the Pink Palace. For the most part, they send all young guys there. Really, I should say that is where they send mostly all young gang bangers. Tons of fights, it's off the hook is what I hear. Don't know why it's called Pink Palace though."

"Well he said I could go any day at any moment. So however it is at the new prison, it's got to be better than this hole. It sure the fuck will be better if they got air conditioning in the rooms there. I'm sick of feeling like I'm in an oven cooking slowly."

"Well Crazy, you kind of made your hole time worse than it should be. You could have got high a couple times off pain pills. Plus there is a ton of sleeping pills just being given away. You refused to accept anything."

"I like getting high just like the next person C.J but I'm not going to do it unless I can pay my way. I don't want nobody coming at me right now or down the road with the attitude that they gave me something for free so I should hook them up. I prefer staying on neutral level with everybody. I don't plan to always be broke C.J, I'll find a way in a hustle or con I am good at. When I do find my way in, I'll not look back C.J. I'm no fool though, I realize people will have all kinds of game when I start to hit. I figure I can kill all the game right now by the very choices I make." We're screaming back and forth to each other because it's already loud as fuck on the walk. C.J. isn't but eight feet from me, but sounds like he is a football field away. In addition, my voice gets hoarse yelling like this all the time.

"Yea I feel that Crazy but I'm not on no game at all. I swear the times I wanted to get high with you; it was all the way because I don't like to get high all by myself. It's a lot better if we get high together, then we can stay up and rec. off each other."

"I get all that C.J., but I just follow a code I set up for myself. It's nothing against you or anyone. It just makes things less compli- cated, if I cannot pay, then I don't do it, plain and simple honky. I don't break from this rule at all C.J., not for friends or nobody. People will respect you better if they see you aren't easily misled. I don't follow other people's ideas at all, unless they can prove to me that my idea could use work. It is what it is, no matter what, I just like to pay my way on the things I get."

If I have to be truthful with myself, it's also because I've heard rumors on the walk that C.J. had a sissy live in his cell out on the yard. Now, they can up and move anybody in a cell with you. They won't mix colors or gangs but everything else is fair game. The thing is though, you don't have to let them stay in the cell with you. They put a sissy in your cell you give that sissy a choice to pack up, get out the cell, and you don't care where he goes. He just got to go, or you'll beat him up. Maybe you even make your point with a hard smack across his face. The word is that C.J lived with this sissy for over a year and a half.

I myself have no issues with sissy's, blacks, Mexicans or anybody. It's just that prison rules are so tight, one wrong choice you can lose all your respect in here. When you lose respect in prison, there is no way at all to get it back. Prison is fucked up like that. You can hold it down for ten years, but make one wrong choice; you will lose that whole ten years you built and earned. You have got to stay on your toes every moment in here. This is our world of prison code.

If a black person, sissy, or Mexican moves in your cell, it dosen't matter that it's unfair, it don't matter you going up for the parole board next month. Nothing at all matters but that moment. The choice you make at that moment will decide if the sharks stay off you in here. You can either move that person, but that is taking the chance of messing up your parole; on the other hand, you let them stay in your cell and the 500 sharks on the yard will mark you as a sissy lover, niger lover, or wet back lover. All extremely bad names to have in prison for a white guy. So all that to say, I ain't getting high with C.J. because I don't want to fuck with my own reputation. Shit is just crazy like that. Rumors will fly and people love to gossip in here, if C.J. loves sissy and where I'm young, people will try to make something into that. I don't really care, but I'm not trying to deal with it.

Well, I hear all the time from C.J and other buddies of mine, how their people on the streets don't understand. I'm so glad I got nobody on the outside because I wouldn't even know how to explain this world to them. How do you describe hell to a person that has never been to hell? No amount of talking could make them get it. No amount of talking can get them to see the fucked-up choices we have to make every day in here. No matter what you do to explain to your loved ones that you're doing your best, they'll never get or understand the cost a prisoner has to pay to do well. In here, you can be coming back from the chow hall or church, and somebody gets it in their mind that they love how you walk or talk. They love how cute you are or young you are, so they got to have you at any cost, that's how they start to think. They might have life in prison, nothing to lose, so they roll up on you and try to rape you. To get this to stop you break the guy's jaw maybe it's even an accident. Just trying to get him off you.

Well, you can't tell the guards he tried to rape you, if you tell the guards you can't go back to any yard at all because, then you're a rat. So you look like a troublemaker who assaulted another inmate. Not only did you assault him, you broke his jaw. Your people on the streets are all baffled. They jump all over you with bullshit like how you must not want to come home, or you would stay out of trouble. They just don't get it at all.

Your people don't realize you almost got raped, now you got to listen to them bitch at you about how they should leave you, and you can't even tell your people what happen. The fucking internal affair's guards read all outgoing mail and incoming mail so you bring it up in a letter, internal affairs will copy it then go lock that other guy up and use your letter as evidence to convict him. Then you are still known as a rat on any yard. Then you'll never stop fighting with that name on you, and you will never stay out of trouble. Everything is like a domino effect in here, and you knock one over you can believe more will fall also.

How do you explain to somebody on the streets, that a guy tried to rape you so you broke his jaw? Then you had to do the convict thing and not tell on it? That it's just another day in your world?

Most people on the streets are cool with ratting or telling on whatever they see that is against the law. Hell some people won't have shit to do with what they seen but they'll still break their leg trying to give their story to the cops. How do you explain your world in prison to people that live like that? That everything they know and think is right, in prison all that shit would get them stabbed or killed. There is no hiding or going home after you rat in here. There is no escape or running. Each choice you make you face the wrath if it goes against prison code. Your people, regardless if they do or don't understand, will either accept it or not. But only real men survive in prison. If your people are real, they won't need much of an explanation. Real never needs hardly anything at all. That's why finding real-ass people is so hard.

About a week later, I am almost done with my hole time, and I'm starting to think I'm going back to R.C.C. When on a Tuesday, about four in the morning—early as a motherfucker—the rats are beating at my door. Yelling at me to pack my stuff up and get changed out in an orange jumpsuit they brought. I don't know what it is about rats always moving us at the butt crack of dawn.

They must have my size wrote down somewhere 'cause, they got the size of this orange suit right. I probably got it wrote down in the laundry room. I know every time I take a shower, they got a clean blue scrub outfit for me, and it's always my size, so I'm sure they wrote it down the first day I got here. I wish that bitch Megan would've come got me again but fuck her.

At any rate, all I have to do is put the jumpsuit on. I had nothing in my cell but books that belong to C.J. I have not been to the store since I've been here. I don't really have anything and don't need anything. (Some deodorant would've been nice I guess. For sure in this hot-ass hole.)

I throw my sheets out in the hallway then I throw my blue scrubs out in the hallway. Not like I'm going to take any of that shit with me. I look over in C.J.'s cell, see he's asleep, but I yell his name to wake him up. I'll be glad to get away from his dumb ass.

C.J. is a hard sleeper, it has always annoyed me that some people can sleep without a care. I don't dream or sleep hard; I used to think something was wrong with me. I'll probably wake the whole walk just to get him up. Not that I care about these cock suckers considering the millions of times they woke me up in here.

As I get older, I realize my thought process is completely different than everybody around me. It took me all the way to when I got to the fish tank for me to learn this. It's not that I'm a dreamer; it's not that I live on a cloud of hope that someday it will all be better. It's just I refuse to settle for less in life. Some people take what they get but I know I can walk away from anything, no matter how much it hurts me, if it isn't best. It's not that I'm cruel or mean or cold hearted. I just want only the best or nothing.

Most people seem to live in the moment, seem to be caught up in what they can get right now rather than getting something better in the future. I am hard wired to always play the long game. I only accept strong people in my life. I push people to their highest potential. They can let me take them there, or I'll ditch them, or they may ditch me.

I have no time for the weak. Weak people, in my honest opinion, can't love the way a person needs to be loved. They're weak in the mind. So the first sign of struggle, what do you think a weak person is going to do? People seem not to see this, or they live in the moment like I said. So rather than see the person they are falling in love with as weak and not at all a keeper, they only see what they want. They only see the person makes them feel good right now.

For me, it's like I am gifted. The veil is lifted away from my eyes, so I see people for who they are. I understand I'll live an antisocial life, a hard life. For me, I'd rather live lonely looking for that one right lover, that one best friend instead of having tons of fake people around me. People that want something, the kind of people I'll invest time and feelings on, but will be gone in a few years. Those people are weak in the mind. That is what weak people do.

I know with certainty that someday I will meet that gangsta chick that thinks and acts like me. And I know the moment will only happen once. I need to be ready and available when it happens, so it don't pass me all the way up. I know for a fact my Bonnie is out there. I'll find her at the right moment.

C. J finally wakes up after I yell at him 25 times. "Yeah, Crazy what you want dog? Why you wake me up Crazy?" he says with his eyes barely open.

"Damn C.J, I have been yellin' at you for twenty minutes. I wanted to give you, your books back. You want these books back don't you?"

"Damn Crazy, you could have just thrown them on my floor. I hate being woken up in here. Hell, the rat would have put them on my bars if you asked him."

"Yeah well you are up now so come up here and get them. I'm sure as hell not going to ask no rat, so fuck that cop out there honky." C. J came up and got the books then went right back to the bed closed his eyes, went back to sleep. No good bye or none of that. That is how it is in here.

Can't blame him though, every time you act nice in here somebody tries to play on it. You learn to be tough no matter if you want to be or not. That's another thing people on the streets don't understand. How are you going to get rehabilitated if you're surrounded by guards who hate you and convicts that only understand being mean and violent? Somewhere in all this madness I'm going to get better? Right.

It takes over an hour for the rats to come back to get me. It is the same routine they did from R.C.C. to over here, put the black box and all the silver on my wrists then ankles. Walking is a slow process with all this on.

It turns out Megan isn't in the property room when we make it down there. Her shift doesn't start till 8am. There are about 15 of us all down here ready to go, some from the yard and some were from the fish tank like me. We all are dressed out in orange jumpsuits. I look around at the other faces, searching but no bitch-ass Tiny.

The people that are from K.S.R. have TVs and more property. It is already sitting out here in the hallway. So I figure they must've got all this ready last night for them. I hate that I won't be seeing Megan again. It's part of it though.

They feed us breakfast down here in the basement in brown paper sacks. Two small nasty bologna sandwiches with an almost rotten apple. Not a thing to drink with it; no mustard or anything for the sandwich. Shit sucks!

They loaded us all on a big bus. Just the same as the Grey Goose. The ride takes almost six hours to get to the Pink Palace. It sucks to see the world through a prison bus window. All the fast-food places, people coming and going. None of them ever have to see the world how I have had to see it. We drive up a huge mountain for two hours. When we pull around the last corner, I get my first look at the Pink Palace.

Chapter 9

MY FIRST REAL TASTE OF MY CON COMING OUT

No one can make you feel inferior without your consent.
—Eleanor Roosevelt

My first thought when I see the Pink Palace is; *it's not fucking pink at all*. Kind of funny now I think about it. It's just, for some reason, it was all set in my mind to see a prison painted pink. Turns out it's the same dull grey that all prisons use, all concrete with prison looking windows. Depressing, in no shape form or fashion can anyone in their right mind say that they enjoyed being at any prison.

R.C.C. and K.S.R. has two fences going around it with guard towers every 200 feet or so. Although some of the towers are way further apart than a football field or two. All prisons in Kentucky are small compared with other states. Other states hold five thousand to eight thousand convicts in one prison. Pink Palace is one of the biggest prisons in Kentucky, and it holds around two thousand people.

I get my shackles and my handcuffs taken off. After that I'm sent to go get my state issued stuff. Since I came from the fish tank, I get a new net bag, new state clothes, socks, boxers, and a pair of state boots. They gave me four long sleeve khaki state shirts with my name and prison number on them and four pair of pants, and I also got four short-sleeve shirts. All khaki clothes that they printed my name on a white cloth tag, they used a machine to hot press the piece of cloth onto the khaki. It reads on my tags, R. Smith 142586. All I did was my hole time at K.S.R. but like C.J said, I am still R.C.C. Now that I have gotten here I am considered an official convict of the system. My time starts now.

It's at this point that I learn why they call it the Pink Palace; these socks and boxers are dyed pink! I don't have a clue why. I just know I'm now the owner of ten pairs of boxers and socks, which are solid pink. This is why it's called the Pink Palace, turns out, they have been passing out pink stuff for a very long time. If you want regular white socks and t-shirts you got to buy them with your own money.

The rats also give me a bed roll, it has two sheets with a wool blanket in it. The wool blanket I hate really bad, it scratches my skin. I know they have real blankets you can buy on canteen of any kind you want. They just can't be black or blue for "security reasons." They say those colors match the rats' uniforms, and they're scared we'll use the material to sew a fake guard uniform. I don't know how yet, but I plan to get a real blanket the first chance I get. Fuck this dumb-ass wool blanket. I wouldn't let my dog lay on this uncomfortable blanket. I'm going to get a real blanket off the top. I don't give a damn if I got to take it from a motherfucker, I'm going to get one, one way or another.

This place is all two-man cells. I don't have a clue who my cell mate is yet. I just know if it's the wrong guy I'll be in the hole or he will be by the end of the night. I would like to go lay down in my bed, just relax for a few hours after that long bus drive. Nonetheless, there is no relaxing in prison. I got to do what I got to do if they put me in a cell with the wrong person. That's just part of the world I am in now. These guards know what's up, they probably pick a bad cell mate for us, so they can get a good laugh at us when we walk in that cell.

After they give me all my khaki clothes, they make me put one of my khaki outfits on with my black state boots. They have to be the thinnest pair of boots I've ever seen in my life. They are better then flip-flops though. We can buy nice tennis shoes, but my list of things I can't buy is way past the limit of anything close at all to what I can afford at the moment.

When I'm done putting my clothes on, they make me put everything else they gave me in this all-white net bag. They also give me two rolls of toilet paper, two-state razors, state soap, a small-ass state tooth brush, and some state tooth paste. I can't wait to hustle up some new hygiene. I get it all in the net bag easy, then they have me go out to a bigger room that has a bench up against the wall. The rats just tell me to come out here, they don't tell me what I'm doing out here though. Every process in prison has always got several convicts involved in it, or going through it with you. The rats always expect us to just follow each other. They figure each convict will explain what is going on. They do this because the rats are lazy and stupid. They find it too much work to keep explaining to each convict what to do, or what to do next. So they rely on us to take care of each other like a herd of cows following the other cows.

This is another fucked-up thing about prison. If someone is anti-social like I am or hated by other convicts and don't want to ask or the others don't want to tell what's going on, what's next, then? I could just say fuck this area I'm in, just wonder off to another area. Then the rats would lock me up in the hole for being in a restricted area. It would be their fault because they should have told me what to do, but at court call the rat would lie and say he did tell me what to do. Only to cover his ass, so he don't get into any trouble. It don't matter that he is lying on you. It don't matter his lie will get you convicted, and nor does it matter that you would probably get hole time. All that matters to the rat is that he keeps his job. So on paper it's got to say he was doing his job; that he told me what to do, but I ignored him. Being the criminal I am. God forbid the rat lose his job. With no doubt that most rats have no other life at all but this.

It turns out they got us in this area to see a caseworker. I guess I will learn who my new cell mate's going to be. I'm not sure why we are seeing the case worker for real. I just heard a few guys saying this is where we see our caseworker. It takes about two hours for a male caseworker to call my name. I am hoping this is fast. That all this is about is to tell me who my cell mate is and where I'll be staying.

I'm getting upset to be honest. It was a long-ass bus ride, then getting me all changed out, now two hours to see the case worker. It is almost one in the afternoon. They have not fed us since this morning! I hate asking the rats for anything; they know they haven't fed us lunch yet. They just want a person to ask. I'm not asking them for shit! I get to the point I feel I need to ask, I will just clock all the way out on them. Start cussing at them, or anything to piss them off. That's how they expect us to act. Most times it feels like you can't get anything done until you behave like that, at least show them you can act like an animal from time to time. That way when you are being good, they reward you because they remember your bad side, see? Everything is a con in prison or some kind of game.

I walk into the caseworker's office. It has room in here for three caseworkers, there's only two caseworkers though. Each caseworker has a desk on both side of the room. A guy in his early forties is the one that called me. The other case worker is a female about sixty years old, maybe older.

I walk over to my caseworker's desk, I sit down in the chair facing him. The chair is on the side of his desk.

"Hello Mr. Smith how are you doing today?"

"Well I got to tell you I haven't been in the system that long, but you have to be the politest person I've met so far. Come to think of it I don't think any rat, caseworker or any staff member has ever asked me how I am doing. You make me a little paranoid, caseworker."

"Mr. Smith I try to be professional as I can, I try to treat people how I would like to be treated."

"Well that is a good motto to go by, I guess, I got a few mottos myself. Not the place for that though, maybe another time down the road. I am doing really well considering my current situation, I am in. How about yourself? How you doing with seeing us convicts all day long? You got a name or will caseworker be okay?"

"You can call me Tony. You don't have to keep calling me case-worker. As to your question though, I have been working here going on about four years. You pretty much got to reteach yourself all new social skills with the kind of environment we're in. But I keep in pretty good spirits. I used to be an addict, Mr. Smith. Fortunately, I cleaned my life up before I got into some serious trouble. I'm grateful for that every day. I try not to judge or get upset at this job or what comes through that door. Part of being a recovering addict is that I realize it could have been me wearing those khaki clothes you're wearing. It could have been me coming through that door."

"I can for sure understand that Tony, I got to say that I admire you a lot. I wouldn't want to be up in here if I got myself together. Working around mostly ass holes seems depressing."

"Well it's just a job Mr. Smith, had to get one somewhere. I honestly want to help and be around people that are like me. I hope my words will help somebody, hopefully through me, people can see it is possible to change. So let me get to this, I have a few standard questions I have to ask you. First, I need to ask you do you have any conflicts on this yard; anybody that you can't be in a cell with. Either because there will be an issue or whatever? Do you have any issue you want to tell me about?"

"I got no conflicts with anyone Tony, I can be put in any cell you want to put me in. I'm not a gang drop out. I get along with everybody."

"How about protective custody? Do you feel you need to be put in the hole, for us to assign you to a protective custody unit Mr. Smith?"

"I don't need any type of protection at all Tony, I won't never be a damn check-in, I'd rather take any type of ass kicking than be a piece of shit, you don't never got to worry about me asking for safety."

"These are just standard questions that I have to ask you Mr. Smith, there is no need to get upset. I have to ask you this to save the prison any type of legal liability. If you went to the yard, then got hurt the first day out there, you can't sue the prison because they set these questions up to cover themselves. You see what I'm saying?"

"Yeah, I see exactly what you are saying Tony. I realize you got to do your job. I'm not upset at all, promise. It is what it is."

"Well I just got one more question Mr. Smith, after that you sign these forms, then we are done with all that okay?"

"Alright, it's all good then. What's your last question Tony?"

"I need to know if you're having any type of suicidal thoughts. Do you feel like hurting yourself Mr. Smith?"

"Those are actually two questions Tony, but it's all good. I don't never feel like committing suicide, or hurting myself. That shit is for the weak people that can't cope with shit around them. I'm doing wonderful inside. I am not even 20 years old yet, I only got a ten-year prison sentence. My life isn't sad enough yet to want to kill myself. Let's hope it never gets sad enough for none of that. All of it goes against every thought I've got about a person being a man or a strong male."

"Okay I understand all that Mr. Smith. I just need you to sign this form showing I asked you these questions, saying you acknowledge them. That you understand them all and I have fully explained it all to you."

I sign the form without looking at the page. Normally, I read every form that is put in front of me. It's just always best to read everything before you sign it. I didn't do this with Tony, mainly because I can judge people very well. Tony isn't trying to dick me around at all. It's not because of him being nice, lots of people you meet are nice, but you got to watch your ass around them even more closely than the ones that are mean. I knew Tony's not trying to dick me around by the vibe I feel. The way he talks and acts towards me. It's a gift I have had since I was little; reading people. So, I trust my gut instincts before anything.

"If I may add something Mr. Smith, you seem to have a very good head on your shoulders. I have seen thousands of kids your age come through here. They catch more prison time out there on the yard. They allow the prison system to make them worse and allow their anger to win. I am not trying to preach to you Mr. Smith, I'm only trying to tell you to go out on the yard, and just do your time as positively as you can. Don't allow the time to do you. Try to get your G.E.D, take advantage of some of the programs they have here."

"Okay Tony, I hear what you're saying. I'm thankful somebody is trying to keep it real with me. I can't say I'll go out there doing programs or working on a G.E.D. All I can say, to keep it real, is I will try it, is the best I can offer. I doubt I'm in the mind frame to be a good boy."

"Let me put it like this, most inmates tell me to kiss their ass, or they tell me whatever I want to hear or rather what they think I want to hear. You are probably one of the few people that didn't do either two things, and I respect that."

"I always try to keep it real Tony, I can't tell you how many times being real has made me speak too blunt towards people. Then they dislike me for it, but that is just a part of who I am. I don't tell people what they want to hear, I tell people what they need to hear regardless of the cost. I tell it to a person the way it needs to be told, no sugar or cream in my words Tony."

"Ha ha ha, I like that Mr. Smith, more people should be like you. Before you go, I forgot to ask you your religion. Do you have a preferred religion that requires you to get any type of special meals? Jewish or Muslim for instance?"

"I don't have any religion at all so just put me down for the regular tray they serve."

"Alright then, that's really all there is this time. You are going to Dorm-2, A-walk, upper floor. You will be in cell 3, in the upper bunk."

"Okay then Tony, I'm out of here right? I just walk to dorm 2 from here?"

"That's correct. I'm your caseworker for Dorm 2, so if you have any more questions down the road you can come ask me. I'm here Mon.—Fri. And always on first shift." I stand, ready to head to my new cell. "I almost forgot, do you have anyone you want to put on your visit list?"

"I got nobody in the world that loves me Tony. I get no visits or phone calls, so stuff should be simple with me. I probably won't need nothing else."

"Be careful with yourself out there. It is easy to get in trouble on the yard, the hard part is staying out of trouble. Don't take the easy road." The whole time I've been talking to Tony I forgot my hunger and just how tired I am. So Tony for a rat isn't that bad a person to talk to.

As I walk out the door, I notice some white guy with a lot of ink work on him looking at me. I play like I don't see it and walk

out the caseworkers' office then turn left to head to the door I have seen other convicts going to when they come off the yard. Before I can make it to the door, the guy who was looking at me runs up to me. I get a bad vibe from him, so I set my net bag down on the floor. I want my hands free if he swings on me.

"Hey, why the hell was you up in that caseworker's office so long? You're in there laughing with him and shit. That caseworker has like three questions he asks everybody then you sign a form and you out of there. What is your issue?"

"Hmm, well I don't got a clue who the hell you are. It don't matter though, for real. Last time I checked, I am a grown-ass man, and I don't answer to you or nobody else. What I do with my time is my business."

"I'll tell you like this, they call me Tat out here on the yard. You better ask a person about me. My reputation speaks for itself, so don't come up in here on your first day with that smart-ass mouth of yours. You young punk! Now let me make this clear with you. The last thing you want youngin is to get me mad or your whole time here is going to be terrible. "

"Okay, here is how it's going to be then, now you done went way too far, I don't let nobody disrespected me. They are moving me to dorm -2 A walk upper. Where you live at Tat?"

"I live exactly on the same walk as you do it seems."

"Well isn't that something? They call me Crazy and I'm going to walk my bag to my cell. You tell me your cell so after I sit my bag down, I'll come to your cell. I'll be happy to show you what a young punk can do his first day here other than run his mouth like you doing. How does that sound for you?" I say staring him dead in the eye.

"Okay fuck it Crazy! I live in cell 7 towards the back. I'll be back over there in just a minute. Then we will see what you all about."

I say nothing else at all to him. I just pick my bag up, turn around and walk to the dorm I am going to live in. I find it a strange a guy on my new walk, that don't even know me, just happens to be down here in the case worker area. Just happens to start shit with me the moment I show up. There are no coincidences in prison. There is a motive for why he's doing what he's doing.

People test you all the time in prison for different reasons. Generally, it's either to try to turn you out or try to extort you. Even if you don't get money in from the streets. It don't matter because they'll make you go to work in the kitchen at $60 a month. Then, they'll extort that from you every state payday. Hell, they may have ten people in the kitchen they're doing that too, so it adds up for them. I don't knock any hustle at all, but that don't mean I'll let it be done to me.

I don't hate the game at all. I respect most hustles. Even when it is tried on me, I still respect it, mainly because when it's tried on me. It gives me the chance to learn it. How can you learn anything in a better way than actually going though it on the front lines?

The key to all game in prison is fighting. Convicts only understand violence. If you won't fight, then you're weak. If you're weak they feel like they can do anything they want to you. There isn't mommy or daddy in prison, nobody to rescue you at all. You want something negative to stop? You got to fight the person that's doing it to you to end it. You really need to fight him before you allow the negative things to happen.

If you let a person extort you one time, or fuck you in the ass one time, or suck a dick one time out of fear, there is no taking any of that back, ever! If you fuck up under pressure, decide to do what they ask and then decide to fight afterwards, it's too late because your problem isn't only with them guys who tried something on you anymore. The whole yard views you as weak just off that one time. Now every person on the yard will give you hell. There is no grey area in prison, there is only the weak and the strong. You have no choice but to show out right where it all starts. Either that or your life is going to become pure hell in prison. If you can't handle that, the option to kill your weak self is always on the table.

I make it to dorm two. Wasn't that far away at all, just down a sidewalk. Turns out they built dorms on top of dorms here, so dorm one is below and dorm two is stacked right on top of it. I walked passed dorm three and four on my way. There is a total of nine, another five dorms on the other side of the prison. I heard dorm five is the hole though, and dorm nine is also a segregation unit. Dorm nine though is somewhere off by itself, and they mostly put check-ins there. They're too weak for the yard. Too weak to kill themselves, so they just sit in the hole looking really stupid.

I had to walk up two huge flights of steps to get up to dorm two. At the top is a small walkway that has a fence all around it from top to bottom. I figure the fence is here so you can't throw anybody off from up here. I say 'figure' cause it's unlike the rats to care but they no doubt did it to save themselves a lawsuit against somebody.

All the dorms are built like this where they are attached to each other. The way it's built, makes the place look a lot smaller than what it is. Just looks like four tall dorms, and that's it. They say the other hole, dorm nine, is all the way on the other side of the prison.

As I walk into the dorm, I can see that the dorm is shaped like a circle. R.C.C. has a tower in the middle but this tower here has glass windows all the way around it. About 20ft off the ground, I can see a rat inside the tower. What isn't glass, is white concrete bricks that go from the floor all the way up about 20ft until it meets the glass. There is no way to get inside the tower but through a locked door in the corner of the main core, out here in the circle when you first enter the dorm. Furthermore, the glass going around the tower from the 20 ft., it goes from there to the roof and the rat can see everything.

There are four wings on the bottom floor with a set of short stairs that land you on a second floor. The second floor has a walkway that wraps half way around on both sides of the dorm. I can see into all the wings because the walls where you enter A-wing is all Plexiglas, also the wing's doors are also. I can see a room in between the wings that looks like a laundry. The four wings on the bottom are referred to as "A-wing" to "D-wing". The upper ones are called "A-upper" through "D-upper". A total of eight wings also the Plexiglas going around the guard tower, the wing doors, and the wing walls that allow the tower to see right into the wings. All of the Plexiglas they say can't be broken at all, in no kind of way, but I don't think nobody is for sure 100% on that.

When I walk in the dorm, I notice several convicts' playing cards. They're at tables that are in the center part of this circle, the core as we like to call it. The core is in the middle next to the tower. You walk down four steps to the core where there are four tables you can play cards at. The tower can still see the tables though. You ain't never out of the rats eyes. Unless you go inside a cell. There are 16 cells on every walk, as you can guess one rat has no way to watch it all. Anything you can think of goes down in the cells. There is also another guard other than the rat inside the tower. We call him the floor guard or flout guard. He is supposed to do rounds every so often, but they never do it until they feel like it. Always the buzz man watches for him and sends the word if the rat comes near the wing.

I notice between A-wing and B-wing there are a couple of offices that look like more than guards' offices. It seems somebody else has an office in this dorm. I'll find out who later, provided I'm not in the hole.

I don't say anything to nobody at all. I just walk over to the office I seen in the corner between A-B wing. One out of the two offices a rat is sitting in. I get my key to my cell and sign a paper saying if I lose the key, I owe 30 dollars. All the doors here are open by a key only. After that I head back over to A-wing then walk up the short set of stairs and go into the wing of my new home. I notice a TV room to my left, and at first I had thought that this was a laundry room. It's about the size of a small bathroom. I can hear the TV blasting out here in the hall way. Up against the wall near the first cell, is a blue telephone we use. I don't use the telephone so it don't matter to me at all. I have nothing on the streets. I don't even exist but for the state issued prison number I have been given.

Between the telephone and the TV room door, there are two small doors. I guess that's got to be the restroom, so I walk in the first door. It turns out that both are the showers for the walk, just two single showers for the whole walk. At least, it's not open shower no more, got a real shower curtain to them also. Haven't seen a shower curtain in almost a year, or close to a year anyway.

I get to my cell, stick the key in the door, and it pops open really easy. When I walk inside I realize the fucking toilet is in the damn cell. The room is like the size of a small bathroom itself. It's going to be a real bitch to take a shit with a cell mate two feet away. Real nice huh? If that isn't bad enough next to the toilet is a sink so I need to wash up in front of him too.

My cell mate is laying in his bed, just looking around at nothing. I get the feeling he has been waiting on me. He is acting or at least, that's how I take it. Don't hurt to be a little paranoid around this fucking place. I don't have friends here. The first thought that comes to me is maybe Tat has something either worked out with this guy or they just friends. Either way I needed to find out if my cell mate is with me or against me. Where I grew up in Ohio, I don't know a single person down here. So I got to pave my roads fast cause, I am on my own.

My cell mate is young like me. He looks close to my height, just a little bigger than me, not in a fat way, but just looks like he has more weight on him than me. He has blonde hair; I could also see that he has a tear drop tattooed right below his left eye. The tear drop is not colored in.

"What's your name honky?" I start out as polite as I know how.

"They call me Justin. I don't got no nickname or none of that. What's your name?"

"They call me Crazy, Justin. My real name is Rick, but really I don't have an issue with which one you call me."

"Well, I'll just call you Crazy, that's pretty simple to remember. Did you just come from the fish tank Crazy?"

"I was at the fish tank at first, got into some trouble with a ratting-ass inmate telling on me about some hooch. They sent me to K.S.R. then court call gave me 60 days in the hole. I hope for real they send that ratting-ass motherfucker here."

"What was his name Crazy? Do you know it?"

"I know his last name and I know his nickname that he goes by or what everybody calls him. I know a couple of his close friends also. If any of them show up here Justin, I promise you honky, I'll roll up on them and make them tell me his ratting-ass real name. However, that's another story for real. I need to have a talk with you really fast. I'll tell you about the ratting-ass Tiny down the road, okay?"

"Yeah that's all good Crazy. So go ahead tell me what's on your mind. Sounds like something is heavy on your mind. You don't got to pause and think about what to say to me Crazy. I'm a real-ass motherfucker. I know you don't know me yet, but you'll find out real fast, I am loyal as fuck. All we got is our word in here. Your word is everything a man is honky."

"Yeah I feel that Justin 'cause I'm a loyal motherfucker also. Nonetheless, you got no reason to be loyal to me for real. You don't know me at all. Well with all that said right there, I'll just cut right to the issue honky. Do you know this guy named Tat? He told me he is on the end of the walk."

"Well here's the thing, I know I don't know you, I know we just met. I just got here like three weeks ago too. Regardless, if I know you or not, we got to live up in this cell together. I'm no fake-ass honky Crazy. I'm not going to lay up in here in this cell, smile at you with some fake-ass smile, then go behind your back talking shit or some crazy shit these weak motherfuckers do. I'm not built like that at all.

"Now as far as Tat at the end of the walk, dude is a fucking predator. That motherfucker always trying to feel out some young white guy that comes off the bus. He is a super fucking fag or some shit.

"When I first got here, I heard he was talking about me to a few people. Turned out I knew the people he was talking to. So they came to me. They up and tell me what dude was on. Then they tell me he is asking people questions about me that he was trying to figure out shit about me.

"It's all some kind of weak-ass mind game that motherfucker likes to try to play, Crazy. I went right to him when he came back to the walk later that day. I rolled right up in his fucking cell just told him to keep my fucking name out his mouth, honky. He hasn't said a word or shit about me since that day. I was wanting him to fight that day, but he said sorry to me like some bitch.

"Truth is, I heard a rumor the other day he does that fag shit as a hustle. He turns motherfuckers out, then I guess he pimps them to everybody. His first game is he tries to see if you're weak or not. If you're not weak, if you'll show him you'll fight, he is always walking away. Why you asking me about him Crazy?"

The whole time Justin is talking I am listening to him while making my bed, tying my sheet to the mat. Then I put my extra clothes in my locker, so I can keep my mind busy.

The cell's has a small metal locker, which stands up to about waist height that we share. It's got a small door on it. The room also has a really tall locker with about five shelves in it. There is a metal table that sits in the middle. Since Justin is on the bottom bunk, he's got a foot locker that slides in and out under the bunk. I get the really tall locker since he gets the Foot Locker. I don't need anything but the small one, but I hope for things to get better I don't ever just accept less in my life. My mind is always plotting and watching, looking for the right scheme, the right hustle or con. I feel I got a path in life. I just have not learned it yet.

"Well to keep it simple Justin, I'm going down to his cell in just a minute. I'm going to knock on his door, as soon as he comes up to the door, as soon as he opens it, before he can even process the next thought, I'm going to steel him hard as I can in his jaw. Then, I'm going to back him up in that cell. Ease all the way up in the cell, then shut the door. I'm going to try my best to beat his face off until I get tired or wore out."

"Damn Crazy, you not been here twenty minutes and already getting ready to show out. What the hell he do to piss you off like that honky?"

"I'm not going to say what he said Justin, but he disrespected me in a foul way where, win or lose, at the end of it, I promise you he'll not call me that name no more, or any name no more at all."

"Well, it looks like I get to show you the first day that we're cell mates that my words are my bond honky. I told you I'm a loyal-ass cell mate; I'm going down there with you Crazy. We can jump him or I can buzz for you, you just tell me what to do, but I promise you I'm not staying in our cell honky. Even if you feel you don't want me down there or not, I'm still coming with you Crazy. I'm not saying you will lose, I'm just saying if you were losing 'cause you slip or whatever, I promise you I won't let him beat you down or none of that shit at all."

I'm paranoid by nature. Mainly because the streets taught me, life is the gutters. Prison taught me people are the sewers. I don't got a clue what Justin will do right here. I don't know if Tat is his friend or not. I just know that until I figure more out, I'm not going to let both in the cell with me.

I figure it like this though, I might as well take Justin with me. See right off the bat what he is all about. See if he is against me or for me. I figure it's best to know this now rather than wait until I fall asleep or something then I'd learn the lesson the hard way. I'd hate to fall asleep and he attacks me with my guard all the way down.

"Alright Justin I'm going down there right now. You can buzz for me honky. I'll leave the door open just a little. So you jump in if I need you. Shit is some real stuff you doing Justin. I have no doubt in this cesspool, I'll get my shot to show my loyalty back to you."

I walk out in the hallway. As I walk towards the back of the walk, Justin whispers to me that I should be careful going in the cell. That the rat out in the core, that is in the tower out there, he watches the walks through the glass at the top of the walk. Rats are always trying to fuck up our fun.

If the rat sees me going in the cell, he will call other rats on his radio. He will send them up here to the walk really fast because he'll think you're either in this cell fighting or fucking. Could be doing drugs or getting a tattoo also. But in any case, I don't want to see what this hole looks like. I just got here, so I'm going to try my best to get away with this. Furthermore, I feel like with all the walks in here that I stand a pretty good shot at not getting caught as long as I act fast.

As I make it to Tats door, I see through the door of his cell that Tat is sitting in a plastic chair in the back of his cell. I also see another white inmate sitting on the edge of the bottom bunk.

Tat's door isn't locked, it's open just a crack. Justin is so close to me that his arm is rubbing me in the side. I notice Justin sneaking looks at the tower guard in the core.

I swing Tat's door open and before Tat can say anything at all, I say to the guy on the bunk, "You get the hell out this cell now!"

"Hey, you don't come to our cell telling us what the hell to do. I don't know who you think you are, but I suggest you turn around, shut that door, and then take your ass back up the hall."

"I'm going to tell you only one more time to remove yourself from this cell. Go down to the TV room or out to the core. You can come back in 30 minutes or so. If you don't leave now, then the problem me and your celly has will be a problem of yours also. Decide motherfucker!" I can tell this guy is really feminine. He reminds me of Tammy, but I can also see his fear in the way his hands are shaking!

"It's okay Missy, you go on up to the TV room. I'll have a talk with Crazy. We met an hour ago, it's all good baby. Crazy and I just had a simple misunderstanding, but nothing big, okay?"

"You sure Tat? 'Cause I don't want to see you get hurt."

"Me and Crazy is only going to have a talk. It's nothing like that at all. So go up there until I come get you. Now, no more questions, go up to the TV room."

"Okay Tat I'll go up there but can I go sit in the core at the table?"

"Yeah, it's all good baby, just get out of here okay?"

I step to the side as Missy leaves the cell. I see that Justin took Tat's door pushed it open all the way to where the door is touching the wall. I didn't even notice Justin do this but I realize now it's a good move. The guard in the tower would notice a half-open door, or just may look to see what's going on.

Tat never moves out of his chair in the back of the cell. He starts to talk really fast as soon as Missy is out the door. Not to where I can't understand him, but enough to where I can tell he's nervous.

"Hey, look here honky, I am not going to front or none of that. I'm going to keep it real with you. I was out of line Crazy, and having a bad day. That's my prison bitch that just walked out a second ago, that stupid bitch got into it with some people at the fish tank. Missy thought they were on that bus load that came down with you.

"So I got all heated cause I'm thinking I'm going to have to beat a guy up then probably have to go to the hole today all because my bitch always got me in some drama. This hustle has got me all stressed-out Crazy. I am sure you can respect the hustle. Realize that every person has bad days.

"I know you don't give a shit about none of this honky. I just feel it's right I give you an explanation so you know. I'm sorry for what I said. I'm no bitch or none of that, it's just I'm a man before I am anything. I know I was in the wrong for what I said."

"Okay Tat, I can for real feel that, I guess people have bad days. I have bad days in here all the time. That you can man up on your bad day and admit you're wrong is some real shit, but it's the 'sorry' that sealed it all Tat. I can fully respect that, I'm sure it took a lot to say sorry."

I notice Justin isn't watching the tower guard over his shoulder all sneaky anymore. No doubt he considers the issue dead now, so there is no reason for me to go into Tat's cell. If there's no reason to go into the cell, then it don't matter at all what the rat is doing in the tower.

"Well now all that's behind us Crazy, I want you to know I run a store up here. I loan food and other stuff for one for two back or two for three back, so if you need to borrow something to eat or hygiene you just ask me. If I'm not in here you can ask my bitch, she'll get it out for you.

"Also, I got to tell you, they gave you a good celly. Me and your celly bumped heads at first—happens sometimes in here honky. It doesn't help that I'm bi-polar so most times I don't even mean it. Any ways, even though we bumped heads in the past, we get along good now. I can tell you your celly is a good honky."

"Yeah, well all that is some real stuff you talking Tat. I also think my celly here is alright. Hell, I just met him a few minutes ago. Already we cool as hell Tat. Really, I'm bluffing my ass off. It would take me weeks to see if I like Justin or not. I don't give my trust out very easy.

"Any ways you know I just came in. They didn't even feed us any lunch, so I'm hungry as hell for real. You got a box of cakes I could borrow?"

"I got several kinds of cakes. You know you get seven days to pay it back right? If you can't pay in seven days, you got to pay triple."

"Yeah, I know I got to get it back in seven days. Do you got either a box of Swiss Rolls or a box of Oatmeal Pies?"

"I got both of them. What one do you want?"

"Go ahead and give me the Swiss Rolls."

Tat pulls the locker box out from under his bed and opens it up to get the box of cakes out. The entire box is full with all kinds of different foods. I also see four or five bags of coffee. Tat pulls out my cakes, pushes the box back under the bed and walks the cakes up to me.

As he reaches out to hand me the cakes, I swing on him fast and hard. I punch Tat right in the jaw.

The cakes go flying to the back of the cell. Tat falls back a few steps and runs into the bunk. If the bunk hadn't stopped him. He would have hit the floor. With his back up against the bunk, he tries to shake that punch off. I got him very good on the side of his jaw.

I don't give him time at all to recover, I step in the cell. I hear my dude Justin outside the door saying *oh shit oh shit oh shit*.

I slam my fist a second time into Tat's eye socket so hard that it feels like my knuckles broke. I know it must feel worse for him. Since my hand hurts now, I take my knee and slam it up into Tat's gut. But it's over for him, he falls to the floor. Then he folds into a fetal position on me.

"You got to be one-week bitch Tat! Who the fuck folds up in a fetal position, bitch? Not even man enough to protect yourself? You man enough to call me a young punk, you man enough to run your fucking mouth, so you would think you would know how to fight or protect your head when you go down. Here let me show you what I mean."

I stand over top of Tat. He's balled up with his arms wrapped around his knees instead of protecting his face or head, so I bring my foot back as far as I can in this small cell. I take all the strength I got and slam my state boot dead into the side of his face. I see a tooth plus a lot of blood fly out his mouth. I get down on my knees, just lean over him then grab the back of his head, turning his face toward me.

"Tat? Tat, pay attention to me now. Hey, you listening to me or not?" I have not been in a lot of fights in my life. Prison just made it all come out where people kept fucking with me. It seems I am pretty good at it. He now make the second person I done broke their teeth out.

"Oh shit, oh shit, my face fucking hurts man!"

"Shut the fuck up Tat or I'm going to hurt you a lot worse than this. Now answer my fucking question, are you paying attention?"

"Yeah, I'm paying attention to you Crazy! I said sorry Crazy! I didn't mean no disrespect for real."

"Good, very good Tat. Here's how this is going to work, I'm going to take everything in your cell. I'm taking all your food and other property. Fuck you Tat. Fuck your sorry or whatever you say."

"Fuck you Crazy! If you think, I'll let you do this. Nobody fucking steals from me!"

I slam his head hard into the floor. The skin on his forehead cracks open like an overripe watermelon and blood is now coming out pretty good. It's a nice cut for real. I'm about to slam his head again, but he starts begging me not to do it.

"Okay Tat I won't do it again under one condition. I need you to listen to me. Are you listening to me?"

"Yes, yes, I swear I'm listening to you! Shit, Crazy, I don't deserve this."

"Okay Tat as I was saying! I'm going to take everything in this cell I want. I'm doing this 'cause you called me a punk. I'm a lot of things in life but being a punk has never been one of them."

"Man, Crazy I said I am sorry honky. I'm telling you I didn't even mean that. You said you accepted my sorry Crazy!" Tat whines.

"What you think Tat? You think a fucking sorry matters? You can disrespect a person and *sorry* is going to clean that up?

"Well I tell you right now, sorry don't mean shit at all. Not once you cross a certain line. Now, I'm taking all this shit. You try to stop me, or if you try to come back on me later, I'm telling you right now I will fucking kill you. I'll show you punk! You want to die Tat? You want to take it there?"

"Shit no I don't want to die Crazy! Man, do you got to rob me though? This is going to ruin me. I'll have no respect at all."

"Stop acting like a bitch Tat. You did this to yourself," I say, disgusted with him and his whining. I stand up start to turn towards the door. Tat is clearly done.

"Hey Justin, you out there honky?" As soon as I say this, Justin steps in front of the door.

"Hell yeah I'm out here Crazy. Sitting out here buzzing for you. I got to tell you, I can see now how you got your nickname. I swear I didn't see that coming. I thought you was forgiving him."

"Nah, I'm not forgiving no bitch that calls me out my name. How about this though, you want to eat good tonight honky? This motherfucker has a ton of fucking food up in here. I'm taking everything."

"Hell yeah I want to eat tonight! It's been a minute since I ate some good food."

"Okay, here's how we do this. You go up there, get his punk ass celly, and tell his celly that Tat told you to come get him. Once you see him headed this way, you just buzz for me up there. Yell my name if it gets hot or a guard is looking. I'm going to get dude's bitch to pack all this to our cell. I'll help him pack it up as he moves it."

"No problem Crazy, I can do that for us. Check this out though, I don't got a TV or none of that shit. Why don't you take his TV also? I'll take the rap for it if the rats shake us down. That's if they notice it don't belong to us, I'll tell them it's mine."

"Okay that's all good then. I'll send the TV to our cell also. We will be eating good tonight and watching some good TV. This is going to be a good night! After two months in the hole I fucking need some love."

In what seems like but a few seconds, the guy that Tat was calling Missy shows up at the cell door.

Tat is still laying on the floor. The cut on his forehead is still bleeding and blood was coming out of his mouth. I'm guessing the blood from his mouth is coming from where his tooth flew out. Tat has this dazed look on his face. I don't feel sorry for him at all. If I would have let him calling me a punk go, then the chances of me being the one on the floor busted up would be pretty high.

When Missy comes into the room, he sees Tat on the floor dazed and bleeding. Like some bitch, Missy starts squealing then runs to Tat's side. He drops to the floor and wraps his arm around Tat's shoulder.

"Missy listen to me. Missy, I need you to look at me and pay real close attention."

"You hurt him, man! Why did you fucking hurt him?! Oh Tat, you said you two were just going to talk baby!"

I don't even try to ask Missy no more questions. I can tell his dumb ass isn't listening. So I take the back of my hand and slap him backhanded like a bitch. My knuckle still hurts like hell, but I did it really hard any ways.

The smack lands perfectly across the side of his face. CRACK! The sound is loud with the door to the cell still all the way pushed open. It sounds like the smack echoed all the way down the hallway. Missy grunts then backs up into the corner on his hands and feet, like some kind of human spider. When he runs out of room behind him, he looks up at me with fear in his eyes.

The good news is, I got his fucking attention now.

"Missy I don't want to hurt you worse. I'm sure you don't want me to beat you up like I've done your boyfriend, right?"

"No, no, no I don't want any issue at all, what do you want?" Missy is talking so fast I can barely understand the bitch. I am not really mad at him though. He didn't say nothing out of the way to me but if his fucking boyfriend left me alone, none of this would have happen.

"Okay Missy, here's the deal. My name is Crazy, your dude right here had an issue with me. As you see Missy, he lost. The bad news Missy is that you are caught in the cross fires. I'm sorry for your luck, but I didn't start this. I'm only the guy who plans to finish it.

"The issue will be over in a second though because you will help me with the last part. You will help me or I will do the same to you I done to him."

"What do I got to do Crazy? I don't want to suck dick. Please don't make me suck your dick! I don't want to suck a dick Crazy, please. You can fuck my ass but I hate sucking dick."

"Are you fucking serious? You can't be fucking serious. Look I want you to take the sheets or any bags in this cell. I want you to fill them up with all the canteen you got. You can also put it in the middle of blankets and tie it off.

"Then, you'll take everything up to my cell. We're going to move fast, or I promise you I'll not only hurt you, but you get me mad enough I'll kill you in this cell. You got that motherfucker?" I add an extra touch of anger. It sounds so real that I even almost believe I'll do it.

"Yes, Yes, I swear I understand! I'll do whatever you say." Missy's eyes are as big as saucers plus tears start to roll down his face.

The truth is I'm not going to kill anyone. I mean I may if I was ever put in a really bad position. I just hope I never will be put in that position. I, for one, would hate to do the time. I am too cold hearted to really care about murder itself. I just know I don't want to do the time. I mean who would want to spend forever in hell. Not me, at least not if I can make the right choice and not get the time or do a crime that didn't give you that time. Either way, I am a good person that can bluff really well. I'll con my way into anything, or try to con my way out of anything.

It is in that moment it comes to me, as me and Missy pack up all this canteen, Tat still on the floor, that I can always have whatever I want. All I had to do is show out a little and then use my mouth to get it. I could con my way into anybody's mind. Fear seems to be the biggest ruler to all people. People will do anything at all you tell them to do, when they're truly under your spell of fear.

Missy's so nervous that he's fumbling all over the place. I could get angry or lose patience with him and pack the items myself. Instead, I take a very nervous and scared Missy, slowly get him to calm down then focus on me and do what I want him to do. To be honest, it is empowering to have this kind of control over a person. That powerful feeling convinces me that being a con is what I want to be. It's what I know, at that moment, I am meant to be.

Chapter 10

PRISON IS WHAT YOU MAKE IT

"Reality is merely an Illusion,
albeit a very persistent one." —Albert Einstein

In life, people live by other people's standards. Everything they do is viewed as bad or good, cruel or nice based upon the views of others. I ask myself every day, who were these people? Why do they get to decide what's right or wrong, so others can follow them? Why do I have to follow them?

You would be amazed how many weak-minded people there are in the world. Criminals who can be tough, that can be shot callers or gang leaders, even these strong people are controlled by what others think.

The strongest people are the ones that are not controlled by what others think is right or wrong. A person who only believes what he chooses to believe is a person who will move any road that is in his way. He alone can help or take care of the people he is loyal too.

Since I understand what the law calls wrong, and I understand what convicts say is wrong; I understand what both sides say is right. And because of that, I understand what is expected out of me in life. Life is basically a con and as a strong white male, I can't allow anything to control me. I have to be smart enough to do what I please in life, not to let the rats catch me doing it. I need to protect myself and the ones I love. To do all that, and to survive, sometimes you got to make your own path. I mean if someone runs up on your mother or wife. What if that person tries to rape or kill one of these women in your life? Are you going to fold, run, call 911, or are you going to man up and protect them?

Even in prison there is a certain standard you have to live by. But if that standard blocks something I want, then I need to learn to trick the convicts around me just like I do for the rest of the world. You'll get nowhere but run over being the nice guy. You should only be nice to your loved ones. In my personal opinion, everybody has that one soul mate. When you find that other half of you that is when you never allow anything to stop that love. Murder, or any limit to protect her or him.

I understand to a lot of people what I believe would make me a monster; I have no issue with that. Part of being strong you have to have thick skin. You can't care about anybody else's thoughts or opinions at all. Who gives a fuck what the world thinks or feels? You do you, I'll do me and my loved ones. Others may not agree with me, but my values are my own. In life, you can spend all of it getting walked on or you can spend it where you do all the walking.

Now I say all that to say this, the day I robbed Tat, the day I made Tat's lover do what I wanted because he feared me, that day I realized that being a con is the most powerful feeling I've ever felt.

I have felt a lot of feelings in my short life, so that is saying a lot to be honest. I learned as a kid how to con, for church people I got them to give me money or food by playing a hungry kid. However, that day in Tat's cell was different. I sized up Tat and sized up Missy and figured out how to control them.

For Missy, it was fear that did it. Missy didn't care if he loved Tat or not. The only thing Missy knew is that he is scared of me, so he obeyed me. With me in the room, Tat didn't even exist to him.

Seeing that control, it clicked for me that being a true con is like being a salesman. All you have to do is find a person's weakness. It could be their guilt you play on by being a hungry kid, for others it might be sex, like with Megan. For some, it could be fear, the promise of love, drugs, or many other things. The key to control though is to find the weakness. When you find that weakness, you fully own that person. I also realized that I never want to be like Missy or some of the people I've met in here. I want and will be that guy who if I walked in that cell and Tat was my lover, without a doubt I'm fighting hard.

It's not always going to be as easy as it was with Missy. It's mostly about patience, maybe stroking that person's ego a little. People are so very transparent that most will tell you anything if you got the right attitude when asking it. Once they start talking, it isn't long before you understand what they want, what motivates them.

All this brought me back to what C.J. had told me when we were in the hole about his con. Writing fags on the streets would be simple. I knew I could do it, that I'd be fucking great at it, but I just wasn't ready yet. I kept giving myself excuses that I didn't have a picture or I didn't have the money to send the magazine people to put up my ad. I had tons of excuses of why. Mainly, I realize I got a good mouth piece, but writing letters all day seems extremely hard, boring and so I keep pushing it off.

Already two months have passed since I beat up Tat; He ended up going to check in. Missy followed behind him. After I did what I did to Tat, other people on the yard started to refuse to pay him back on the stuff he loaned. Guys were making Missy do sexual things and not only was Tat not getting anything for Missy doing it. He couldn't stop any of it or help him. Nobody had any respect for him at all. This is how prison is: sharks and fish. You don't get to decide what you are. Your peers decide after they try you. Tat got ate, so from now on every shark keeps tearing more chunks out of him until he folds and begged the rats to help him.

After about a month of this treatment, Tat had to ask the rats to protect him, so they put him in the hole. Then they moved him to protective custody at Kentucky State Penitentiary. All the check-ins are housed over there together and do their time like that. Missy followed behind Tat one week later. I'm surprised that he waited that long. I was even more surprised both didn't blame me for their lives going to shit and then rat on me to try to get some revenge. I was honestly expecting Tat or Missy to rat on me about the TV. They may still have told, but the rat that one of them told might not give a fuck about no TV.

In these two months, Justin and I have just been laying back. We ate all the food we got off Tat in the first two weeks. We still have the TV, plus we also got a radio from his cell.

I learned Justin grew up in Louisville, Kentucky. He's white trash. He grew up with a Gangsta-ass mom, but she was locked up a lot. Justin didn't grow up in trailer parks, but he did grow up in the projects. His mom is cool-ass people though. He writes her as often as he can.

He is street smart, brave and extremely loyal; the kind of loyalty that's rare to find inside prison or out. In other words, Justin is just like me. He caught a 20-year sentence for robbery. He robbed a bank but a bank security guard shot him in the side, bad robbery that day.

You got to understand something about me. The only people I don't con are the ones I love. The issue is that if I'm going to love you and be loyal to you, then I demand loyalty and love back because I give the best love. I have a strong belief on what love means. Very few people are capable of loving the way I do. I see people for who they are and that is why I have hardly any friends.

I'm going to tell you right now, there isn't a million ways to love. Love is a very simple emotion, but few can give it the correct way. Instead, people justify their weak-ass shit. They use their theories on love to justify not loving all the way.

My way of loving I know is the correct way. Regardless if I get called a monster or not, to me love is unconditional at all times. You don't ever try to change, control, manipulate or run your lover's or friends' lives. You don't run or leave because you can't do these things to them. The people I love do no wrong. The people I love can make any choice they want, and I will love them the same. Good, bad or whatever, in my eyes there is only the love I feel for them. I will kill, steel, rape, and even give my own life up to help to save my lover or the people I love. There is no wrong in my eyes to love. The only wrong I see is people aren't strong enough to be what they need to be for their lovers or friends.

Justin is so loyal, if I am standing somewhere talking to a person and that person starts getting rude or just loud, he'll fire off a punch before you can blink a fucking eye. He's loyal, and he don't like to lose so if he even thinks you're about to swing; he swings first because it's best to get the first shot. So we're always in the winning corner.

The only problem with this is that some people are just emotional people that speak loud or use their hands to describe everything. They don't have any issue nor do they intend to start a fight. They just speak that way.

For others, it's a bluff, sort of how I con by telling a person I'll kill them to get them to listen. For these guys who aggressively talk is a con in its own way. They may realize they're doing it, or they may not. Who gives a fuck really?

Either way, they are talking to you in a way that makes you believe they're ready to fight. They have learned they can bluff their way through confrontations, by controlling the conversation through fear. They hope if you see all this, or feel it, you'll back down either because you're scared of them, or because you're scared of getting in trouble. So they talk loud and use gestures that appear aggressive. You would be amazed at how many people I've seen back down by just fearing what is being said to them.

The problem with Justin punching these types is that most men who act like this, I would say over half of them, learned it as their own personal survival gear. They don't like to fight at all, so they learned a way to keep people off them. Most of them are bitches that have learned how to blend in. There are lots of people in prison that talk loud or have a good talking game but in the end, they're weak. They will fold up like a lawn chair soon as you smack them. All they are is mouth and hot air.

On the other hand, I got a lot of really fucked up ways of looking at things in life. I fully understand some of my views, and opinions make people feel like I'm speaking about them, or they just feel I'm too blunt. After they hear what I have to say, they not only dislike me altogether, they stay away from me—which is fine by me.

I'm trying to teach Justin we don't need to beat those people up. Justin is my only friend, I got right now. He is my number-one honky. I don't want him to feel stupid. I say all that because I hate to speak of my friends in a bad way. I also don't think you should change people you love. However, if it's to help them then, it is okay to try to push them to their highest potential. The number-one thing that most people are fake about is that if they can't control or change their loved ones, they walk away from them. People have to accept and not judge their loved ones. If they refuse to change, or you can't change them, you still love them no matter what.

What Justin doesn't realize is he don't need to beat everybody up. He could use his mind to learn to trick these people out of stuff. Nevertheless, Justin is all balls and loyalty.

Now, this would be perfect if I wanted to con him. I'm a con man after all. But I'm just as loyal back, so I refuse to con my friends. My worry is that Justin could be too easily conned because he's so loyal. He gives that loyalty to the wrong person, and they'll take advantage. So I'm trying to teach Justin how to get what he wants without beating a person up, or at least using that method as a last resort. Justin is young like me, but like a lot of people, Justin doesn't use his head.

Before I showed up, Justin was making his way in prison by extorting weak inmates. His method was to run up in their cell, beat them up, and take anything of any value.

Justin's problem was he did no research on who he ran up on. At least two times I know of, he didn't even have to beat them up. They were so scared they would have given it up with no issue. This issue of not doing the research cost us really bad.

Justin run up in a cell with two black guys in it. Justin's theory is that since they are both young like us and both only about a hundred pounds soaking wet, they will be easy. He figured it is okay to beat up a person 75 or 80 pounds smaller than him because there's two of them. If you add them both together they weigh 200 pounds, so that makes it very fair in his theory, so nothing wrong with beating up a smaller guy. Easy money is the best money, right?

Hell I'm 140lbs at my best, so these black guys made me feel like I'm a big guy. Anyway, Justin goes in there on them showing out at first winning the fight. Then one of the small guys picked up a can of food that is sitting on the table and hits Justin with it so hard in the back of the head that Justin goes down. I think Justin is knocked out behind it, but he wakes up from it so fast I couldn't tell. Don't matter though, Justin is so light headed from the blow to the head that he needed help real bad.

I'm at the door buzzing for him. The good news behind all this is that the guy Justin was focused on had so much damage to his face already that both his eyes are almost swollen shut. When I did my last look up at the tower guard and the core guard, I see the rats aren't looking so I ran into the cell. The skinny black fuck with the can sees me coming in. He tries to take the side of my head off with that can. He throws it like a damn pool ball at my head.

Luck or whatever being on my side, Justin came back to his feet so fast, he is kind of swaying a little bit so he grabs the guy with the can food to catch his balance. This throws off the black guy so, the can shoots by me an easy five feet away. The can food flies by me, out into the hallway, then slams against the wall out there so hard it blows up when it hits. Thank goodness that fucking thing didn't hit me.

After that, things start happening really fast, but it feels like slow motion. I'm on the black dude that threw the can. I punch him so hard in his left temple that he falls back into Justin. The other black guy can't really see, but he's swinging hay maker punches at Justin. (I don't see how he even took all he did and still hasn't passed out at all. I got to say both of these two small fucks weren't easy as they looked!)

About then, Justin realizes I'm in the cell. He doesn't ask me to go back to buzz the door or none of that bullshit. Justin is always good at reading me. We make a decent team like that. Justin knows I'm not going to leave the cell, not after the hit he took. I know for real he is still dizzy.

So Justin turns around to hit the other black guy with a three piece that's sloppy; he still isn't at full strength. Nonetheless, it does the job because the three punches are all the black guy can take. Those three punches knock him out. I am surprised, he took all he did.

Meanwhile, in the time it took to do this, I receive two good hard punches to my rib cage. This skinny black fuck might be 100 pounds, but it is like his hands are lightning. They are not only fast they have power in them you wouldn't at all think is there. I take the two hits pretty well though (lost my breath a little bit to be honest) but I'm able to hit him back with a perfect combination of left and right hook punches. Each punch slams into the side of his head about four seconds apart.

It's the second hit to his temple on the left side that does the trick. He falls like a sack of rotten potatoes—right to the fucking floor. My rib cage hurts a lot. This motherfucker has punches that feel like bricks hitting you. Justin still looks dazed. This is a good fight for real.

We were thinking this was going to be very easy but to be fair Justin picked them on the sole fact they were small. We heard both went to the store every week also. Justin got good information they both had a lot of stuff in their cell. So we thought this was going to be very easy with a nice payoff. Obviously, the information he got was lacking some serious detail. Just how much is the real question, but I'm so juiced and hyped up, I can't think clearly when I am like this.

Turns out it's the best fight we've had so far, but I need to correct myself. I said Justin's hustle is extortion, but I've seen Justin extort probably three people, and they requested protective custody soon after. But Justin's real hustle is robbery. This is how I got caught up in this new hustle of mine. Tat was just a fluke cause, he disrespected me. Justin talked me into doing more and so far every bit of it is high on my scale of life.

There are all types of ways to steal in prison. Here at Pink Palace, you can slip a razor blade next to the lock while a person's door is open. You could be at their door talking to them and just slide the razor blade in under the lock. When the door shuts, all you got to do is slide an ID card down the crack of the door really fast over the part where you stuck the razor to block the lock. I don't get how all it works or why it does, really I don't even care to be honest, I just know it works. Here's the thing though, it's a coward's way of stealing.

I'm in prison for trying to steal. I tried to do it when no one was home but here's why that is different. The person on the streets would rat on me in a fucking heartbeat. They would more than likely not miss a court date either. I'm not saying all would do that, some may kill me or try to kill me. Some may shoot my ass the moment, I kick the door in.

The point is I don't have a clue who is going to be a Gangsta about it or not. So it's best to do it all with the thought of not being seen. Not at all getting caught like I did. It's about keeping your freedom outside these walls. Everybody knows that the less evidence they got on you makes a better shot at no case on you.

Now for prison though it's different. Being a rat is the worst thing you could ever be. Telling on somebody will seal your fate in prison to where you'll never walk another general population yard ever. So I can't use the excuse I robbed him while he was at the chow hall because I was afraid he would rat on me if he saw me do it. That's the coward's way. Don't get me wrong now, lots of people still do it that way in here. You might come back from medical or chow hall and everything in your cell would be gone. Then you can't let it go or it will keep going down. You got to track down who did it or just pick a person who you think did it. I'm just saying this isn't my way.

As far as Justin and me, we agreed we will be gangsta about our shit. If we take a bag, we going to do it with the person right there. If we rob a cell, we going to do it while at least one of them is home, in the cell.

I'm not saying I'm proud of myself acting like this. The truth is I'm not at all proud of myself, not because I feel robbery is wrong. I'm ashamed because I believe I'm above this nickel and dime shit. I should have got ahold of a better hustle by now, one that would've helped me make a lot more and get more than I am making now. I've always been hard on myself like this my whole life. I don't at all think like the average person. Never is enough just 'enough'. I know I have it in me to do great shit, I just feel I'm on a journey looking for what it is still. I don't play cards or bet on any sports in prison, I don't socialize or nothing like that, I daydream and plot all day. The issue right now is I got caught up a little in the chaos around me and it fuels my mind the daily dose of hate it needs. So like an addict I am chasing my fix not my dream.

Gangsta or not, the only people we've ever robbed on our walk is Tat and Missy. I've not done nobody else on this walk since I don't really like to shit in my own backyard for real. The two black guys that we robbed, they live on our walk but they were my honky's idea so I went with it because he goes with all my ideas.

We always robbed people on different walks, we even went into other dorms. As you can imagine with 2,000 or so convicts, it's not hard to sneak around. These inbreed dumb ass, country redneck fucks are too stupid to remember who lives where. Maybe if a person stands out or maybe if you cussed the rat out, he may remember a face or two. Basically, if you fuck with the rats, they'll remember you because the dumb ass rat is looking to fuck with you back now. They're extremely childish like that.

Point is, I've never been caught going into another dorm or another walk. To be honest it's too easy since, as long as you haven't pissed the rats off, they for real don't give a shit what you do. They just trying to do their eight hours and go on home. (They not acting like this though because they cool, they acting like this because they don't want piss or shit thrown on them or somebody to lose control and just smack the shit out of one of them.) The Ro-bo rats go out their way to fuck with people. You don't want to ever get on their radar of a Ro-bo rat because they take everything personal and they are control freaks

By staying off our own walk, we feel pretty safe when we're in our own cell. No one on our walk has any beef with us. When we are in the cell we can relax. Now we got to worry about the two black guys. Robbing them went against my thinking but it is what it is.

But like I was saying before, Justin never dose research on people we rob. I sort of just fell in this pattern with Justin, mainly because he's been robbing people since before I got here. Justin only did it every 2 months or so. Here lately about one time every three weeks just so we can pay all our bills back, with a little extra for ourselves hopefully.

Well, to be fair, we didn't go in blind but our only research on anybody is to watch them. If they had nice shoes, sunglasses, a watch, maybe a necklace on or any other jewelry, this set our radar all the way off. That's all the research we needed or did for real. But we forgot the rules. Everything in life needs rules or as I like to call it, a plan on how to do what you do. Once you got that plan you shouldn't step outside of it. I try to find the best plan but I've just let that go here lately.

Even in the streets I grew up in, the gutters I came from, the rules were the same. There were certain gang leaders, certain drug dealers, certain people, you just don't fuck with in the trailer parks or projects or on the streets. It can cost you your life, so you learn who these people are, fast. The truth is I knew this like the back of my hand. I'm not sure if I am just under estimating prison or if I just felt prison rules are different, I'm not sure why I am acting naïve like this. Maybe it is just the Gangsta in me; you get to a point you don't care what the consequences are. You're tired of stinking, tired of being hungry every night. You're just sick of it all. So you just say fuck it all. Do whatever at whatever level you can take it to. Prison is one place you can lose yourself like this easily. Lose touch with yourself and reality, real fast.

But whatever the reason, I learned this lesson the same way I learned all my lessons in jail or the fish tank, the hard way. About three days passed since we robbed the two skinny black guys. On that third day all hell broke loose on me and Justin. Turns out the two black guys we robbed are in a gang, one of the biggest gangs on this yard; they are called Bloods.

The day it happened, Justin and I are kicked back, watching the TV in our cell. We just cooked a real good meal off the 200 dollars' worth of food we took from the two black guys. Our door is open just a crack to let the air circulate. When out of nowhere our cell door swings open and about six black guys come flying into the cell.

Two of the six guys that run into our cell, I see right off the bat are the two black guys we just robbed. I don't know yet that they're Bloods, I figure this out afterwards. Everybody assumes I knew or that Justin did, we don't want to look stupid so we just play it like we knew but just didn't give a fuck.

When they run in our cell, three of them are on Justin first because he was sitting on the bottom bunk near the door. I'm sitting in the back of the cell, on the plastic chair that all cells have. It didn't matter though, three of them are on me pretty fast. The only good news is that these cells are real small so all three can't really get on me, because the cell isn't wide enough. For the first time, I am loving my small cell. Just happens to be I love something in the worst time. Probably no doubt shows I've got a morbid mind.

I hit one of them real hard in the jaw. That's all I really get in to be honest. Justin isn't doing very well either. They've already got him where he's lying on his side on the bunk. One of the black dudes got in the bunk with him and is straddling Justin's hips holding him down while another guy is for the most part using Justin's face as a punching bag. I feel terrible I can't help him.

I fall to the floor real hard when I feel something hit me in the head, I feel light headed. I realize some of the hits I'm taking should have knocked me out. The only reason I'm not knocked out is that the fear of passing out is more powerful, or at least I think this is why. I feel a shoe or boot or something hit me so hard in the forehead, that I feel my forehead slam into the concrete floor so hard that I feel my forehead splits open. *That's going to leave a mark.* Then somebody hits me so hard in my jaw that it feels like a damn sledge hammer. That is my last thought before everything went dark on me.

It only feels like a few seconds later when I hear somebody's voice screaming in my head. It seems so loud that it feels like whoever it is, is yelling at me on a fucking bull horn or some shit. For real, I wish he would shut up and let me sleep a little longer.

"Hey honky, wake the hell up! Wake the hell up or we going to throw a bucket of water on you honky plus I will put ice in it so it is ice fucking cold. "

My eyes pop open all the way! Not only does it feel like he is yelling at me, the lights to the room seem so bright that it makes my head ache like hell. I am lying flat on my back with my legs straight out. My legs are under the bunk, the top half of me is the only thing sticking out.

I must have took a good ass kicking, however it went down. This white dude in front of me I don't know who he is. He is a big white guy. I can see a swastika in the middle of his neck.

One of my first thoughts is that I don't want to ever show weakness. So at this moment, I really don't want to look weak in front of this skin head. People use that shit against you. So asking for an aspirin is out the question. Telling him to tone it down some, shut the lights out or any of that I'm not going to say. I'm not going to let it be known how bad my body hurts. I need to bluff my way out, even make it seem like I am ready for another fight.

The white dude looks at me pretty intent. He starts to yell again or at least it feels like he is yelling.

"Damn honky you took one hell of an ass beating. I got to say you and your dude here have got to be brave as a motherfucker to rob two damn monkeys in the Bloods. You two honkies got a set of nuts."

I wasn't going to tell him we didn't know they were in a gang. I figure I would rather be told I got courage than be called fucking stupid. Justin won't speak on it either, Justin hates to be looked at or talked to like he is stupid. So I know he won't bring it up.

I push up off the ground and put my back against the wall. I see the plastic chair is all the way at the front door. Another white guy, that looked like a skin head also, is sitting in the chair. I don't even know how the chair got there.

There are two other white dudes helping Justin sit up. I don't know any of them at all. I don't know how my cell has gotten to look like the New Jersey turnpike. Whatever happened, this hasn't at all brought the law down on us. That by itself is probably a miracle. I am just trying to run it in my head where the hell did all these white guys come from?

I look at the white guy in front of me, lots of muscle and blonde hair and probably six feet tall or so. Time to see who he is.

"Who are you honky? What you guys doing up in our cell?" Before he could even answer I turn and yell at Justin, "Hey Justin you good brother? You alive over there?"

"Yeah, Crazy I'm all good bro. It will take a lot more than that to kill me out. I guess we pissed somebody off."

"My name is Ryan, honky and I'm up in your cell because I saw the monkeys packing your stuff out of your cell.

"I've heard about you before on several issues Crazy. I've also heard about your dude Justin here. News travels fast in prison, you two honkies are always into something. I know you two are young, solid honkies, but you got a lot to learn or you two going to get killed in here. You two got more heart than you got sense. I mean no disrespect by that.

"Anyways, I stopped the monkeys form stealing from you. I kind of came at it late though, I think they got everything but your TV and your clothes. I didn't see none of it till the end.

"I got some other bad news for you Crazy that needs to be spoke on now before we talk about anything else."

The way Ryan is looking at me told me this isn't going to be good at all. I was fresh out of ideas what it could be. What else could be any worse than my day so far?

"Okay Ryan before you get to whatever, let me first tell you honky, I don't know you. It is real as hell that you stepped in and kept it 100 with us. I'll bring this up again later, but for now go ahead tell me the bad news. I can tell it's going to be terrible."

"Well it's not all that Crazy, it's just terrible because what needs to be done is going to hurt like hell. My dude over there at the door, he's got a sewing needle and some thread. Although for what he needs to do he'll use dental floss. You're going to need a few stitches Crazy, on your forehead, or it will never close. If it don't close, you'll get busted sooner or later, or it'll get infected or both. That's never good for nobody, brings heat to the walk. You can't go to medical for it either."

Medical will report it to the rats. So you're stuck with only getting some convicts medical help.

"You telling me that your guy over there is going to stick me with a fucking sewing needle in my forehead to close my cut? That he is going to run dental floss threw my fore head a few times with the needle going in and out of my skin, no telling how many times?"

"Yes, that's what I'm saying to you Crazy."

Chapter 11

A TRUE CON MAN CAN TALK HIMSELF OUT OF ANYTHING!!

If you are blind to the warning signs of a scheming mind you will be taken for a ride every time.—Ashley Bennett

Ryan's speaking to me so I am trying to listen. I am really trying, it is just that when somebody is telling you they going to stick you in the head with a fucking sewing needle; it's real hard to fucking focus. I am also still bleeding pretty badly. Although I'm slowing it down somewhat with the toilet paper that I have crammed into the cut. I have to keep changing it a lot though.

At this moment I'm not sure if those fucking blacks are Crips or Bloods, I'm a little confused because I'm so dazed. I thought they were Crips, but I heard Ryan call them Bloods, I don't remember why I was thinking they were Crips.

I'm worried about Justin. I want to check on him to make sure he's cool. It's just I can't really focus my eyes at all. Now that I am sitting here and thinking about it, everybody in the room sounds real far away. I think I need to vomit or something. Just a moment ago everybody sounded loud as hell. Now they all seem far away. I don't know what's going on.

"Hey honky, hey! Snap the fuck out of it Crazy!"

I'm pretty sure that is Ryan or someone trying to talk to me. For real I don't give a damn who it is, I just need to lay down. Take at least an hour nap, that sounds like that would be good right now.

"Hey! Hey, Crazy! I'm going to smack you dead in the face honky if you don't answer me. Snap the fuck out of it Crazy!"

Well to be honest I got to admit I was not listening to him. The thought of getting hit really has my attention though, not that I'm going to admit that to him ever. Nonetheless, I am not going to let him smack me like I am some kind of bitch. So he's got my attention now.

"What? Damn Ryan, why you yelling at me? I'm sitting right here in front of you." I can't tell but I must be yelling at him because he motions for me to lower my voice. All I can hear is the ringing in my ears, so I make an effort to tone it down.

"Crazy, you save that shit for another person. You just now passed out on me. I need you to understand my dude Aaron over there is coming in here to close that cut on your forehead. We don't need you to wake up in shock, not knowing what's going on at all; either you'd jump really fast when you come awake and cause the needle to do more damage, or you'll try to swing on my dude. I'm not going to have you freaking out on me. You got what I am saying so far Crazy?"

"Yeah, I got what you saying. I'm all good Ryan. Ready for whatever, down for anything at all; let's do this."

"Well, you think you are ready Crazy? I'm telling you right now young honky, I don't care how tough you think you are this is going to hurt really badly," Ryan says softly.

Aaron says, "Hey Ryan we need to get this on the road. That cut is bleeding real badly on him, so it needs to be closed before he ends up losing too much blood. Otherwise, he'll pass out on us all over again."

"Okay Aaron, you the doctor honky. Come on over here and try to put humpty dumpty back together," Ryan then starts laughing at his own joke, then he steps aside to let Aaron in front of me.

"I'm glad I'm just sitting over here bleeding all over myself while you crack jokes. I know you *think* you got a sense of fucking humor. That's all good, but can we get this moving?"

Ryan stops laughing and says, "Well Crazy, we can't offer no pain pills at the moment so a sense of humor is all we got to help you through this pain. Sometimes a little joke will help take your mind off things."

"Okay I got the needle ready, and I have enough dental floss to stitch the cut right. He'll need a ball cap or something to keep his forehead covered, so the rats won't see the cut at all." Aaron says all this while poking and looking at the cut.

"That's all good. I'll get out of your hair to let have as much space as you need. You do your doctor shit on him, and I'll go get the ball cap for him to wear, or something for him to put on," Ryan says moving to the door.

As I watch Ryan walk out of the cell, I notice Justin near the door just sitting there with his head in his lap. I want to ask him what is up with him, but I just can't keep my eyes off this fucking sewing needle that Aaron was rubbing with an alcohol pad. I also notice though that the other two white guys that were helping Justin are gone as well. I didn't hear or see them roll out.

"Jesus fucking Christ Aaron, isn't that needle really fucking fat? Are you supposed to sew with something that round?"

"It's all we got Crazy, it's not like we can go to the store and get us the real deal. We work with what we got in here."

"I mean, I get all that honky. I'm grateful that you are helping me. It's just I'm saying with a needle that fat, won't that punch huge round holes in my skin as you go? How you know it will work? "

"Look Crazy, I've done this a few times, just be glad you're not the first guy I worked on. Enough talking though, we need to get that cut closed. Get over here and sit right in front of me. It's time to man-up. You want to play the fucking game? Well, this is all part of our lifestyle. Now you get to learn what happens when you lose a fight. Hopefully, this will hurt bad enough to where you won't ever want to lose again."

"Fuck it, I get it." I move towards the spot where he indicated I need to be. Aaron is sitting on the bunk in the middle, he wants me to sit on the floor right between his legs facing him. Fucked-up position I'm in right now. I got to get this cut closed though. It's not bleeding as bad as it was, but I've stalled long enough on it. As Aaron told me, I need to just man up!

Aaron leans over top of me, pulls the toilet paper out of my cut. He then puts his finger at the top of the cut, with the same hand he puts another finger on the bottom of it. Moving his fingers in like a scissors' sort of way, both fingers are pushing into where the cut pulls apart and opens. This hurts like a motherfucker. Jesus, the pain by itself makes me want to pass out again. I barely hold on for real. I only hold on 'cause I get angry at myself for acting like a pussy.

"I got to pour some water into your cut. It's got some dirt in it, so I got to wash that out then I'll close it. Here we go Crazy, ready or not!" Aaron stands and moves around me to get to the sink, when he sits he has a cup of water in his hand. He is using my drinking cup. Fast as lightning he opens the cut again then pours the water into it directly washing out the blood and dirt. When the water hits the cut, it don't at all feel like water. It feels like a million little needles poking the shit out of me. This shit hurts, but I am starting to get used to the pain.

"See that wasn't so bad, Crazy. All clean now." Aaron sits there smiling at me, and I know he knows it was terrible.

"Now listen to me Crazy, I need you to make sure that when this needle pokes your skin you don't jump or move at all. I'm going to pull hard on it to bring the cut together. By looking at how deep your cut is, I'm guessing I'll need to poke four times at the top. Then four times at the bottom to bring it all the way closed. It could be five times both ways, we'll see as we go. Do you fully understand? Don't move at all. Got it?"

"Yeah, I got it Aaron. I'm all good, I won't move at all. I can handle it all honky."

"Alright then here we go."

The first stab makes me close my eyes tightly shut. I don't want to look weak. I really do try not to but nonetheless, tear drops escape. Just a couple that I couldn't hold back for nothing. I don't know what to feel or think, I know I've been through a lot in my life, but this right here is the top of the list for the most painful.

The funny part is that it didn't even hurt this bad when that fucker did this to my head to begin with. By the time Aaron was in his fourth stab—two in the top, two in the bottom—I feel like just passing out. And, he's only halfway done!

"Hey snap out of that pussy shit Crazy!"

I am so relieved to hear Justin talk that I'm not even upset he just insulted me. Justin hasn't spoken since this shit went down. Had me nervous for a minute cause he was putting off vibes like he is feeling guilty about something.

"You're alive honky? That's what I'm talking about, I thought you was dead over there Justin."

Aaron stops stitching and says, "Hey hold still Crazy, I told you no moving at all."

"We can talk later, let Aaron finish on you. I'm not dead over here though. I'm not as bad as you got it, I just got my jaw real fucked up. It is hard to talk for real. Probably be a huge knot on the outside of my jaw tomorrow. Got to lay low for a few days. By the way, that looks like it hurts to be real with you."

I don't say anything at all. I'm not trying to mess Aaron up. But I still give Justin the middle finger. He knows this shit don't fucking feel good.

"All done Crazy! All it took was Justin to distract you. As soon as he started talking, you went from pale white like a ghost, to your color coming back. I'll be real crazy, that is a very nasty cut. I give you plenty of points for how you just held it together. I'm telling you some honkies would've at least cried while I did that or made a few moans or something."

"All the way real Aaron? I think the only reason I didn't fully break down into sobbing is I maybe was in shock. I probably still am for real. I may not show it, but this cut hurts really bad."

"That shit is going to hurt like lava was tossed on your forehead tomorrow. Right now ain't nothing, I'm telling you wait until tomorrow gets here." Aaron says all this while washing the sewing needle down with an alcohol pad.

"That's cool" I say and turn to Justin. "I'll be laid up in this cell here with you. I won't tell nobody you cried about your jaw, as long as you keep it a secret what I do tomorrow about my cut."

Justin starts laughing, "Ha ha ha, we are going to be like two old people up in this cell for the next week. Won't be able to do shit Crazy."

"Hell you probably not even going to be able to eat for a few days when that jaw fully swells up tomorrow."

"Yeah thanks for reminding me about that, Aaron. Not that I feel like eating right now any ways. I probably will tomorrow though."

"Here's the hat Crazy, it's not really a hat. I couldn't find no hat. I found this bucket hat though."

Ryan is just standing in front of the door waving this ridiculous looking bucket hat around.

"Long as it keeps me out the hole, I guess it really don't matter at all. I don't care about the hole, but I love getting away with anything I can. I love that feeling I get when I get one over on the rats."

"Yeah I guess that's the truth. By the way, the smiley face on your forehead looks very good. Good job Dr. Aaron, couldn't have done it better myself." Even though I just met these two guys I feel a real good connection. Most times I hate everybody for no reason at all.

"Yeah, you laugh now Ryan, wait until you need some dental floss action. We'll see if you're making jokes then."

"Ha ha ha, yeah I may make jokes, but Aaron here is the best with the sewing needle.

"Now try this bucket hat on and see how it looks on you. Hopefully, it's not too tight so it don't press on the stiches."

I catch the hat he throws at me with my good hand. My other hand is hurting really bad. I'm not sure how my left hand got messed up. It must've been from the punches I threw, or maybe he stomped on it. Either way my left hand is killing me too.

"Oh yeah and Crazy, I need to come pull that dental floss out in about 8–10 days. It won't fall out on its own."

"It's all good. For real, I'm just grateful for Ryan and your help. I don't know how I would have fixed the cut on my own forehead. You two honkies have kept it real."

"Just so you know, and you also need to hear this Justin, me and my dude Aaron, this is all we know; we only know how to keep it real. Me and Aaron been playing this game a long time. You two honkies are young. We realize you guys haven't picked a side. It's all good though. I'm not here to be your daddy. I'm just trying to give you some advice, not some fake-ass advice, some real-ass advice. These nigger's don't got no love for no honkies. They'll try to use us anyway they can, they'll try to extort a brother or they'll try to fuck a white guy. There might be a couple good ones, but the rest of them only understands violence. They got it in their minds us whites are scared of them.

"So, let me tell you two something, it don't matter where you grew up. It don't matter if you got black people married in your family on the streets, this is prison, honkies. This place has its own rules and codes. If you don't got pride in your skin color, then what could you have pride in? You stand for something or fall for anything. It's simple as that. You got to love yourself before you can love anything else."

Aaron stands up and moves toward the door. "Aaron and I are out of here; we're going to head back to our wing. But just so you two fully understand, that shit isn't over. Those black guys? You might be confused all to hell, but those are Bloods. Their gang leader isn't going to let them let it go so you two watch your back. We were just so happening to be coming up here to collect some money. So it was just by luck we could help.

"We're part of a group called Nazi Low-Riders, if you two honkies need our help, there is a good amount of us here and the other white gangs back us. Regardless, my dude Aaron will come back in 8 to 10 days to take that dental floss out your head. You two keep it real and be careful."

"Yeah, we'll always keep it real. It's good hearing what you just said. We will for sure be on the lookout for them. Motherfuckers won't get a second chance to run up in here like that. Me and Justin going to be watching for it. We'll heal up then probably go beat them up again, or we'll do something. Whatever we do though, keeping it real will always be number one on our list."

I watched them walk up to the top of the walk to get out of here, not sure what wing they're on. I could tell Ryan was a little upset that I just didn't jump on the idea of joining them. I could read his subtle meaning in his words. He was trying to tell us he'll make the problem go away with the Bloods; that if he and his group couldn't do it, he has other white groups on his side to help.

"Hey Justin, why you not talking at all player? I know your jaw is hurting, but I still never heard you be this quiet."

"Shit Crazy, you didn't hear that fucking hand out those damn idiots is trying to give us? All that shit about fucking pride and how we need to watch our back. Like we're a bunch of bitches in here that can't take care of some issue on our own."

"Shit Justin, that's why I love you brother. You think just like I do. Your fucking crazy like me and don't give a fuck about anything."

"Well then, you know why I wasn't talking. I'm not listening to that shit. I mean I got pride I'm white. I've always had pride, but that don't mean I got to be racist to have pride."

"Yeah, I feel you on that. We don't need to go all racist to show our pride." I sit down to think and then it comes to me, "We should start our own shit up. Call our group what the fuck we really are."

"I can't wait to hear this, what are we really?

"We're the fucking Dirty White Boys, Justin. We're the D.W.B for life brother!"

"Yeah, okay, I feel that shit Crazy. I've heard that before though. I think some other trailer-park, white gutter-trash boys call themselves that. Not sure if any are here though. I have also heard some other white boys from the city calling themselves that. I am not 100% sure about them, but I don't think they are crazy way out their racist. I'm pretty sure I've heard they're just really prideful in being white. They know what side they're on in a race war, but in any other times, they just do them."

"Well I don't give a fuck if any are here. I'm from the gutters so you don't get no dirtier than I am. A person can't lay claim on being called dirty any ways. So we're the fucking Dirty White Boys Justin! Not nothing but pure fucking dirty. Even though you're from the city Justin, you have had one struggle after the next your whole life. So you know what it feels like on what I'm sayin'. Plus, we're going to go get each one of them six that ran up in here. We'll catch them motherfuckers when they're in their cells as soon as we heal. We'll set us a fucking war off on our own. We going to get our lick back."

"You damn right Crazy! Show these motherfuckers how us real DWB's get dirty. Show 'em we don't give a fuck. Just realize this though Crazy, give it some time first so the heat on the whole, issue can go down a little first.

The next three days go by really smooth. We don't see any of those six black guys in the chow hall or anywhere else. It's like everybody is lying low and waiting to see how Justin, and I act on what happened.

For real, that is their worst decision, they are too cocky. Just because there are several of them and only two of us. They figure they have the upper hand no matter what way we go. Really all they are doing is letting us heal and giving me time to figure out how to con the white gangs into turning on the Bloods without us owing anyone or joining any of the white groups. I'm thinking that I can stage a fall out with the two. After all, I have convinced myself I'm a great con, so what better con could there be? I'll turn one group on my enemy's without either party knowing it and even if the Bloods do figure it out, it will be too late because the bigger white gangs will destroy their group.

In these three days, I've been keeping my ears open. I've been listening to information from both sides. My first step to con them is I have to learn more about what's going on. I need to find a way in so that as an outsider, I can convince the white gangs that they're getting disrespected somehow. I need to make all this sound real when I bring it to the bigger white groups, or they may turn on me instead. I already have it in my mind that I'll tell the white gangs, I am doing this because Ryan and Aaron helped me. They stitched my forehead all the way back together. I'll make it look like I'm repaying the favor. Then the bigger groups will stroke Ryan's and Aaron's dicks for helping Justin and I. That cancels the two of them out also. They'll feel like helping us brought them mad respect. So then Ryan and Aaron won't feel like we owe them.

If it works right, the war will remove a lot of Bloods from the yard. With the Bloods getting hit badly in the war, they'll have no time to focus on us. If any of the six remain in the middle of this, then Justin and I will pick them off one at a time, so the white gangs will feel like we're helping them. The hard part is to get that key information I need. I see all this as a win for Justin and I, as long as I can fish out enough dirt to kick it off.

Putting my con skills to work on other cons so they don't even realize what is happening, that's what a real con is. It's about being the best. Everybody calls themselves a fucking con, but they don't have a clue what that means. I was born to be the con man, I've always known this is what I have in me. I've realized I could con at a young age, and now I've been conning for a fucking decade. This isn't me being cocky. This isn't me saying I'm better than anybody else. I just realize my talent in life. I understand my calling, I don't ever run from it. I embrace it with open arms. This talent of mine is going to smash my enemies in front of me. My talent is going to put me and Justin in the winner's circle. How could I ever become the top con if I care what others think and most important of all, how can I become the top con if I am scared to bring him out to play?

By the fifth day, my forehead has no pain at all and Justin's jaw is healed, for the most part. It had swelled real badly for about the first three days, then on the fourth it started to go down. Now the swellings almost gone altogether. We were starting to feel like our old selves.

During all this, I started talking to a couple white dudes in the chow hall. Yesterday, I asked these white boys where I could buy some weed. They are what I call wiggers, they got it in their mind they are black, or want to be. I found these two idiots for a good reason. They hang with a few of the Bloods, also I heard they were trying to get into the gang. The whites done disowned them. The blacks really got no respect for them because how could anyone have any respect for two idiots that are unhappy with who they are.

These two try so hard to fit in. They are desperate for a person to talk to them because hardly anybody ever does. They try way too hard for a person to like them. Justin and I are on neutral ground with them. We're not in a white gang, so they feel they can talk to us, that it's not disrespecting any blacks they hang with. These two idiots don't realize the blacks have made them their "do-boys"—as in "do this" and "do that". The blacks won't never make these two idiots part of the Bloods. Nonetheless, if the bloods have branded them weak and that their only use is to be a 'do boy' then that means give me time I will unlock these two cause weak people always fold with the right words that throws them into confusion.

So far, what I have tricked out of these two dumb-ass do-boys is that their names are Donny and Joe. Their nicknames are Ren and Stimpy. (That should tell you everything you need to know for real.) Nonetheless, a simple fact is that most times lower do-boys know more than maybe a L.T.U or so cause all the errands they do teach them info.

Donny is the one called Ren. He has solid red hair. He is only about five foot five but cut up and stocky. He has bucked teeth with at least a million freckles upon his face. He wears his pants all the way down past his ass. He has solid green eyes; It's like he has Scottish in him. It's said he can fight well. He looks and acts like your typical school bully. I would put him in his late twenties.

Joe as you probably figured out is called Stimpy. He is every bit of six foot two. He is tall as fuck but unlike Ren, Stimpy is really slim, not cut up at all. He has black hair with blue eyes. He also wears his pants down past his ass. I don't have a clue if he can fight or not, I don't think anybody has ever seen him in a fight. But I'll tell you what, if the cops chase these two idiots, they'll trip over their baggy pants that are down around their knees and get caught. Stimpy is also in his late twenties.

Ren and Stimpy are best friends. They live in a cell together, been cellys for years. Neither one of them realizes they'll never be Bloods because that would make them family. The gang wants them as do-boys and you don't treat family like that so they stay do-boys.

Here's the thing about gangs; gang leaders rarely get their hands dirty. Most times they made it high in their gang because they did a ton of dirt in the early stages. So becoming the leader is like becoming the boss. They don't have to do the dirt any more, and they call the shots to everything. Those shots get passed down their ranks to their generals, lieutenants, and so on.

It's always the new recruits who get the shit jobs risking them more time in prison. These lower rank fucks are called soldiers or pecker woods, just depends on the gang. All white-boy gangs have generals as the highest rank. The generals call all the shots. In the black gangs that white guys can get into, their lower recruits are normally called soldiers. Pecker woods are new recruits for the white gangs, most of the time.

Some of this I already knew, some of it I didn't know at all. I learned all this in the last five days, mostly from Stimpy. He talks a lot. Ren is kind of paranoid and quiet.

I'm asking Ren and Stimpy about buying weed because I am trying to find a hook that involves money. If anything can set a war off between two gangs, it would be money for sure. Neither of these two idiots know what I'm doing. I'm trying to learn who controls what out on the yard. I want to know if anybody is just allowed to deal drugs. Information is power, and I don't care who a person is in prison or how top rank they may be. If you ask random people, and make the question just seem like you are curious or stupid; twist the question a little, you can learn anybody in prison behind their back without it being told to them. Sooner or later, you maybe will find some good info out. So if they ever come at you wrong, you can come back even harder yourself.

Ren and Stimpy are really dumb, or at least not on my level. I have this talent that I've been working on. It's where my mind can break down what a person says. I can do this in a flash. My mind breaks it down, then spits it out a new way to twist the whole conversation. I can do this on any subject, on any level. I don't care if a person with a college degree is talking to me about what he got his degree in, I can talk to him in a way he'll believe I have some knowledge on what is being spoken on. I have a sixth sense, a freaky connection to where I can read a person mentally. Mostly, it's me understanding body language and listening. I listen so well that I basically take what the person says, spin it a little, then I speak exactly what he just said right back at him. Plus I'll add a little extra information for the person to grab hold of. I'll have them thinking I get everything they say, and I'm adding to the conversation. The reality is, half the fucking time I don't have a clue what the fuck people are saying. I just got a talent of being a con man. I aim at someday being the best at it. Hell, even my most truthful moments, I'm fully bull-shitting my way through.

I sit down with Ren. The metal tables in the chow hall are square, so there's room for four people. Ren is on my left side, Stimpy is on my right, and Justin is right across from me. I remember how the tales at R.C.C. are wooden tables. These are metal tables, they also have a metal stool you sit on that is bolted to the table, and the table is bolted to the floor.

The chow hall has about 50 tables. Actually, there are two chow halls. The other chow hall is next door, it's for dorms three and four. The rats let us out of our wings one at a time, the yard rats call on the radio when the chow hall is at max limit. When enough tables open, the rat will call over the radio and tell the dorm officers to let another wing out. As soon as your tray is empty, the fucking rats will roll up on your table, tell you that you got to roll out. They don't want this shit to take ten hours every meal. They don't like us to just sit and talk after the tray is empty. If you sit there too long, they'll run you off whether the tray is done or not. The rats like to prove they're in control, but the reality is that they only have the amount of control we give them.

The whole chow hall setup is long, extremely loud, and stressful. Without fail there is always a line. Then there is also the issue of trying to get a table open when there are four of us trying to eat together. Certain people will try to buck in the line, to get a spot in the middle or towards the front. Some buck just to test a person out. You either fight or you look weak to everybody. Looking weak in here is like a shark bleeding out. It attracts some pretty unwanted attention from all the other sharks.

The blacks sit at the back of the chow hall, the whites sit in the front. Certain tables on the white side are for specific gangs only, so some tables, even on my side, I can't sit in. Ren and Stimpy sit on the black side. I might be trailer park trash, but for a fact, I'm not an idiot. I'm not going to sit in an area where there's a hundred blacks. Where I'm the only damn white guy or maybe Justin goes with me, so maybe two white guys. Fuck that! Talk about standing out like a sore thumb.

Ren and Stimpy aren't even allowed on the white side. Mostly, all the whites have disowned them altogether because they hang with black guys. For my plan to work, I need Ren and Stimpy feeling comfortable, so I sit on the borderline. Where we sit, Ren's back is almost touching the black person behind him. Normally, we sit around a table in the middle of the white table section. As we all sit down at the table, I can tell my dude Justin is feeling uncomfortable sitting so close on the border. He feels like this brings unwanted attention to us or that is what I think he's going through.

Justin trusts me though, so he follows me to the table. Justin is smart, but he lets me lead when it comes to this shit. He isn't on my level of skills, he is nowhere near my level when it comes to conning people. He just doesn't have the patience. Justin's whole idea of fixing something is beating the person up, so he realizes I can fix things better. This is the pattern we're comfortable with. He allows me to handle the talking, because he has seen first-hand my talent and respects it. So here we sit today. I realize I am extremely young. That I need to go through about 200 lessons, then go through around 200 issues to build my conning skills up.

Justin doesn't know what I'm up to. He just knows I'm plotting on something. He knows I'm trying to start something. Justin is real brave, he doesn't really care what goes down. So I figure I'll tell him tonight as long as everything goes well here at this little talk today. I should have the answer I need to start a war in a minute. At least, I really hope so. My con man inside is trying to break the doors down. I'm so excited to see if my plot works. Every little win feeds the con inside.

As Ren is putting salt on his food, I ask him, "Can you find me some weed or not?" I can feel Ren trying to pull away, paranoid all the time.

"Crazy you never spoke to me before, why you asking me this? I'm not trying to say nothing bad, I'm just trying to figure what's up."

"Damn Ren, I feel insulted. It's like you trying to say I'm plotting on you. You that fucking paranoid?"

"Hey I'm not fucking paranoid at all Crazy, I'm just real cautious with my surroundings is all."

"Stimpy, does this guy act like this all the fucking time? Over just a simple fucking joint a person wants to buy?"

"Yeah he's cautious around everybody Crazy. Hell, sometimes he even treats me that way."

"Okay then Ren I'll tell you what, you act paranoid all you want. I'll just take my money elsewhere. It's really no big deal. The only thing me and Justin are trying to do is smooth over some bad vibes. We had a small fight with some Bloods. Me and Justin figured if we bring our money over here to you, that smooth's it out with them. At least, we'd hoped it would.

"Any ways, I just thought you and Stimpy here were Bloods yourself, so I figure we could deal with you to kill a vibe that was all only a misunderstanding."

"Ha ha ha, you call running into two of my brothers' cell, beating them up real bad, and then robbing them for everything they got a misunderstanding?"

As I sit here and ponder this idiot's question, I notice how he didn't make any comment when I called him a Blood. I know he isn't a Blood. For him not to come out and say, he isn't one, lets me know these idiots whole weakness is that they're dying to be something they'll never be. If I stroke his ego hard enough about being a Blood, I may get him to lower his guard. I might be able to learn something from him. On the other hand, if we just keep talking maybe Stimpy will slip up. Stimpy is the slower one.

"Yeah Ren I do call it a misunderstanding. What else do you call it when you got no clue both people are Bloods? Since I didn't know, the misunderstanding is very obvious. If I would've known Ren, do you think I want to die? I wouldn't have run in that cell if I knew all that. Justin wouldn't have either. We're brave ass honkies, but we're not trying to go against the best gang on the yard."

"Well Crazy that's why they got this little word called *research*. It wouldn't have been hard to find out, all you had to do is ask around. Anybody would've told you about who they are. Who they roll with."

"See that's what I'm talking about, right there. You just spoke some real shit, that's why I'm now talking to you. You say I've never spoken to you. Well Ren, if I did speak to you before, I would have had firsthand information on what both those two were, who better to tell me that than you and Stimpy over here? You two, I've heard from everybody, are Bloods. Hell, you could've told me real easy. I realize me and Justin's mistake, not doing any research got us into this. So I'm trying to make new friends, Ren. That's why I'm talking to you."

"Well, you never came and asked us Crazy. If you would've, I would have told you. Stimpy would have told you also."

"Okay, well that's the past. Now I'm trying to turn over a new leaf, adding new people to my friend list. That's why me and Justin are trying to come ask you two. Me and Justin are loners just like you and Stimpy here. We hardly ever talk to anybody at all Ren, that's why we didn't know those two are Bloods. We don't talk to nobody else. Surely you can understand that Ren? Stimpy? What it's like to be loners. What it's like that nobody at all understand you or how you think and feel."

"So what you trying to say? I understand everything you're saying. I just got the feeling you want more than just buying some weed. Do you want me and Stimpy to go back to our brothers? Try to fix this whole issue that you and your dude here started?"

"Look Ren, I'm just going to keep it all the way 100 with you. Your dude Stimpy seems real cool. However, you on the other hand, are starting to creep me all the way the fuck out."

"Oh is that right Crazy? What am I doing that is creeping you out?" Ren says this while looking around the room, anywhere but at me.

"Well see, I told you I just wanted to buy some fucking weed. I didn't say nothing about you fixing nothing. You're so fucking paranoid towards people that you keep reaching to the stars for hidden ideas or hidden plots. I've tried to explain it to you already, you're not at all listening. Either tell me you don't want to sell or let me in. The whole paranoid shit is beyond creepy."

For emphasis, I turn to my dude Justin and ask, "Hey, Justin did you ask Ren or Stimpy to handle any issue for us at all?"

"Nah, Crazy, I didn't ask neither of these two anything. I'm just here for your moral support. I've never even asked either one about any weed, but I would like to get some. It's not worth all these questions though Crazy. Ren is treating us like we're some kind of yaps or something."

"Hey man you two aren't acting fair at all. I done told you I'm not at all paranoid, I'm just a real cautious person. I didn't say you asked for help on the issue, I am just being real nice. Simply tossing the offer out there."

"Look Ren, I'm going to go out on a limb here. I like you, and I do understand why you act paranoid. I like Stimpy here also. Justin and I have never done anything to either of you two. We've done nothing to ever lose your trust or earn your trust. So there's no need for you to act like this towards us. You got to give us a shot first, or tell us to get lost.

"Look Crazy, I like you also, I'm sorry I panic all the time. You seem like good people. Justin here is always real quiet but seems like a good dude. I can get you both weed. How much you two looking for?"

I can't even tell if I'm happy or just relieved to finally hear this idiot say he'll go get us some weed. But now it gets harder; my next question will balance this whole thing out. What I got to say will make this con work or break my scheme. Somehow I need to convince this idiot what I'm going to say is true. This will either put us into another fight by tonight or get me what I need to make this happen. The best cons are the ones that take the highest risk. This is going to be as risky as it gets, everything I have to say is a bluff.

"See that's what I'm talking about Ren. Now was that really so hard to trust me and my dude here?"

"Come on Crazy you not slow. Trust takes time in prison or anywhere. You know all this. Every white dude here hates me, they hate Stimpy also. So I stay watchful for our safety is all."

"Well I'm glad you say that. I need to tell you something that is going to take some trust. I'm sure Stimpy will have no issue trusting me. I really don't see you having an issue either considering if I'm lying to you with what I'm getting ready to tell you. The harm that would come to me, and Justin would be unstoppable. So I'm sure even you will be able to see I got no reason at all to lie.

"The two black guys me and Justin had the whole issue with Ren. I was talking to them the other day. Now I got to say I like the skinny one better. They call him Young Dubbs or Dubbs. His friend who lives in the cell with him is called Gangsta.

"I fully broke it down to these two, Ren, that I'm sorry. We didn't target them for any specific reason at all. My dude Justin and I was only hungry. We got desperate, picked the wrong cell.

We should've have done research. I told Dubbs that every good lesson is learned through a bad mistake. Sometimes through a terrible mistake."

"Yeah, what did they say about all that? I can only imagine how Gangsta is taking it. You have no idea who Gangsta is Crazy, he given that nickname because he fully earned it." Ren is a fucking coward or he is nerves stay bad. It seems as soon as we brought Gangsta up, he has started to shake in the hands a little bit. He also cant seem to stop fidgeting with stuff.

All this is just me starting my con. About two days ago I had found out through Aaron who the blacks were that we robbed and what their names were. I've never spoken to either of these black guys. I'm not only bluffing a whole lot here, I'm flat out fucking lying to these two idiots. I got to say that I really like Ren's last question though. It lets me know he believes I am desperate enough to run to Dubbs and Gangsta.

My next lie is going to by my fucking lie of the year. I need to find out about the drug money, who controls it. Find the money and you'll find a con. There's a root of evil behind all money in prison. I'm looking for these two idiots to tell me something. Ren is too paranoid at the moment to tell me anything good, so I may have to play this for another day or two to gain Ren's trust. That is, if me and Justin last that long without getting hurt or hurting someone else. It all depends on Ren and Stimpy trusting me and not taking this talk to nobody else. For sure, they can't take it back to the Bloods.

"Look Ren I fully understand what you are saying to me. The thing is, I do know who Gangsta is. Gangsta told me he's got to show out harder, at least harder than most other Bloods. Gangsta's uncle is the leader to the whole group, so Gangsta told us his uncle expects a lot more out of him. That's why he came at me and Justin so hard, that's why I got this damn dental floss in my head. So I do realize who they are. Dubbs is married to Gangsta's sister, so Dubbs is also family to them.

"Shit, I feel so stupid. I fucked up so bad that me, and Justin hit a cell that happens to be the fucking leaders of the Bloods' family."

"Hey, hey, Crazy keep that shit down. We got other people all around us that don't need to hear all that. Hardly anybody knows that."

"Well, it's your fault I got to say all this. If you wasn't so paranoid about people, I could get right to the point. However, I feel I got to explain myself to you just so you'll calm the fuck down some."

"Yeah, I see that now, it's all good though. I'm listening, get to the fucking point. The guards getting ready to run us out of here."

This fucking guy is so slow! Most of what I just said is common knowledge on the yard. I mean me and Justin didn't know back then, didn't give a fuck who they was really, but we would have heard it too if we slowed down some. We still don't give a fuck who they are but the point is that for my con to work, Justin did some digging and asked a few friends, or people he talks to, about Dubbs and Gangsta. Justin did all this while I worked on other stuff. Justin says the whole fucking yard knows these two are related to the leader of the Bloods.

The only hard part was to figure out the exact relationship. That part took a little bit of work. That is what is making my con work now. The fact that Gangsta is the nephew to the leader isn't common knowledge at all. Justin told me a Crip that knew them all on the streets, knew all this. Who better to know a Blood then its sworn enemy, a Crip. It turns out, they all are from Lexington, Kentucky so this Crip knew them very well.

"Well, I done got to the point already. I told you Dubbs and Gangsta have got to do things harder than the rest to show they just as tough as the leader of the gang. Show everyone they not getting special treatment. Dubbs wanted to call it even when we talked. Gangsta, on the other hand, felt like because they didn't get everything back when they robbed us, so me and Justin should work that off.

"Me and Justin owed forty dollars, plus we ate like twenty dollars in the three days before they came into our cell. So we didn't have around 60 dollars of the stuff we took from them. We offered to pay that off with the TV we got in our cell. They didn't get that when they came in on us. So in the end, me and Gangsta worked it all out. Dubbs and Gangsta sent me to you guys. They warned me you are really paranoid. Dubbs said it's because you like blacks more than whites. That you're real leery of white guys. I would have said my true intentions before now. But it's just that I wanted to build my own level of trust with you. That way you don't feel you got to give it to me just because they said so."

"I respect that a lot, I'd do anything for my brothers. If you had just told me they sent you and why they sent you, I would have gone with it. But I wouldn't have had any respect for you or any feelings of friendship. I really like how you beat around the bush to earn my trust. That means a lot to me. So tell me, what did Gangsta work out with you and Justin?"

Keeping my voice low, I say "Well we can go get him on the yard if you like. We can get out of this kitchen or you can trust me.

I figure this is a shot for all of us to earn something, but if you run to them they may take that as you can't never think on your own. So it could make you look bad."

"I don't need to go get them Crazy. I can't see why you would be lying about something Gangsta said. You might have the nickname Crazy, but you're not that crazy, ha ha ha, get it?"

"Any ways, he wants me and Justin to get weed from you, sell it all for them for six months for free. Then give all the money we make to them. Me and Justin make nothing. Then we're even."

"I don't get it, we have two pecker woods that sell for us."

Chapter 12

VICTORY AWAITS ALL TRUE CONS

The tallest oak in the forest was once just a little nut that held its ground. —Unknown

We all lean in, none of us want anyone else to overhear what we're talking about. In low voices, we continue the conversation.

"Well I'm pretty sure I didn't misunderstand Gangsta. Unless you got a clue what he meant Stimpy? Maybe you or Ren are going to have to go ask him."

"Listen to what I am going to tell you, Stimpy and I don't want to go run to Dubbs or Gangsta. This could be our chance to prove we can do things on our own. I can't see one reason why you would lie about this. We'll figure this out together."

On normal days that is the truth about not seeing one reason why I would lie to him. What he thinks isn't hard to understand. He believes the bloods will kill me if I'm lying about this. His mind can't go where mine is at. So he doesn't see it at all, and that makes my plot work better.

"So let me ask you both a question, when you two spoke to Gangsta and Dubbs are you sure you heard what they said right?"

"What kind of language are you speaking, Ren? What do you mean did we hear it right? Help me out here." It's getting hard for me to keep the annoyance out of my voice.

"Well Crazy, it's real simple if you ask me. Me and Stimpy have had the job of picking up two pounds of weed for our higher-up brothers. We got this job because we're white. One time a month we pick it up then deliver it to the same two pecker woods. We also pick up the money the pecker woods made throughout the month. They have to pay us for the weed. The higher ups give the two pecker woods a deal, they charge six thousand dollars for a pound. Those fuckers can make ten thousand or better. No doubt they make everything they can out of it. Any ways, since the two are part of the Aryan Brotherhood; everybody thought two white guys talking to them is the safest shot at it all going down right.

"Any ways, are you sure that Gangsta said to sell the dope or did he say take the dope to the sellers? I don't believe in coincidences at all, me and Stimpy been getting a lot of heat. The two pecker woods we take it to, act like we not supposed to be talking to them. They act all paranoid every time we meet. You think I'm paranoid, Crazy? You should see how these two act. Gangsta would know if we're catching heat. He probably wants you two to deliver it now then bring the cash back to us. The peckerwoods would not be so paranoid around you two. It's a genius plan of Gangsta's for real."

Now that I have Ren running his mouth, I can't get him to shut up. I think I'm onto something here, but I need more information. I don't get everything Ren is saying, but I can say for a fact that he is on my side now. I learned way back when I was a young con, that when you are trying to con somebody the hardest part is to get that first bit of information out of them. Once you open them up and they give up a small crumb you can rub that crumb in their face. Let them understand that they done gave up a crumb so there is no going back now—might as well give it all up. The hard part is getting that crumb. I learned that probably around 12 years old.

As I thought, Ren's weakness is his devotion to the Bloods and wanting to be one of them. The Bloods don't see it but Ren's and Stimpy's desire to fit in and their need to be turned a Blood have made them a loose cannon. They see their dream is maybe, finally in front of them that they don't see through my bullshit. The Bloods have pushed these two so far that it has turned them desperate. This is better than I hoped for, for real. The whole con I'm trying to pull over on these two idiots is fully depending on their desperate need to become a Blood, and it appears it's working, fully.

"Well Ren, it probably is a genius plan of Gangsta's, I'm not no mastermind like these guys. I can see now though, if you're getting heat from being around two pecker woods, with you two being Bloods, this is how it needs to be fixed. Get you two all the way away from those pecker woods.

"Now that I think it all over, I'm sure Gangsta said to take the dope to the sellers, I just was not paying attention. I heard sell or sellers, so I thought he meant to sell the weed. You being so smart, you just fixed a cluster fuck I was going to do." I turn to Justin now who's been following the conversation, "Hey Justin you remember if he said sell dope or take it to the sellers?"

"I'm pretty sure it's like you think it is. I think you, and I messed up. I just heard the word sell like you said Crazy and we just went with that. It's an easy mistake to make we should have had Gangsta repeat it." Justin is looking nervous as fuck. I can't put it together why he is acting so damn agitated.

"Yeah, that's what I thought too." I turn back to the two idiots, "So Ren, if we take it to these two pecker woods, me and Justin pick it up from you or pick it up from Gangsta? Then we take it to these pecker woods so the heat comes off you and Stimpy?"

"Well it's kind of crazy Gangsta sent you. This has got to be what he meant for sure, there is way too many coincidences to all this. We pick weed up tomorrow, and we're supposed to deliver it the same day. Then suddenly here you two are. I'm positive this is what Gangsta wanted.

"You'll pick it up from us. I mean for real, it's no loss to us even if Gangsta didn't mean for you to deliver it. The weed will still be delivered even if you do find out later Gangsta said something all-the-way different. It's all good 'cause Gangsta will, either way, be proud of us for coming up with the idea. That seals the deal, it's a win-win. We get points with Gangsta and you get to work off your debt.

"But if you did hear them wrong, we'll fix it with them for you. To tell you the truth, even if you didn't hear him right and it is for you two to sell it but not deliver, this is better any ways. Once he sees the heat is off me and Stimpy, he will keep it like this with you two just being the delivery guys. It makes more sense, for real. I can't see why they would want you two to sell when you two are loners. Two pounds are a lot of product so it takes a lot of connections to sell it all. You got to know a lot of people." We're onto something here, and I'm finding it hard to hide my excitement.

"Yeah, all that sounds about right. We would much rather just deliver the two pounds than to have to sell it. That's a lot of fucking work. Besides that's a lot of fucking heat trying to sell all that weed. It's like you said, me and Justin can count everybody we know on one hand. So who we take this two pounds to?

"You'll find this funny, at least you'll find their nicknames funny. They are both real blood brothers, not just brothers through the gang, but real family from birth. Their nicknames are Bulldog and Mad Dog and both act or look just like their nicknames.

"Bulldog is the younger brother, he's in his mid-twenties or so. He's built like a huge bulldog. He's extremely loyal to his brother, also like a real bulldog. He is highly dangerous and will kill you without thinking about it. Bulldog ain't nothing but about five foot five inches tall, but I promise you Crazy, Justin, don't let none of that fool you. He isn't ever getting out of prison. He's got nothing at all to lose. Half of the time he has a knife on him, he ain't afraid to use it either.

"His brother is about thirty years old or so, he is the worst of the two. He stays mad all the time for no reason at all. Sometimes he'll just start cussing you out. The only person that has ever had any control over him is his brother. If that's even possible. Mad Dog has more time than his brother so he's not getting out either. He's way more dangerous. All he does is work out all day so he's built real big. Both of them are bald headed and both look crazy as fuck. I don't or Stimpy does either, know their real names. I haven't never heard anyone say any thing but their nick names."

"Well Ren I'll be sure to take a knife with me. These two sound like a nice sunny day in the park. I do got one question or maybe two questions then we'll be ready to roll."

"Yeah, okay but hurry up Crazy, the guard has looked over here already twice. That rat will try to run us out any moment."

"Okay Ren, I don't got an issue with picking the weed up at all. I don't have an issue with picking up the money. I know Justin will help me carry it." I look over at Justin for confirmation.

"Shit Crazy, you know I got you honky. I don't give a fuck one way or the other. I'm down for whatever."

"Well okay Ren here's my question. Is it all cash we pick up or something else?"

"You'll meet Mad Dog and Bulldog in the property room. The property room rat is cool. Mad Dog and Bulldog will have at least seven to ten net bags, normally they're packed with bags of coffee. You can take two or three trips to get the net bags, just hurry up and try to avoid the yard rats all together. He'll have at least eight to ten-thousand dollars in cash hid in the net bags. Just leave the net bags closed, don't bang the net bags around. Those bags of coffee can't be crushed or none of that. Be careful with them because they use all them on the table as a form of money."

"Okay all that sounds real good, one last question. When you spoke about Mad Dog and Bulldog, you made a comment that they're loyal to each other to the max. You kind of left out that they're loyal to their Aryan Brothers. Is there a reason you left that out Ren? It just sounds like there is more to this story. I only want to make sure me and Justin are safe." I notice Ren immediately shoots Stimpy a paranoid look. I catch the worry in his face. This time Stimpy speaks first.

"Damn Ren, you told them all this already. I mean they are trying to make it right with Gangsta and Dubbs, I don't see Gangsta sending them to us if he felt a threat from them."

"Yeah, you got a good point. Besides, they probably need to know so they can avoid the other people in Mad Dog's and Bulldog's group."

"What the fuck you two talking about? Do you mind speaking where me and Justin can understand you?"

"Let's get out of this kitchen first. We can finish the rest of our talk on the walk back to our dorm. What I'm going to tell you is very real and has to stay between us. Besides, we have been in this kitchen too long."

"Yeah, well I need to get out of here any ways. This khaki state shirt is got me so hot I feel like I done sweated a bucket of sweat under it."

We get up to leave then walk our trays up to the front to throw them through a small window. Four convicts work back there clearing trays off. The state pays them two dollars a day for eight hours of hard labor. People try to say slavery is over. They should come to prison, in here it is far from over. They work a person to the ground, then pay them 18—40 dollars a month, it's all bullshit!

As we walk, I notice Justin trying to peel his khaki shirt off his chest where it is sticking to him from sweat. I don't understand the dress code. We have to wear our full khaki uniform everywhere, all day unless we're on the yard. On the yard, we can wear our white T-shirts, grey shorts or grey sweat pants. Other than that, we have to stay fully dressed in khaki pants, khaki shirt, and khaki belt. Can't ever untuck our shirts. We also have these khaki shirts buttoned up all the way to the top, or damn near. All summer long we sweat.

I guess it all balances out though, because in the winter time, we freeze. We wear long sleeve khaki shirts with a thin khaki coat. If you want gloves or a toboggan, you got to buy it for yourself. You can freeze to death for all the state cares.

As I am getting near the top of the kitchen, I see Justin trying to get my attention, so I slow down and allow him to walk up next to me. He whispers into my ear.

"What the fuck you doing Crazy? We'll be in fights 24/7! I don't give a shit but I'm just saying it's a pointless project because we'll never get the chance to enjoy it."

"Calm down Justin, it's not like you think at all. I'm trying to get these two idiots to tell me information. I think we're about to get the key piece in a minute. I'm not looking to rob them, I'm looking for a way to turn the Aryan brothers on them. I'm looking for a way to start a war. The Aryans can take care of our enemies for us without anyone even noticing they are doing it for us, or that I set it all up. Don't sweat it, I'll fix all this honky."

"So that's why you had me go find all that information out about Gangsta and Dubbs. What about Ren and Stimpy? What happens to these two guys?"

"It's part of life. We need to sacrifice them to the Aryan brothers. Let the Aryans know whatever we found out is through these two idiots. It's us or them, and I pick me and you all the way honky. I'm going to get these Bloods off us. They should have just gave me that ass kicking then leave me alone. They can't make it simple for us. They want us to sweat it. They want us to stay paranoid, not knowing when they may come back or even where they'll get us again. Two can play that game all the way. I don't stay paranoid, I plot how I can get them and I'm close now."

"Shit Crazy, you are crazy as fuck for real! It don't matter at all, I done got it in my mind. I'll ride this boat wherever with you. You like a brother to me Crazy."

"I'm not as crazy as you think Justin. I'm just being what life made me. I'm both hard and soft; I'm mean and kind also. You got no idea the way I think. I could take a man's life or make a person part of my life. I'm your enemy or your friend forever, it just all depends on the vibes I get from a person. Am I wrong for acting the way life made me? Don't all kids and adults act according to how they were raised?"

Rather than answer me, Justin starts to walk and says, "Let's go finish this, honky. Now that I understand more, I'm down all the way Crazy." Justin slides his tray in the slot. Ren and Stimpy done made it outside already. As I slide my tray in the slot, the ratting ass cop pulls up on me.

"Hey inmate, come here and let me pat you down." I don't have anything on me, so I don't give a shit what the rat does.

"Hey turnkey I'm not an inmate, I'm a convict to the max. You should watch your mouth rat."

"Yeah, yeah you're all convict, with your, what…? Two months in prison or maybe four months in?"

"Just pat me down and let's get this over with turnkey."

As the rat is patting me down, I notice Justin at the door keeping Ren and Stimpy busy. Justin is a lot smarter than he gives himself credit for. His instinct told him to talk to those idiots, so their minds don't think about what I said too much. He does shit all the time he don't even realize. It always helps us but he always claims he don't know that he's helping. I don't think I have ever seen him own up to helping.

"Alright inmate, you're good but next time you and your buddies better not take this long in the chow hall."

I just walk off. If I comment on what he says, it will be a smart-ass comment of mine, then he'll make a smart-ass comment back. Then I'll end up in the hole because I'll really cuss him out good after that. I can't afford to go to the hole right now. Besides, people may call it a slick check move. On top of all that I can't let him see my forehead. Since my back was towards him, so he can pat me down I was safe. I got too much going on to go to the hole.

Justin told me the other day what "slick check" is. The way Justin explained it to me, it is when a person owes or is about to get into it with somebody, then stages a fallout with the rats. The person can after that play it like they got locked in the hole by accident, but really they were scared or couldn't pay their debt. So it's like protective custody (check-in), but not. At least, that's what Justin tells me. I do know getting told that you slick checked means a fight right there or people will believe it. Even then they may still believe it if the facts are too high against you. You get that name on you, they'll run you off the yard.

As I walk outside I hear Justin saying something about a hamburger and chicken sandwich. This honky has the weirdest fuckin' eating habits. I can't really say nothing though, I got some weird stuff I enjoy also—hell, I like pickles and ice cream. That's like some pregnant female shit right there.

"You talking about that famous sandwich you love Justin?"

"Yeah Crazy, I was telling Ren and Stimpy that you put a bone-less piece of grilled chicken on top of a nicely cooked hamburger, then put pickles and mayo on it. It's the best ever!"

Justin is speaking to Ren and Stimpy like they're old friends of ours. Right after I told him, I'm going to sacrifice them both. Whether Justin realizes it or not, he's as cold hearted as I am and he is as soulless as they come. Men used to be warriors long ago but nowadays most men are pussies and worthless. Men have lost their nuts and gave them to the females. I love females and I'm not a sexist, but I believe it's the man's job to protect his woman. How can he do this if he's a bitch? Seems like more cowards are born every day, or more than in the past. I don't care what any right-wing feminist group yells, men have roles and women have roles. That's why we are built differently, so we can balance each other.

Stimpy says, "Man that sandwich sounds so good. I wish I could be at home now with the grill going and chicken and hamburgers on it. That would-be real nice huh?"

"You damn right, it would be. The only things that you are forgetting would be a nice cold beer and the music on real loud," Ren agrees.

"Don't leave out a half-naked woman Ren! One that's cute and short and thick, not boney at all," Justin says.

"Yeah, that's what I'm talking about, Justin. A woman who is about five foot even and about 130 lbs. or so, would be perfect," I say, finishing the fantasy.

"You don't know nothing about that Crazy. You what, 19 or 20 years old?"

"I'm 19 years old, but it don't matter. I've never dated tall or boney women. Why would I want a bitch that stands above me? I know more about this then you Ren!"

"Ha ha ha, you're real funny Crazy, I'm a lot older than you. It don't matter though, we will just agree to disagree. We need to move on to another subject before we make it back to the dorms."

"Okay that's cool. Tell me what's on your mind. " I try to say this with no emotion in my voice.

"Well it's real simple. It's just this stays with us four and don't leave our circle," we all nod our heads. "You want to make it right with Gangsta? Well if you speak about what I'm going to say you'll make not only Gangsta your enemy your whole life, you will make the entire gang of his your enemy. You won't never be able to fix it. Every yard you go to, you will be considered an enemy of the Bloods."

"Okay we get all that. We are just here to make things better. We're not trying to repeat nothing you say, we're not like that at all. We are real as they come."

"Yeah, just like Crazy says, also I don't even really talk to too many people any ways.""

"Okay that's good, I do believe you. I know you both will keep your word."

For real, the way Ren is speaking to me, I want to smack the shit out of him. Ren sounds like some little bitch that is scared to death of his own gang. For Ren to tell me, I'll make the Bloods on every yard my enemy? That shit really burns through me. I had to bite my lip on that.

Ren acts like a person is a bitch because he is one. I wouldn't give a fuck about being nobody's enemy. I get to a new yard I'll deal with whatever issue that goes down when I get there. I've never had a fear button inside me. I don't give a shit about nothing. I've always figured I'm this way because I don't have nothing to care about or anything to love. I guess until I find something to care about, I won't never know if this is true, or if I'm just doomed to be hateful and mean sound real depressing.

Ren is finally ready to say what is on his mind. "So here is how it is, Mad Dog and Bulldog get the weed from us like I told you. That cannot be told to anybody ever."

"What are you talking about Ren?" He's being dramatic and it's pissing me off. "You need to hurry up, we're almost at your dorm. What's the secret about those two selling?"

"The Aryan Brothers think Mad Dog, and Bulldog get the weed from a dirty cop. They're telling the Aryans that it's 7,000 dollars a pound, but we sell it for 6,000 dollars. Bulldog worked a deal with the Bloods that he would sell the Bloods' weed for them as long as the Bloods give him the best deal. A pound can go for 10,000 dollars if we wanted it to, so 6,000 dollars is unheard of. It's a wonderful deal that Bulldog jumped right on. Bulldog uses the Aryans to sell it and gets a 1,000 dollars on the side.

"So as you can piece together, Bulldog's brother went along with the whole deal. Backed him up all the way. The only catch is, the other Aryans don't know what the two brothers are doing." Ren pauses a minute to let that sink in. "It's extremely funny if you ask me. These racist fucks hate blacks. While they sit over there and hate, they don't even realize they're getting tricked and selling our drugs for us, making our money for us. On top of that they're getting used by their own two pecker woods for extra money. Isn't that the funniest shit ever? Crazy? Justin?"

Crazy answers, "Yeah that shit is pretty funny for real, I can't believe the higher-ups in the Aryans are this slow that they haven't caught on to it all."

"Well it's not that they're slow. It's just they trust Bulldog and Mad Dog. They believe they get it from a dirty cop. The high ups got no reason to question the two brothers. We've been doing this for two years now.

Stimpy whispers to us, "Before I head into my dorm, or before we do, we need you to remember one thing; when you take this weed tomorrow and pick up the money. If you see Aryans around, hold back until they leave the area. Even if it takes you six trips to get the bags back to the dorm, every trip you will avoid every white guy you can. Don't let none of them see you pick the bags up or drop the weed off. This way, we avoid any fights.

"We Bloods don't give a shit about none of these racist fucks. Hands down, we'd win any battle, but why battle when we got all this money coming in? Us Bloods don't even get no heat. The Aryans do all the work for us, take all the heat, and we just sit back and collect."

"Shit you Bloods are crazy as fuck. Man I'll be glad to get my deal done with Gangsta and get out the way again," I say watching Ren.

"Well just do good and remember everything I told you. We'll see you and Justin tomorrow."

As I watch Ren and Stimpy walk into their dorm, I think to myself that these idiots that call themselves Bloods, just told me information that could set a war off on every yard in Kentucky. I can't care less about any Bloods. I, for real, could have called it fair after they jumped me. However, life isn't that easy and the Bloods not only jumped me, they feel they have to destroy me and make me their bitch. Because of that thought of theirs, they pushed me to this. They didn't only bring my con-man out, they brought the monster out of me. I realized to a certain limit some of this is my fault for robbing people first. But we are way past all that now.

"What are we going to do Crazy? We going to sacrifice the two crazy-ass pecker wood brothers also?"

"I mean, I'll discuss it with you, but I see no way around it. If this is going to work, we got to fuck over the two brothers and Ren and Stimpy."

"Shit Crazy, don't you see that this is creating more enemies?"

"Yeah I see that Justin, but we can deal with Ren and Stimpy. We can even deal with Mad Dog and Bulldog. But we can't deal with a whole gang. My way, we beat one enemy that is huge and yeah, we make four or five simple fights down the road, but we may never see none of these guys again. We just got to play it out. Nonetheless, we got the beast off us, then all that's left is a few pests on the side."

Chapter 13

WAR IS EVERYWHERE AROUND ME!

"I love good sense above all,
perhaps because I have none." —Gustave Flaubert

As Justin and I walk into the dorm, I realize I need to talk to Ryan or Aaron. It can't wait till tomorrow. The stitches in my forehead have to come out now because I'll probably get into at least one fight behind all this. I can't afford to get hit in my forehead, especially with stitches in it. Justin will need to make sure he don't take too many hits to the face, or at least to his jaw.

"Hey Justin, on what walk do Ryan and Aaron live?"

"They live over on D walk up stairs, but why you want to holler at them?"

"I have had these stiches in for five days. They need to come out, *now*. You know we'll get into at least one good fight out of this. I can't afford to get hit on the forehead, honky. If the cut gets ripped back open with the right hit, that could take me out the fight. I don't ever plan to lose, at least not if I can help it." That is my worst fear, getting knocked out. Then you can't protect yourself from the person.

"Well, honky, if you learn to fight better you wouldn't have these issues."

"Ha ha ha…whatever Justin. I fight real good, honky, and you know it. It don't matter though because even the best fighters take a hit or two. This shit is going to get serious. We need to prepare ourselves for the worst."

"What does that mean? You trying to say something?"

"Yeah I mean something, honky. After we talk to Ryan and Aaron, and I get these stiches pulled out, we need to go holler at the dude three cells down from us."

"You talking about the big fat guy? The one called Heavy?"

"Yeah that's who I'm talking about. I had a talk with him back in the day. He has a couple of homemade shanks."

"God damn Crazy! What you going to do with a fucking knife?"

"Look, I'm not trying to be in prison forever. I don't see myself doing forever in here, but I'm a gangsta before I'm anything. We need to strap up and protect ourselves. I'll be damned if six people jump on me again. If that shit happens again, I'm stabbing the first one that swings on me. I'm in this shit to win, Justin. I can't stop what will happen. All I am saying is let's hope it don't happen, but does it hurt to be ready if it does? We made a decision to run in that cell, to rob those two black guys. Now we got to man up and fix what we started. I may be a lot of things, but I'll never be a coward."

"Yeah I feel all that honky, I just think we should use our hands. Getting a knife is taking this to another level."

"I feel what you saying, I just don't know if you see what is getting ready to happen. Mad Dog and Bulldog are extremely dangerous. They not ever getting out of prison. Those two honkies are crazy as fuck and I'm not going to let nobody gig me and I just stand there. If either one of those two come at me and pull a shank, I'm going to pull mine out and gig that motherfucker before he gigs me. I hope it don't come to that, but if it does we can get away with it. We'll do it in a cell where no one can see. I'm not going to die up in here. Now, you with me honky, or not?"

"Shit Crazy, you know I'm with you. I just try to be the voice of reason because you are crazy as fuck, for real. Either way it goes, we're in this to the end. I'll get a shank too. Don't never misunderstand me, I don't care at all what we do. I just try to also be the voice of reason, that's all." As I listen to Justin talk I get to thinking I wish my dude Country or J-bird was here. I wonder where they went.

"Yeah, I know you do. You my number-one honky. I'm cool with how you do things for real."

"Let's get up here to D-Wing Upper and talk to Ryan. We just need to avoid the rat, but it's all good honky."

The rat don't pay any attention, so getting to D-Upper isn't hard at all. Now, I just need to find out what cells Ryan and Aaron are in. There's about eight guys in the TV room, so I open the TV room door.

Before I can ask, Justin grabs me by my arm to get my attention. When I turn my face in his direction, he whispers to me that he needs to take a piss and grab something out of our cell, that he really wants me to wait for him, so he can listen to what is said. I can't argue about none of that. Plus, no matter what I say, he is knee-deep in all of this. So really he does need to know everything that is said, so I agree to what he is asking of me.

"I'll be up here in the TV room waiting on you Justin, try to hurry up honkey." As I watch Justin go out the wing door, I think to myself; at least, I can make myself of some use as I wait. I can try to find out where Ryan and Aaron live.

So as I open the TV room door, it keeps nagging at me, what the hell is the 'something' that Justin wants to get? I didn't ask and probably won't ask because it makes it look like I don't trust him.

"Hey, anybody in here know what cell Ryan or Aaron live in?"

A big fat white boy with a lot of tats on his face, sitting in the corner by himself, is the one that yells back at me, "Yeah, Ryan and his celly are in cell five. His celly's name is Aaron, they live together honky."

So, Ryan and Aaron are cell mates. No doubt it helps a person's time to have the right cell mate. Hell we spend more time with our cell mates then most married couples spend together.

"Oh, okay good-looking honky!"

It seems like twenty minutes have went by, I am starting to get inpatient. Then Justin finally pops his head in the TV room. "I'm ready." I tell Justin it is cell five.

By the time I shut the TV room door, Justin already walked off and is at cell five knocking. As soon as I catch up to him the cell door swings open and Ryan steps out, "Hey, what you two young honkies doing over here on my walk?"

"I need to speak to you and Aaron. Are you two busy?" I try to say this with the most serious looking face I can. I don't want these guys to think I'm running any type of game.

"Nah, we not busy at all, we just laid back watching some TV." He eyes Justin, then asks me, "Does Justin also need to holler at me and Aaron too?"

"No Justin is just riding with me, he only come along to say hello. You know my dude don't talk a whole lot."

"I try to speak only when I got something useful to say. Other then that, I try to listen more than speak. You learn a lot more in life this way. Justin has this big smile on his face where you really don't know if he is bullshitting you, or if he is serious or not."

"If everybody did that, the world would no doubt be a better place." Ryan says this to Justin but is staring at me like he's trying to send a message. I get this vibe that runs deep in me that Ryan doesn't trust Justin. I just can't think of why, or if I am missing something. I get the feeling Ryan knows something about my dude that I don't know. Down the road, I'm going to find a way to get Ryan to talk to me about this. First, get my plan going and see how the next 72 hours goes.

"Let us come up in your cell, you guarding this door like we're your enemy honky." I learned in my early stages that as a good con, you must learn how to apply humor to certain issues or problems.

"I'm not guarding the door Crazy, I am just seeing what is on your mind first. Looks like you want to talk about something important so you two come on in here and sit down. I can only imagine with how crazy you are, what you want to talk about. To be put a better way Crazy and I mean no disrespect, I'm just keeping it real, but I'm saying nothing you could say could surprise me.

Ryan walks right to the top of his bed and sits down. Aaron is laying down in the top bunk. He is wearing a pair of headphones, watching some movie. Their cell looks the same as ours. Toilet in the front and a bunk bed in the corner, and with the two metal lockers against the wall with a table in the middle of the lockers to sit your TV on. Right across the bunk. Then right between all this is your plastic chair pulled to the back, against the wall.

Ryan and Aaron must be hustling really hard, or they got people on the streets that love them. They both got a TV set, I also see two coolers under the bed. There's a nice Sony cd player sitting on the table. I notice they have real sheets and blankets on their beds. Aaron jumps down from the top bunk, then sits in the plastic chair in the back of the cell.

I find it so funny to say 'real sheets'. It makes it sound like I am calling his sheets fake. I bet when I get out people will barely understand me, but fake sheets are plain white state sheets. Real sheets are made with cotton and have color to them. It's just I'll have to explain this every time I say fake or real sheets.

"Hey don't you be up in our cell checking shit out, Crazy. I know all about how you two like to steal," Aaron says, joking. I know he means it though. I can't blame him or get upset about it. It does in a small way make me feel like a piece of shit. Nevertheless, I choose this path and there's no need to call it anything else, I try any ways.

"Come on Aaron! You got to give us more credit than that. We may steal from time to time (I call it robbery), but we would never do that to you two honkies."

Aaron kind of smiles at me, "Well we hope not. And I don't really think you would, Crazy. I am just playing with you. Any ways, tell us why you two over here."

"I need these stiches out. It's been five days, and I feel fine. They are ready to come out Aaron, or at least I hope they are."

"Hmm, okay come over and sit down in front of me. Let me check it out."

Ryan grabs a cooler under the bed and pushes it in front of Aaron. "There you go, sit down on the cooler and let me see if they can come out or not okay?"

As I sit down on the cooler, I notice Justin watching these two real close. I get the impression, he hates these two for some reason or another. So now I know the feelings they feel are both sides. Shit has me paranoid.

Aaron pokes and pulls on the skin on my forehead. I just sit here and hope like hell they can come out. I'm running on so much adrenalin between Justin and all this shit getting ready to come out, that I don't even feel anything Aaron is doing.

"Well good news and bad news. The good news is, I can pull them out. The bad news is that it will leave one hell of a scar, honky."

"I don't give a shit about a scar Aaron. I just would like them out because they itch like hell all the time." I figure to lie is best for me at the moment to get what I want.

"Yeah, the itching is where it's healing. It may hurt a little or a lot when I pull them out. Just depends on when you were healing, how far the stiches went into your skin."

"I'm cool with that, I'm just grateful for your help."

"Ryan can you get in my locker? You know where I keep the tweezers at right?"

"Yeah, I know where you put them, I've only been your celly for two years."

"What you going to use the tweezers for?" I ask, getting worried, but really not knowing why prison has fucked my head up a lot where I got some fucked-up trust issues.

"Well, I plan to use them to pull these out. The dental floss gets stuck in the skin sometimes, then I have to pull hard. That may tear the skin so make sure you sit still. As I told you already, it just depends on how deep they went."

Ryan gives Aaron the tweezers, he starts working on my forehead. The moment he hands over the tweezers, I can see Ryan's kind of eye balling Justin. My intuition is telling me Ryan has something up his sleeve. It could be my imagination, but Ryan seemed like he was putting off a kind of negative vibe.

"Hey Ryan, what's on your mind honky? I see you looking at my dude. Tell me what's up with you!" I figure he won't tell me it, but I want him to know that I'm on top of it, and I know something is up.

Aaron just pulls a stitch out that was stuck to my skin. When he pulled on it real hard, it felt like I was hit on the head with an iron. I get a little light headed from it. Pain, violence, and patience are the top three things every convict learns real fucking fast. It breaks you or turns you into a monster.

"Damn Crazy, that stitch was locked in there so tight that it took a chunk of skin just to get it all the way out."

"Yeah, I kind of put that together for real. Shit hurt like a motherfucker honky. Just to keep it 100, I hope no more are stuck in there like that."

"It's not that anything is on my mind Crazy. Well maybe there is just a little bit," Ryan looks over at Justin then me when he says this.

"Ryan, we talked about this already and agreed not to get in their business at all," Aaron says as he keeps working.

"Yeah I get that. I had no intention of saying a word, but it bothers me a good honky would deal with two fucking yaps."

"What you talking about right here?" I really couldn't keep the anger out all the way. I hate that because I train myself over and over to master my emotions and feelings.

"Well, I have seen you and Justin at dinnertime sitting with those two fucking wannabe-fucking-black pieces of shit, Ren and Stimpy. Why would you want to sit with them two dick suckers? All they are, are the black man's punks? Now the rest of what I know about your dude, Crazy, this isn't the time or place."

Then Aaron looks over at Justin and says, "everything sooner or later comes out to the light."

"Well I'll tell you why—ahhhh! MotherFUCKER! Damn, what was that Aaron?"

"You had another piece of dental floss that was stuck under the skin. I had to pull so hard that it's cutting you real bad. You'll still need to wear that bucket hat for a few more days, and this'll be sore as hell. The good news is that they are minor cuts. They'll heal on their own in due time. Just hold still for a few more moments. It's almost all the way done honky."

"It's all good Aaron and I don't mean to bitch about it, I'm just grateful you did this for me honky." The pain was a little more manageable, and it's important they understand me, so I press on, "That brings us back to our main topic, I don't give a shit about Ren or Stimpy." I decide to let the whole Justin issue go until I get my plot and plan rolling. I refuse to allow my emotions fuck my entire plan and work up.

"Yeah, I don't give a shit about them either. I probably dislike them for a different reason than you guys," Justin agrees. I also notice Justin agrees to this, but he never spoke up when Ryan or

Aaron said what they did to him. It's either he's scared of them or what they know.

"What you talking about? Why you say you dislike 'em but sit and eat with 'em?"

"Well, I dislike them because they're cowards. They don't know how to man up and make their gang take them in. They so fucking weak, they accept being do-boys. I have no respect for people that weak. As far as why me and Crazy sat with them, I'll just let Crazy tell you honkies about that." Justin says all this real fast with some anger. He never speaks so he must feel pretty strongly about these two.

"Yeah, well Justin, I don't like them because they are weak, but I also have no respect for a white guy that has no pride in his own race."

"Yeah, I can feel that Ryan. I mean me and Justin are not really racist, but we still got pride in ourselves. Justin and I are Dirty White Boys, Ryan."

"Ha ha ha, yeah you two are for sure that Crazy. You two grimy as fuck, for real. Although Justin here is riding dirty as hell."

"Well it's kind of funny you say that Ryan. We've been sitting with Ren and Stimpy because we were trying to gain their trust." Ryan and Aaron exchange a look, they're not sure where this is going so I explain more. "Me and Justin wanted to do you a favor back so we're researching some stuff. We did gain those two idiots' trust, we got some information that is really messed up. It don't matter how messed up it is though, it's got to be exposed. Honestly, didn't think we were going to get the mother-load of info, but if I'm right, then that's what we got."

"So let me see if I got this right, Crazy. You saying that you and Justin been sitting with the two yaps this whole time because you two crazy-ass honkies been plotting on them?"

"Yeah, that about sums it up for real Ryan. We feel it's only fair for what you and Aaron have done for us. We also think it's just loyal of us."

"Well that's some real shit. Justin you may be quite a lot, but you're a real motherfucker too." He looked at Justin like he was seeing him for the first time. "So what is this information you got? By the way Justin, just to keep it real to you, I know your secret and I hope you become clean before it becomes too late.

"Well here's the thing Ryan, we going to give you two all the credit." I pause not knowing how he's going to take this. Plus, I am trying so fucking hard not to bite off his comments towards my dude, but it makes me madder Justin says nothing.

"But...?" he prompts.

"But, the only issue is me and Justin want to tell this to a higher rank Aryan while we tell you two."

"Well hell, that's not an issue. Two cells down is the captain of the Aryans. Their general is locked up in the hole at the Castle in Eddyville. You want me to go get the captain?"

"Yeah, can you go get him for us? I feel this is something he needs to know real badly."

"Damn Crazy, this sounds like you got some dangerous information. So be warned Crazy, and I say this with lots of respect, Bill-Bill is extremely dangerous. Be real for sure your path you take and be ready to man upon whatever you do or say."

"Well I guess it could be dangerous, but it's all how the Aryans take it. Nonetheless, I am a man before I'm anything. I will own up to anything I say or do, honky"

"Alright, I'll go get him right now. Aaron can stay here and finish your forehead. It looks like he's almost done with it. Any ways I'll be right back guys."

Ryan leaves to get the captain but all I can really focus on is these damn stitches coming out. I swear it hurts worse coming out then going in.

I'm glad to be getting them out, for real. It's only a matter of time before some rat sees the stitches and wants to know what happened. When that rat patted me down in the chow hall, he made me take my bucket hat off. He just patted my hat to make sure I got nothing in it but it could've been bad. The key to prison is just being a little smart. I never turned around so the rat didn't see the stiches at all. The truth is that over half the rats are dumb. They grew up being bullied. They are scared and for sure, they're bitches. They are not street smart at all and have little common sense. So if your swagger is anything at all, you will have no issue tricking a rat or playing them to the left. I mean, really, who the fuck wants to be a correctional officer? The issue is that rats are run by anger. Killing them with kindness fucks their head up better than anything else you can do.

"You got to sit still, I got one last stich to come out honky. Here comes Ryan."

"Justin, Crazy, this is Bill right here. You guys can call him Bill-Bill."

"Hey what's up with you Bill-Bill? My name's Justin, honky"

"Well my name is Crazy, but I can't turn around right now honky."

"Well hold on a second, Crazy. This last stich is almost out." Aaron pulls my last stitch out, at least this last one hasn't hurt that bad. "There you go Crazy, it's all over. You'll have a terrible scar but, unless you get power-drived in the head again, it will stay closed."

"You can move over there if you want but put your back up against the metal locker." Aaron points at the locker. I move where Aaron suggested I move, then I sit down and see that Ryan sat down on his bed. Bill-Bill sat down next to him. Bill-Bill looked scary as fuck. This honky is enormous, has muscles in spots I never even knew you could get muscles. Like behind his neck, in the back part of the head. I can almost see what looks like one huge roll of muscles stuck back there.

Besides Bill-Bill's muscles, he has a well shaved head and no hair on his face at all except his eye brows. He's just sitting there staring at me with these two cold eyes. Bill-Bill is wearing a wife beater muscle shirt and pair of grey shorts. His shoes looked brand new. He has racial tats everywhere, all kinds of different ones.

"What do you want to talk about young honky?"

I just ignore Bill-Bill because I want to make sure Justin is good. Plus, to lay out messages without words is the best form of conning. Sometimes without words you let people know you don't jump, when they say jump or other messages can be said if you know how to do it.

"Hey Justin, you want to sit down over here?"

"Yeah I need to sit down, but I'll just sit down over here by the door honky."

That's why I say Justin is smart. He knows I'm telling him to sit down because it would make everybody in the room uncomfortable with us sitting and him standing. More important though,

Justin just let me know he don't trust any of these guys around us. He isn't going to sit over here with me. He's doing this to let me know if it pops off into anything in this cell he'll have my back all the way. Besides, this way he's in a good position, real close to the door like that. If anything popped off in here, it would be best we get out in the hallway. No way can we fight these three big-ass honkies in this small cell.

Bill-Bill looks to be about forty something years old. By the look of all his prison tats, I would say he has been here for a long time. Also, I'm sure it's no easy feat making it to Captain of the Aryans.

The Aryans are a brutal group. Strong, proud white boys who are fully racist. Back in the day, what I hear from a few people, when there was more blacks in prison than whites, way back in the 1970s or so, the blacks were killing out the white boys. They were beating them up or raping them. Some good white boys in California or somewhere got together and started giving the fight back to the blacks.

Now fast-forward to where I sit right now, you have tons of white groups. Aryan Nation is the Aryan Brothers right-hand man. Then you have the Aryan Circle that is trying to take off. When a honky can't get into the Aryan Brothers or Nation, they go to the Aryan Circle. The Aryan Brothers and Nation are both old school and they're two of the oldest groups in prison, the Brothers and Nation has tons of rules: 1) They don't do any heavy drugs. 2) They fully believe in being sober at all times, just in case war brakes off (they won't be high and get took out too fast). 3) They don't mess with homosexuals. 4) They don't listen to black music and 5) They don't mess with blacks at all. The Aryan Nation is the same way.

Your newer generation of kids coming into prison, like me, we refuse to stop taking pills or things that get us high. As a result, the first two Aryan groups won't fuck with the type of white boys that get high. The Aryan Circle was created for kids in my generation. I myself, have had no interest in any of it. Mainly cause I don't like anyone telling me what to do.

Besides the Aryan Groups, you have your Nazi groups of different kinds. Ryan and Aaron are in one of the bigger Nazi groups. The Nazi Low Riders are, for real, pretty big. Then you got your Nazi skinhead groups. They're all loud and do stupid shit all the time. It's the Aryan Brothers and Nation though that hold the title for the top honkies running the prison system. Another reason I don't have any interests in gangs. Gangs are like your family and you got to know each other pretty deep. As the con man I am, I realize its best to never, ever let anybody fully get to know you. They can use what they know against you.

"Well Bill-Bill, I got a story to tell you. First, I want to tell you why I'm giving you this information. About five days ago six Bloods jumped me and my celly, Justin. None of that matters for real, Bill-Bill, because me and Justin stay in shit. This is just how we live at the time. So, for real, the Bloods can suck our dicks. They can jump us as many times as they want. That's just part of the game I play. You can believe I'm going to get my lick back somehow or another."

"Yeah, I've heard about you Crazy. I've heard about Justin here also. About a month ago I was going to send somebody to talk to you two, just a simple talk. You are both really young and real new to the system. You don't realize you can't hit certain cells and beat a person up and steal their shit like you two do. Not without researching who the person is. The person you hit could be under the Aryan's protection. You need permission to do that. Hell they may be under any gangs' protection and you're lucky you haven't made several gangs mad at you so far.

"Any ways, as you two can see; we didn't come talk to you. We felt like, for real, it is a win-win for us. You two run in a cell and beat a person up and steal their shit. That certain person under my protection, they come and cry to me or somebody under me. We lie and say we warned you two young guys. Times are getting harder with these young guys. So we tell the person to pay a little more. It helps us squeeze more out of the cowards. We tell the person you robbed. That for the extra money, we promise it won't happen no more."

"Hell Bill-Bill, you're a con just like me." He looked a little surprised at that so I added, "I don't mean no disrespect at all."

"Crazy everybody in prison is a con to a certain degree. The only ones that aren't cons, are the weak and worthless ones that get locked up for weak charges. The rest of us are trying to get better at being a con. Just like on the streets, some cons in here are real slow or stupid, some are half and half at it. Others think they're good, but don't got a dollar in their cell to prove it. Then you got your cons, your real true cons that most people can't even tell they're being tricked because this type of con is so good at it. These con artists call the shots behind the scenes. All the way being real with you two, this type of con is like a rare bug. They are extremely intelligent but can act slow or smart depending on what he needs for the con. He or she blends in wherever and is extremely cold hearted. If he or she can love at all. It would have to be their soul mate. I would bet these two would be fucking powerful together.

"So I take no offense to the word *con*, Crazy. I'm a con in every way. I also am a convict in every way. So, what was you saying Crazy?"

"Well I was just saying I got into it with the Bloods. Me and Justin ran into a cell, beat two black guys up then robbed them. We didn't realize they were Bloods for real." I pause for a moment to see if he reacts. He just sits there looking at me so I keep going.

"Well, those six black guys ran up in our cell, as you could guess they messed us up real bad. We both got knocked out. Although Ryan and Aaron didn't see us getting jumped or see the black guys run in our cell. They did see our stuff getting packed out the cell. I know if Ryan and Aaron would've seen anything before that. They wouldn't have let six blacks jump on us two white boys.

"The majority of me and Justin's stuff was either the stuff we took from others or stuff we took from those two black guys. The good news for us is that Ryan and Aaron talked to them six. They got the rest of our stuff from getting took; that helped a lot to be honest. Bill-Bill, because of them, we still got our TV in our cell. As a hustler, everything we get is all off the land so any blow is hard for us. As you said yourself Bill-Bill, we're new to the system. I have nobody but me and my friends in prison. So I'm trying to find a way to survive. I know it will come to me, I'll find my path. For now, I'm not proud of what I do, but I got very little to choose from.

"Anyway, Ryan and Aaron saw that I needed stiches real bad. On top of all that I couldn't go to the medical office. Medical would've locked me up in the hole then the rats would have come checked my celly. The rats would have taken one look at his jaw and locked him straight up also. Aaron put in these stitches he was just taking out, and fixed it so no one wound up in the hole. So me and Justin felt we owed Ryan and Aaron, even though these two honkies say we don't, we still feel we do 'cause it means a lot to us what these two have done for us. Aaron just took the stiches out my forehead, he has never charged me anything. So, Bill-Bill, to get to the point, me and Justin was trying to pay these two back. As I told you already, everything we got is off the land, so I set out to try to get some useful information that I could give Ryan and Aaron. Something for their whole group. Just something they could know about their enemy. I was raised; knowledge and Intel is everything. So I figured I could get something small they could use as leverage when needed.

"To make a long story short Bill-Bill, I didn't get any good information for their group. I did get some about your group, though so I figured I had to tell you. I just wanted to tell you under the understanding I had done all this as payback for a favor that was so needed. I did it for these two honkies right here."

"Yeah, yeah, I get you did whatever you did because what Ryan and Aaron did for you. I also get, and I'm sure they do as well, that what you two found out cleans up your ties with Ryan and Aaron. That they can't come back and say you owe." Bill- Bill looks at me so intense that you would think he could look into your soul when he says all that.

"That's correct. Me and Justin aren't saying these two are the kind to come back and hold it over us. It's nothing like that at all. We just think fair is fair."

"Okay I got all that. But now *you* listen to *me* real, real close. Before you let whatever you're going to say come out your mouth, make damn sure none of it is a lie. I'm not your toy Crazy and trust me when I tell you that you don't want me as your enemy. You better be ready to own up to what you say." He is looking at me but then paused, turned and looked Justin right in the eye. "That all goes for you too Justin."

"Yeah, we'll own up to anything we say Bill- Bill. We're not liars, me and Justin might be a lot of things, but we haven't told any lies to anybody."

"Look Crazy don't get no complex on me, I haven't told you anything I wouldn't tell anybody I deal with. To give you your own words back, little honky, fair is fair. I'm just being real with you and letting you know what's up."

"Okay, so let me tell you right out what I learned. We've been talking to these two yaps named Ren and Stimpy. It took us a little while to get their trust, but in the end we learned that the higher-up Bloods give Ren and Stimpy two pounds of weed, the weed you think is coming from a guard. Ren and Stimpy sneaks the two pounds over to Mad Dog and Bulldog in the property room for six thousand a pound. The two of them resell it for seven thousand a pound, give the six to Ren and Stimpy and pocket an extra grand for their trouble." I said all that in a rush because I'm not sure how Bill-Bill is going to take it. I figured it was like my life, just better to never hold back.

"So let me make sure I got this right, you trying to say my two brothers, Mad-Dog and Bulldog are not getting the weed from a guard? That they really getting it from the fucking niggers? Then, if that insult is not bad enough on its own, you're saying that my two brothers are hustling me and the rest of our brothers out of a thousand dollars a month? Is this right? Because I'll tell you right now this is going to turn out really bad. So think about what you're saying Crazy!"

"I don't need to think about nothing Bill-Bill. What you say is how it's being played out every month. Now as far as all this turning real bad, I am all the way prepared for it."

"You would make a good brother for real. I would even be willing to train you myself, but that's a subject for down the road though. Let's get back to the subject here at hand.

"You're sure it's those two faggot-ass wiggers, Ren and Stimpy, that not only gave you this information, but also that they've been the ones doing the delivery service? These two faggots have been acting like us Aryans are a bunch of bitches and idiots!"

"Yeah, that's what I'm saying to you Bill-Bill."

"Okay this is how this is going to play out. Not to insult you two at all, but we're going to yank Ren and Stimpy up tomorrow. I would normally wait on somebody higher up to make this decision but on this issue, I will be covered to handle it how I see fit."

"Hold on a minute Bill-Bill, if you're getting ready to say we pull Ren and Stimpy in a cell so you can hear it for yourself, I got a better plan for you. Ren and Stimpy are going to give me and Justin the two pounds of weed tomorrow. We talked these two idiots into believing we're the new delivery. Plus, we suppose to pick the money up from Mad Dog and Bulldog."

"Hmm, well this is even better than I thought." I am surprised how controlled Bill-Bill is but then he's been doing this a long time. He seems more tired than angry, maybe he is just disappointed in his brothers. "Okay this is how we play this. I already know that Mad Dog and Bulldog got eight bags of canteen and a thousand in cash. Tomorrow, you will bring the weed to me when you pick it up. I'll wait until late tomorrow, and then I'll have the money, Bulldog and Mad Dog all brought to a cell on this walk. I'll also have Ren and Stimpy brought up here and put into a cell.

"I understand you two did this as a favor. Regardless, I'll give you and Justin a pound of the weed. Ryan and Aaron, you two can have the other pound out of a favor for these two. As long as all this is true, because if it's all true I don't want those niggers' weed."

"Hell, that's all the way good-looking Bill-Bill," Aaron says, obviously pleased with the prospect. Apparently, the Nazi Low-riders have no issue with taking the niggers' weed. It goes to show you that some of these guys only become racist in prison.

"Yeah for sure Bill-Bill! Thank you very much. Thank you a lot." I probably sounded like an idiot, but I couldn't help it because a pound of weed is a lot in my world.

"It's all good but I'm not done so hold on. Crazy, I want you and your celly to fight Ren and Stimpy. Afterwards, I'll have a little extra for those two wiggers. I'll handle Mad Dog and Bulldog myself. My brothers are my responsibility. But everything else is your responsibility."

"What are you talking about Bill-Bill?"

"You're saying two of my foot soldiers are stabbing me in the back right? You're saying Mad Dog, and Bulldog are stabbing their whole race in the back. To me, that's pretty fucking serious! To make matters worse, from what you're saying, Mad Dog and Bulldog really have no reason for what they're doing. Risk your life to make an extra thousand dollars? Maybe they're just thrill seekers, I don't know. But I got to ask why two good honkies would do this."

"Look Bill-Bill I don't mean no disrespect, I'm only trying to do the right thing here. I really do understand your struggle in not wanting to believe Mad Dog and Bulldog would do this. I'm sure nobody wants to believe somebody close to them would be the one to harm them. Regardless, if you want to believe me or not, I'm giving you some real information. What you do with it is up to you."

"Hold up for a second, Crazy. You're so young that sometimes you don't see the whole picture. Unlike you, I've been in prison for twenty years. I've seen a lot of things in all this time and every time I think I won't see anything worse, something comes along that is a great deal worse than the last time. It's not that I don't believe you, I've seen people do worse for a lot less than them two. The problem isn't whether I trust you and Justin or not."

"Well, what is the issue Bill-Bill? I went through a lot of work to get this information. If you don't want it, that's cool, we'll move along."

"Things in prison are never that simple. You're making one hell of an accusation. You don't get to just say what you want. In prison, you got to man up behind your words. I asked before you spoke up if you would stand behind what you said. Now, like I said, Mad Dog and Bulldog are my responsibility but as far as Ren and Stimpy goes they're your responsibly."

"What are you trying to say right here Bill-Bill?"

"It's very easy to see what I am saying. You and Justin are putting out information that could start a lot of trouble. What I'm saying is tomorrow, before anything negative happens at all, or before I make any decisions at all, you and Justin are going to do your part. You two involved yourself. So much as I'm grateful if this all turns out to be true, I still need to go at this smooth."

"I don't have any issue with none of what you're saying. Justin and I may be young like you say. Nonetheless, Bill-Bill, we involved ourselves because we felt we needed to pay back Ryan and Aaron here. Now if you telling me we need to go a step further here, we got no issue at all with that."

"Well, as I said, it's very simple. You say Ren and Stimpy told you this, so tomorrow you and Justin are going to pull Ren and Stimpy into a room. Me and my lieutenant will join you in the cell. You and Justin are then going to make Ren and Stimpy tell me what they said."

"Alright, no big issue at all. I am not at all naïve Bill-Bill. Ren and Stimpy are loyal to the Bloods, so it's not going to be easy for us to get them to talk to you and your lieutenant. It don't matter though, because I'll do whatever it takes. What about the weed? You don't want us to pick that up now?"

"That's what I'm saying here Crazy. You and Justin will pull up on Ren and Stimpy at breakfast time. Fuck the weed at the moment, we'll get these two to talk first. Don't worry Crazy, you two will get your weed."

"What about Mad Dog and Bulldog, Bill-Bill?"

"If all this turns out as you say it is, then as for Mad Dog and Bulldog, I will handle them. That's all that needs to be said about that."

"Alright then Bill-Bill. Ryan and Aaron, seems like all will come out tomorrow. Me and Justin are going back to our wing. We'll see you guys at breakfast time."

"Crazy, You will see me and my lieutenant, Ryan and Aaron won't be there."

"Okay that's all good, we're out of here though." I head to the door but I see Justin hesitate.

"Bill-Bill, what if Crazy or I can't get Ren or Stimpy to open up? Can't get them to tell us again?" Justin looks only at Bill-Bill when he asked this question. It feels like fire between them.

"Well, I have faith in you two. You two got them to talk already, that was the hard part. It's easier to get somebody to talk by using violence, Justin. They'll talk if you fuck them up good enough. Lord, you get the vibe Bill-Bill is also saying that to Justin.

"But to answer your question, Ren and Stimpy are your responsibility. If they don't talk and admit to what you say they said, then it will be up to you to decide what to do next. I will still investigate what you said, even without Ren and Stimpy talking. This shouldn't be hard to figure out so let's just save it for tomorrow. We'll figure it all out at breakfast time. I'm not worried if they talk. It all this proves to be a lie is what I'm concerned about Justin, cause I will kill you and Crazy for these types of lies."

With that, Justin and I roll on out the door. We will need shanks more than ever now.

As Justin and I walk across the core, I can feel Justin's tension. The plan has changed but even good cons sometimes need a little fixing up. When you deal with several different personalities, it's obvious that those different personalities will have their own challenges.

As long as the result is the same, I really don't care how many different hoops I got to go through to get to it. Ren and Stimpy are a means to an end, I have no feelings at all towards what I will have to do to them. I'm pretty sure Justin don't care either. Justin has a twenty-year sentence for armed robbery, he took a store with a gun. His only fear is never getting out of prison.

I'm deep in thought when we get back to our wing, but there's no time to sit and think. When we walk onto our wing, we can tell something is up, and it doesn't take long to see what's going on.

As we walk past the first cell, we can see at least four people in the room. There's a white guy in the back of the cell, he's crying and sobbing. It looks like he done took a good beating. There's a black guy raping the white guy, which is why he's crying so much. I can tell the other three white guys in the room were waiting until their turn. All of them had their shirts off so they may have already all took a turn. One of the white dudes steps out of the cell.

"Hey Crazy, we got this cute young boy in here. You want some of him? He is fresh also Crazy. Just came off the bus, and he was not gay at all. We popped his cherry an hour ago."

I've spoken to this guy maybe three times on the walk. His black hair always looks greasy, and he's got beady eyes like a raven. They call him Mike, I think.

"I'm all good Mike. I don't fuck around."

"Well how about you, Justin? You want some of this boy in here?"

"No more please! Please no more!" We can hear the kid all the way out in the hall. One of the guys tell at him, you wanted to smoke weed huh, well now, you pay up by taking this dick.

"Doesn't sound like he likes it Mike," Justin says. "Don't matter any ways, I'm not in the game at all."

"My name isn't Mike, my name is Todd and it don't matter if he likes it or not. He does what he's told to do. He wanted to smoke tons of joints and not even ask to pay. Now he's my bitch."

"Well that's all good Todd, you guys have fun, but me and Justin going to talk to Heavy down here."

"Yeah, yeah, but if either of you change your minds, you let me know or I'll put you on him. He also gives great head. This is prison Crazy, you know smoking somebody else's weed right off the bus, is the oldest trick of them all to turn a person out. Don't matter if he likes it or not. Sooner or later he'll get with the program or kill himself. "

Sometimes I wonder if something is wrong with Justin and I. That black guy was hurting that white guy pretty bad. He was raping him, slamming in and out of the white guy's ass. I could hear the boy's whimpering. He is sobbing so bad that his voice is hoarse. Neither one of us try and help the dude, we don't care what's going on. It's just another day in prison. We have seen so much we are numb all the way inside.

Maybe Justin is just good at masking his feelings. For me, I feel nothing at all. I'm all the way numb inside. Either I'm a monster, or life has turned me into a monster. However, in here it doesn't matter. It's how you survive. You either become the prey or the predator. I thought for a long time, *is that just a cop out*, but seeing the white kid I know it's not.

The world would only judge me as a monster if I did something gruesome when I get out. The world doesn't care about my life in here. But kill someone on the outside, or walk away when someone's being raped, and I would be a monster, a story they'd write about. People would read it and shake their heads wondering how anyone could be so cold. But if I could ever ask the people that write those stories, my one question would be, how do you expect a person to walk through hell and not be touched by it?

Prison has programs but to do a program is extremely hard. Other convicts mess with you and the rats can't see or stop everything. Hell, sometimes they do see it and walk away and still others, it's them that mess with you. It really don't matter to me. I live day to day. I've been on my own for so long that it's easy for me to make whatever decision I need to. I'm not hurting anybody that cares about me or loves me. I'm 100% loyal to the few that are loyal to me. If the state has taught me anything in these violent places, they put me in. I will kill or do what is needed to protect my love ones. I know how much a gift it is, so I'll fight like hell for it.

I can see Heavy and his roommate through the window on the door. He is laying down, his roommate was standing up going through the locker in the back of the cell.

Justin knocks on the door pretty loud, and they act like they can't see us standing out here. Heavy finally gets up off the bottom bunk. His roommate keeps going through the locker.

"Hey what's up Crazy, Justin? What you two up to tonight?"

Heavy is like 320 pounds. He is a big fat white guy with a lot of prison tats on him. I've heard a rumor he has been caught three times with a fresh tat. Don't know if it's true or not but I think he is addicted to getting them. Lots of people get addicted to something or another in prison—anything to ease the time. Even the strongest men need something to help keep depression from taking over. Listen to some of them in here, they will say that's not true, but I bet you they are writing or doing something.

Convicts are the best at hiding all our feelings. Weakness can never be seen, *ever*. If you get a letter in the mail saying your kids died or the wife wants a divorce after 15 years of marriage because she can't handle being alone, you don't react. Through it all, whatever life throws at you. You stay and look tough, never shed a tear. So if getting tattooed helps you take the edge off, go for it. If getting to the cell and putting the covers over your head and crying helps go for it. But don't at all let another convict see you. They feed off any weakness that they can use against you.

"We not up to anything Heavy, we want to talk to you about some quick business is all. Can we come in or what?"

"Shit, I don't care if you come in or not. You know you can come down here and kick it with me anytime you want, you too Justin. You two come on in."

I let Heavy make it to the bunk, and then I sit down and put my back up against the metal locker. All the rooms are set up the same, so I go to my normal spot upon the floor right at the end of the bunk. Justin took his normal spot by the doorway. Heavy's celly is still looking through the locker and hasn't said a word.

"This is my cell mate. Everybody just calls him Harley. As you guys can see Harley has the munchies and can't decide what to eat."

"Fuck you Heavy, I don't got the munchies at all. That piece of shit weed was worthless. I'm trying to decide on something sweet or should I make a meal."

"Yeah, yeah Harley that's your story, tell it how you want to tell it. Why don't you just grab a Texas cinnamon bun and come sit down? When Crazy and Justin roll out, maybe then you'll have your answer of what you want."

"Yeah that sounds good Heavy, a Texas cinnamon bun sounds like heaven."

As Harley grabs the Texas cinnamon bun, looking at it like the Holy Grail, I take a look around their cell. Heavy and Harley are living pretty good. There are two TV's in here, at least four pairs of headphones that are nice. They have a fan and two nice hotpots for cooking.

I've never tried to rob Heavy, mainly because he is too huge. I have no doubt in my mind I would have to stab him. I'm not ever trying to go through that, I have no picks. I don't believe anyone would want to be trapped in a room with a big-ass Kodiak bear! At least not without a weapon. Kind of ironic though, because I told myself that I wouldn't pick a shank up ever. I'm not trying to get more time, but here I am getting a shank. I'm pretty sure Justin has never picked one up for the same reason as me. Nothing ever works in prison as you plan it to.

"So what's up honkies? Tell me what Harley and I can do for y'all?"

I heard him but I let my thoughts wander off for a moment. Harley done took a seat in the chair in the back of the cell next to the locker he was going through. He's just sitting there in a dreamy state, enjoying the shit out of every bite he takes of the cinnamon bun.

"Yeah there's no doubt in my mind, this honky is high as hell," I say out loud.

"Damn Crazy, you wouldn't bust a honky out would you?"

"The way I see it Harley, it's only us convicts in here. So it's all good to talk about it. Besides, I'm not busting you out, I'm just saying you got some serious denial issues if you don't think you're high honky."

"Ha ha ha ha ha ha, this honky has got to be the most sensitive person I've ever met, ha ha ha."

"Shit isn't even that funny, Harley. I mean, I didn't even crack a joke. You can't laugh at your own jokes anyway."

"Man fuck this shit! I'm not even high at all really. Bust one of them joints out Heavy, we'll all smoke together and then talk about whatever."

"You two honkies cool with what Harley just said? Or is that something you two don't do?"

"Shit I'm game. I don't even give a fuck."

"How about you Justin? You like to smoke?"

"Yeah, I love it even more when it's free."

Everybody in the room laughs at this. Justin has always got some witty comebacks when you can really get him to talk.

"Well what you waiting on Heavy? Fire that motherfucker up, player."

As soon as Heavy lights the joint, we hear several really loud sirens going off.

"Shit, put that shit out Heavy! Damn what the hell is that?"

"Get those shanks out you was talking about, Heavy! This may be bad."

"Damn Crazy what the hell you talking about?"

"Look Heavy I'll give you the quick version, but I got a bad feeling about the sirens going off. So to protect ourselves, get the shanks out. If we don't need them tonight, then no harm done right? I'll tell you this much, between getting raped or badly hurt, I pick gigging the shit out a motherfucker."

"Okay Crazy, I'll get them out. It won't be very hard, they just hid up under Harley's locker, well really taped to the bottom of his locker."

"Okay here's the fast version. You live on this walk, and you know me and Justin have robbed people."

"Ha ha, hell yeah we know you two rob people. You two are why we got the hustle we got. Me and Harley are good at taking shit apart that the prison builds, so we make a great living out of the shanks we make."

"Well, that's great you two learned to hustle, and make a good living in prison all because of me and Justin. As much as I would love to talk about your hustle, Heavy, I feel we need to have another talk."

"It's all good! Harley get the shanks out while we hear what he's got to say."

"Well it's real simple. The Bloods have been fucking over the Aryan Brothers. A war is about to start. I don't know if that's why the sirens are going off, but if a war is starting, I would like to be able to protect myself. I'm not trying to be in the middle of a riot. With not a damn thing to help me and everybody around me is strapped."

"Why do I feel like you're holding something back?"

"Probably because I am Heavy. It don't matter though, really you and Harley have as much information as I'm going to give out. Just be grateful, if that is what's going on. I hipped you before you walked right in the middle of a war, clueless."

"Okay that's cool, really I'm just curious." Then to Harley, "You got them yet?"

"Just about got them out. It's just hard to hold the locker up and put my hand under it, and reach for them."

"Well hell, why didn't you just ask one of us for help? It don't matter." Clearly he won't be able to wedge his fat ass in the back of the cell so he turns back to me, "Crazy will you help him out?"

"Yeah I got it honky, I'll hold the locker up."

"Harley, you staying in this cell. If it is a riot, you way too high to join. Your safest bet is in this cell. They can only get to you if they break the glass out on the door to the cell. That won't be easy if they do try to put the locker in front of the window. So they can't reach in and unlock it. "

"Yeah, I think I'll have to sit this one out, Heavy. As much as I don't want to, but I didn't think I was high at all. Now my head is spinning. Okay I got them Crazy, you can put the locker down now."

"Wow what you got in that locker? Sheets of metal? That damn locker is heavy as hell."

"Ha ha ha, nah it's just a lot of can foods and soda pops," Harley says grinning.

"Damn you guys got at least 15 shanks in that bag."

"That's how we roll Justin. The more shanks we get the more money we can make. We normally sell about 15 shanks every two weeks."

"Turn that damn TV down Harley," Heavy says. "I hear something out in the hallway."

Harley put the TV on mute, and we can hear screaming all up and down the hallway.

"Damn Justin, how you don't hear that?"

"Well shit Heavy, over the loud-ass sirens and your TV, I can't hear shit."

"Give us a shank, Heavy!"

"Hell, it sounds like we'll all need one. I'm thinking what you just told me Crazy, was an understatement."

"Here's your shank Crazy, and here's yours Justin. I'll keep one also and leave the rest with Harley."

"Damn, this is real fucking nice honky. It's extremely sharp. You filed this down very good," I say admiring his work.

"Yeah, this shank probably take a person's head off," Justin says.

"Yea, well I'm glad you two love them, now you see why I make such good money. Plus you two honkies are fucked up bad. I hear world war 3 out in front of my cell and all you two care about it how nice the shanks are."

"Well let's head out in the hallway and see what we dirty white boys can get into. I only care about the shanks Heavy, because it gives my mind something to focus on."

"Damn Heavy, why you want to come any ways? This isn't your battle."

"Crazy, I got 75 years in prison, and it's 85%, so I got to do like 64 years flat. Harley over there has life without. He'll sit this one out, but you, me, and Justin are going to see what we can get into. Besides, this may not be your problem either. We'll just go see what's going on. If I die tonight Crazy, I got an early parole. "

"If it's the war I think it is, I don't know how it got started this early but me, and Justin are going to go find Ren and Stimpy. I'm sure we'll get some answers from them."

"Well I'm going to join you two then. That cool with you Justin?"

"Hell yeah, it's cool with me! The three of us is better than two."

We head out into the hallway. There are fights everywhere, you can tell it's a race war. Every person in the hallway is white on black or black on white. At least, as far as I can see, maybe it will be different when we get off the walk.

"Shut that door!" Heavy yells.

It's total chaos, for real. In the back of the hallway, I can see at least three white guys getting raped. There is at least four or five black guys dead or dying all the way from the middle of the walk to the front. Blood is everywhere, on the walls, doors, and smeared on the floor. It is clear the blacks had the back of the walk and the whites had the rest. That was good for us white boys, at least for this walk it is. Who knows what's up with the rest of the walks.

"Come on, let's get off this walk and go find Ren and Stimpy." Even though I say this with confidence, I don't have a clue where Ren and Stimpy live at.

"Yeah, that sounds good." Heavy says in a barley whisper as he keeps trying to jump over puddles of blood, or something.

As we enter the core, we can see it is worse here than in the hallway. Somebody has started several fires that are going pretty good inside metal trash cans. I can hear a female voice screaming real loud.

"God damn Crazy look over there!" Justin screams.

"Yeah I see it Justin. I'm not helping her ratting ass. She should have thought about this before choosing a male prison as her job. Soon as we help her, the whole group will turn on us."

"Jesus Christ, there is at least nine white guys in line to take a turn on her."

"Yeah, I see that, it's a shame, she was real cute. I'm sure after they get done with her, she'll have scars everywhere."

"The issue is Justin, we can't beat all the guys off her. It's impossible for us to get 10-15 guys off her without us getting raped or killed."

The guard in the tower has a bean bag shot gun, he's sitting up there trying to shoot the convicts off the female guard, but several inmates took mops and stuck them into the slot the guard is shooting out of. I'm not sure how they did that, the gun slot is about nine feet up. I see at least three inmates holding onto the sticks, so the rat can't push them back out. Also there is at least five convicts watching over these three holding the mop so nobody would jump on them. The rat in the tower is stuck. No way to come out but through the core. I also realize it is worse than I thought for the female. They have a whole system set up so nobody can help her at all. Not without serious weapons or a high number of people.

"Shit watch out Justin!" I yell. There are two black guys sneaking up on him, but before I could even help Justin; Heavy hits one of them with the handle of his shank. He got him good, right on top the head. The black guy falls right to the floor.

Justin had his shank put in his back pocket, so he swung at the other black guy. The black guy blocked it but with Justin's other hand, he came in with a really nice upper cut. It connected right under the black guy's chin and his eyes rolled to the back of his head, he crashed to the floor.

"Damn Justin, you knocked that motherfucker out with one hit," Heavy says, amazed.

"Just because I'm quiet, don't mean I'm not a good fighter, player."

"Ha ha ha, isn't that the fucking truth!" Heavy laughs.

"So where we headed to Crazy?" Justin asks.

"Ren and Stimpy live in the next dorm over, so let's head outside."

"Sounds like a plan, hopefully it won't be as crazy over there as it is over here," Justin says and we head to the door.

Chapter 14

TRUE EVIL ALWAYS COMES OUT WHEN A PERSON FEELS IN DANGER

"There is always a 'But' in this imperfect world." —Anne Brunte

As soon as we get outside, two white dudes run up on us. I don't know them, but I recognized them as Aryans.

"Hey, you Crazy right?"

"Yeah, that's me. What's up?"

"Bill-Bill wants to talk to you real fast. He's over here on d-lower right now."

"Is that cool with you two?" I want to make sure I give Justin and Heavy a choice.

"Yeah, we both cool going over there for a second."

"Look at them idiots taking can foods over there and trying to smash the tower windows out," Justin says with a shit-eating grin on his face.

"Shit, if those niggers get hold of the guard tower, they'll have control over the whole dorm," one of the Aryans says to the other then they both look at us.

"Hurry up! We need to tell Bill-Bill about this," the two Aryans say together. I was thinking about asking them why they got to use the word 'Nigger' So much, but I'm sure every gang love to insult the next one, so I don't ask.

We put some speed to getting there, mainly because I can see the panicked look on these two white dudes' faces. As we enter d-lower, I can see the entire wing is white. There are at least 200 white dudes up and down the hallway.

Bill-Bill is all the way in the back. He is the top rank, so they protect him to the max. If they lose him, there is a guy who would take his spot. But in the middle of a riot, any type of change like that could cost them.

"Well hello again Crazy! How you doing tonight?" He's in a extremely good mood, considering everything is going on. Either that, or he's putting on a good front. In any case, I decide to meet his cool with my own. I learned as a child, any real con man act with being coy and nice to get what he wants.

"I'm doing good Bill-Bill. It's a little bit wild out there honky. Walking through the core was like walking through a war."

"Ha ha ha, yeah I would say it is Crazy. How you Justin?"

"Well Bill-Bill, considering some guys are getting raped out there and I haven't been touched. I'm doing pretty damn good!" Justin says.

"That's good to hear. I see you guys brought along big Heavy."

"So what's the deal Bill-Bill? You know what's going on?" Cool is great, but I figure its best to get right to the point.

"Oh I would say I do."

"Well, you want to tell us about it Bill-Bill?"

"Mad Dog and Bulldog saw you two eating with the wiggers. When the two wiggers came back from chow, Mad Dog ran up on them and asked what the deal was with you four eating together. At least, this is the information I get. Any ways, Mad Dog and Bulldog figured it all out. They're under the Bloods' protection. I want those two dead, but the Bloods refuse. They refuse to give them two turn coats back to me, so we'll fight until the rats can stop us, or until I get Mad Dog and Bulldog. Anyway, you were right about everything, Crazy. Nonetheless, I told you that Ren and Stimpy are your responsibility."

"Yeah, well we were headed over to that dorm to see if we could find'em."

"Sir, if I could interrupt for just a moment I need to tell you something important."

"Yeah, go ahead and tell me Larry!" Larry is one of the white guys who come got us. I would have never known that if Bill-Bill didn't just say their name. It wasn't like they were going to tell me.

"Out in the core sir, at least nine blacks are throwing can foods at the tower window. I'm not sure if they can break it or not, but I figured you need to know."

"Okay Larry, go to D-Upper and get about 15 good soldiers. Go out there and stop them from doing it, use whatever force you need to."

Larry takes off, and I watch as he makes his way out D-lower. In addition to the 200 white guys I see in the hallway down here, there is at least five white dudes in every cell. Every one of them ready to go to war as soon as Bill-Bill tells them to.

"So here's the deal," Bill-Bill says. "I've collected all the white dudes that are 100% with me. We've got about 400 of us, some upstairs and some down here. Our plan is simple, we're all going to head over to the next dorm. At least 3 whole wings are controlled by Bloods. They'll see us coming buy they will think we're real stupid-ass white boys. They got at least 600 Bloods or blacks, they will stay in their wings until we attack. When we attack one wing, the other two wings will come out and hit us from behind, push us onto the wing. We would lose with this plan, but I don't plan to lose. So being pushed unto the walk isn't what I'm going to let them do."

"So what's the catch Bill-Bill?" I ask.

"We're going to stay out in the core when we go in. The guard in the tower is working for me. I know he's scared as hell, and he knows his only way out is with me. I can't take over his dorm without his help. So while we run around the core and act like we lost our minds, I'm going to slip into the tower. I'll tell him my plan really fast, with his help I'll lock down all the wings. Then I'll have one wing at a time opened up. As I said, I plan to win. They don't know the guard in the tower belongs to me. So for their stupidly, they will pay the price. "

"Jesus, Bill-Bill, with the others locked down, your 400 soldiers will be taking on 200 or less at a time. That's brilliant!" I say, really impressed.

"Yep, that's the plan. I'll find Mad Dog and Bulldog, and I'm going to see them dead by midnight tonight. If this all works, after they're dead, I plan on smoking a cigar and watching you, and Justin beat the shit out of those two wiggers. See, I got a mother-fucker down there holding our door open. So we can't be locked down, do you think they did that?"

"What happens if we find all four of them on the first wing we attack?" Justin asks." Also, I'm not sure if they holding the doors open or not, but we'll find out."

"It don't matter honky, we'll still attack all three wings. This type of disrespect needs to be addressed. In the future when we ask about a person, they'll not deny us again." Bill-Bill says angrily.

"Well, when do we head over there Bill-Bill?" I ask.

"We're taking apart lockers right now. We are trying to make a shank for everybody. Then we'll head over there."

"Hell Bill-Bill I got at least 13 shanks in my cell," says Heavy.

"You head over and get them, I'll send 10 people with you. Hurry up though. Where is your celly Heavy?"

"He is too high to join us Bill-Bill."

"That is the very reason we don't get high. We weren't expecting no fucking war but it don't matter because it's here. We're all prepared and clear headed, we are also ready to die, kill or whatever," Bill-Bill says looking around at his men and making sure they understand the significance.

"Okay let's head back up to our wing, Heavy. You know me and Justin coming with you."

"That's good looking for real guys. I know its total chaos on our wing."

"Shit, you don't need to say 'good looking' to us. You the one that did us a favor and come with us. Besides, you hooked us up with a good shank." I can see the tension in him and as I look around it's clear he's not the only one that's feeling it.

"Jack, grab 10 people to go with Heavy and them," Bill-Bill says.

"Yes, Sir, Bill-Bill! Do you want me to go or stay?"

"You go with them, this is real important. We need shanks!"

While Jack goes to grab some more soldiers, Bill-Bill tells us that Jack is his lieutenant and second in command. Jack is like the jolly green giant. He's at least 6' 7" or 6' 8" and he has got to be about 280 pounds, all muscle. His size alone probably scares the shit out of most people, but he also has two tear drops under his left eye that are filled in. I don't see any other tats but those two tats are enough. A filled in tear drop means you had to kill somebody, so Jack here has two people under his belt. If this shit gets as fucked up as I think it will tonight, jack may have more people under his belt.

"Alright guys, let's head to your wing," Jack says. He has collected ten other good size honkies. They must want these shanks real bad.

As we head out into the core, the scene shocks even me. There are many bodies bleeding, several are either dead or dying. The guys who were throwing can foods are all gone and, for real, the guard in the tower looks grateful for that. This is probably why the rat has not locked our dorms down. That and Bill-Bill done won this guard over, plus Bill-Bill gets a person to hold the door open, but the guard could at least try.

As we hit the middle of the core though, the other guys stop, and I could hear them whisper "shit", real low. I follow their eyes and see what has got them all spooked up. Sticking out of the slot where they was putting mops earlier, is the female guard's head. Someone stuffed it into the slot and blood is dripping from it and running in lines down the wall to where the rest of the body sits. A mop head is up her pussy and her tits are gone. The word *RAT* is cut real deep across her stomach. Nobody comments on it, but I can see now why everybody left the core and went to the wings.

Nobody is trying to get blamed for this out here. Then again, maybe they are just taking a break.

In the wings, mostly everybody has clicked up and taken over one wing or another. They're all tearing lockers apart and everything else they can tear up in there. I don't know how the fucking sprinkler system hasn't went off yet, there is a huge cloud of smoke every-damn-where. Worthless-ass system, for real. We'll all burn to fucking death or die of smoke inhalation before it goes off. There are at least three trash can fires burning. Still no fucking sprinklers going off, I wonder what it will take to set it off.

I see Jack looking through the glass in our wing. There are at least 50 people out in the hallways. I can see white dudes and black guys. They took blue sheets and hung them from door to door in the middle of the wing on a homemade rope, so we couldn't see from the middle on back. All the dead people or dying people we saw earlier are gone, and it looks like some kind of truce now, cause it's not black on white anymore.

"What we do right here Jack?" I ask.

"Most of these guys are Crips, Crazy. They are not too hard to get along with. We'll play it smooth. You six stay here. You, me, Justin and Heavy along with the other four of my soldiers are going in. If shit goes south in here, you six run back to Bill-Bill. Let him know what's up. I'm hoping they'll see you six out here, and they'll play fair, because they'll know you'll go get more people than they got."

As soon as we step onto the wing, two big black guys come out the first cell, and then a white dude comes out the next.

"Hey, Red is that you?" I ask

"Damn Crazy, I haven't seen you since the Tank. I just got here two weeks ago. I didn't even know you were here, dawg."

"Damn Red what you doing up in here?"

"Shit, these are my people right here. What you doing up in here, with the skin heads? I never took you for the racist type, Crazy."

"I live on this wing right here. My dude Heavy is trying to pick up his celly and a couple of objects out of his cell. As far as the other white dudes with me, I got a score to settle. Sometimes you got to ride the beast."

"What cell was you Heavy?" Red asks.

"I was in cell five Red," Heavy points at his cell door. "It's one door before the sheets." No, the cell with a guy still in it, he is my cell. He is probably asleep or passed out. Either way, I'm going to take him with me.

"Shit, we been trying to bust the window to that cell for over an hour. The motherfucker in there just keeps smoking weed and laughing at us." Red gives us this look like were all supposed to be mad with him. "So I can tell you right now Heavy, he isn't asleep at all or even close to it. I would guess he is high as a motherfucker with all the weed he has been blowing.

"Shit, I knew I shouldn't have left that weed with Harley. Look Red, I'm sorry about all that. Harley is just real high, he don't mean no disrespect. I left the fucking weed in the cell, thinking Harley had the common damn sense not to smoke anymore. That he would want to come down from his buzz to protect himself. Right in the middle of a war, and this honky is blowing weed!"

"It don't fucking matter, Heavy. You go get him and whatever objects you want. Just leave the cell door open. When the rats come up in here, all deep to break this up. We will need cells to hide in, to block the mace and bean bag guns. Plus, we caught us a couple of guards outside, so we need cells to hide our hostages. So go on back there and get him." Red is tapping his foot, fidgeting with a string in his hand, while clenching his jaw. "Fucking weird-o."

As Heavy walks to cell five, I see Red looking at me real tough. "What's up Red? Why you looking at me so tough? " Plus, he is still clenching his jaw, but I'm not going to speak on that.

"I'm just trying to figure out your game, Crazy. You are a slick-ass honky for real. You come up in here with a giant. You're not part of their group, but here they are backing you up." As Red says all this, he's working knots out of his long red hair. I don't see the string anywhere, so he got rid of it or something and moved to his hair. Seems he is getting ready to blow or something. I can't figure his mood swings out.

"I don't got no game here, I'm just trying to be me. These people helped me out, so I'm trying to keep it real back," I try hard to keep the anger out of my tone, cause I don't like this motherfucker trying to question me, but I go with it so my plan don't go south because of my anger.

"Helped you out you say? Huh?" Red looks annoyed.

"I don't care if you believe me or not, Red. I don't owe you no explanation, but since I know you a little. It's no big deal, I'll show you what's up. But after I show you, I want you to tell me what's up with all these questions."

In life, adding your personal feelings to any con will almost always make the con not work, but being in control of your feelings is the hardest job a real con will go though. I let this run all threw my mind while I deal with Red.

With that said, I take my bucket hat off, toss it on the ground. It's not like I need it anymore, hell it makes the scar itch worse any ways. Judging by the expression on Red's face the scar must be looking badly. Hell I just got the floss took out, so I'm pretty sure it swelled up real good.

"Yeah, I heard something about that," Red says, "I just didn't know it was you that got busted up like that. You fought our number-one enemy honky. For that by itself, I got love for you."

I give him a look to let him know that now it's his turn.

"Okay, so come with me for a second. I want you to come to the back for just a second." Red explains all this completely calm now. This honkey went from one mood to the next in 2 damn seconds, bi-polar motherfucker. Shit like this makes me nervous as fuck. For sure, when we're in the middle of a riot. I think about telling Red no, but I don't want to turn this into more than it already is. Then I think about asking Justin to come with me, but I feel that is disloyal. If I go back there and get into it with them, I will be outnumbered and asking Justin along would send him to the same fate as me. That shit isn't fair at all and I can't see nothing real about that. If I'm going to get my ass kicked, I might as well keep it 100 by not pulling anybody else down with me.

"Jack, I'm going to go back here for just a moment, I won't be long at all. If I am, just head back over, I'll be right behind you guys."

"Nah, we'll just wait on you. The Captain told me to come with you, so I'm sure that means leave with you. I'll wait about 20 minutes at the most, and then I'm coming back there." Jack says this last part more to Red than me, looking him dead in the eyes. These guys might be racists but these honkies are all about loyalty. Didn't surprise me Jack wouldn't leave without me.

"I'm back guys and I got Harley with me. I brought all the shanks also. We ready to go or what?" Heavy looks around wanting an answer from anyone.

Harley is barely standing; shit must be some good-ass weed. Harley is a real small guy like me, maybe even smaller. He's got these dark black eyes that make me think of a raven. He's probably in his early to mid-twenties. Half of his face is tattooed with a Harley bike. That's how he got his nickname. Lots of young dudes get tats on their faces, so they don't look as cute and look a tough as they can. Being cute in prison isn't good. Hell I even see ugly guys get them all up and down their bodies. Just so they can look tough. All mind tricks in here.

"We're not ready to go Heavy. I'm headed back behind this curtain with Red. I'll be back in 20 minutes or so. Just wait here with Justin and Jack and all of them," I say trying to keep it light.

"Shit Crazy why can't we go with you?" Heavy looks all worried, then just for a minute, he reminds me of a big teddy bear. I really want to bust out in laughter. I only don't cause Heavy will feel insulted.

"It's not a big deal at all Heavy, I know Red from my past. We're wasting time even talking about all this. Justin, I'll be back soon."

I say this not giving anyone time to answer, cause I just start walking away. I don't say shit to Red, he knows what's up, and he can follow. As we go through the sheets, Red tells me to hold up a second while he dips behind the curtain. He isn't gone that long before he pokes his head out. I thought in the past that I didn't like this creep, but its moving up to hate.

"Come on back now Crazy." Red just starts walking to the back cell and opens it.

I look in the cell, smells like sex, and see a black female guard getting raped doggie style. A second guy is standing in front, making her suck his dick. This is the part of prison I hate. If I speak up, they'll say she's nothing but a rat, so I'm stuck with maintaining eye contact, no matter how hard it is, but I lose my cool.

"Why the hell would I want to see this Red?" I question, pissed that he's wasting my time with this bullshit. If there wasn't 50 fucking crips' on the walk I'd help her, rat or no rat.

"Hey don't get mad at me Crazy. In the other cell is another chick. This is why I asked you what you were doing with the skin heads. I know they not going to fuck a black chick. They got no fucking idea what they're missing. Look at how her ass jiggles and bounces every time he slams into her. No white chick's ass can do that. Any ways, as a gift, you can have one. You got to hurry up though." Red is just staring at the black chick when he speaks, looking like he is ready for a turn.

"I hate Gangsta. Crazy, you robbing him is so fucking good. We just saving the chicks for people in our click, but you are a special circumstance.

"Okay let me see the other chick," I say trying not to sound discussed.

Red walks across the small hallway then opens the cell. There is a young woman in her early twenties in the room. She is a tiny woman with an hourglass body. She is light skin, just sitting on the bed naked and crying. Nobody else is in the room. I know if I don't go in this room, it will spread everywhere that I'm scared to hurt a rat.

"Okay this is it for me right here," I slap Red on the back, I head into the cell. "Close the damn door Red. You not watching me do my thing. I'm not on that gay shit."

"Fuck you Crazy, I'm no fucking homo either." Red slams the door hard.

There is a towel hung over the window on the door so nobody can see in, good! As soon as I turn around the female back pedals to the corner across the room and starts to beg me, "No more please, oh God no more!" It has always amazed me when somebody is in danger, they find comfort in the corner of rooms. The mind is a tricky bitch.

I notice now her left eye is real swelled up and she has bruises all in between her legs and on her wrists. One of her wrists is cut. A creature that is truly defeated. The world does it all the time.

"I'm not going to rape you, I prefer a woman who wants me. Some of these guys are never, in their life, getting out of prison. This is the only way they'll ever feel a woman again. I'm sorry for what's happening to you, but I try not to judge. I don't know what I would do if I was never getting out. It would probably turn me into an animal too." I can tell she's not listening. I'm just trying to kill time so it looks good, and I figure it gives her a rest. "Any ways, what did you do to your wrist?" I'm trying to lighten the tension. I can't show weakness but at the same time it's fucked up, they're treating her like this. On the other hand, I can't see why a women would want to work in a place like this.

She holds her arm up in a daze and looks at her wrist, "I tried to kill myself. I don't want to live no more." She says this with a lot more tears coming out. Dealing with a crying woman is not my thing. Mainly cause I don't have a clue how to deal with it.

"You don't mean that at all, you'll get past all this and get stronger in the future behind it." It sounds pretty lame, but I don't know what else to say. I've always been taught that crying is weak, so I feel weird with her crying like that. I have been stomped, beat, left by my parents and though it all I knew I wasn't allowed to cry. So I don't know what to do here.

"No, no, no I won't at all. You try to get better after 30 or more people rape you. You think you'll get better behind that? You want to help me, then help me kill myself. You see what they did to that other guard? Oh fuck, Helen…they…"

I figure she's talking about the guard in the core. "No I probably wouldn't for real, but I got an ass hole little lady, that would take all my pride away from me." This sounds worse, and I can tell by looking at her that I'm not helping but hell, it's not like I've been trained to do this.

"They raped my ass, my mouth, my… If I'm going to die, at least I want to be the one to do it, not these fucking animals! Please!" She says, looking right into my soul, the tears gone, replaced with hate. "Do you think I want my tits or head cut off while I'm alive and feeling it all?"

I walk to the bed and sit down on the corner of it, and I just stare at the floor. I'm so out of my league here. I don't have a clue what I'm supposed to do, but I want to help her.

She squats down in front of me, she's not letting me off the hook, "Please don't make me beg. I don't want them to torture me after they get tired of raping me, I just need to go."

"What's your name?"

"Heather, I'm only 20, but I'm not stupid; I know I'm not getting out of here alive! I don't want to hurt anymore! These fucking animals…" she breaks down and starts sobbing again…"Even if I do make it out of here, this pain will be a life sentence."

I pull the shank out from behind my shirt and look deep within her eyes. I've never seen so much sorrow, so much pain in my life. I've also never killed before. I'm beyond confused. She's right, I know she's right. They'll never let her live and there's no way I can get her off this wing. Fuck! They will torture her until she breaks. I don't understand why I care, but in over my head or not. I've made my mind up.

"Turn around and put your back towards me." The look of relief in her eyes makes up my mind even more. She turns around fast then backs up against me. I put my arm around her to move her closer. She's shaking all over.

"You sure you want to die, Heather? There's no changing this, you are shaking all over."

"Yes! Just do it fast. My way out here is the only relief I'll get. "

I put the shank against her neck, slowly grab her chin with my other hand. With one good stroke, I pull her chin hard towards the door and take the shank the other way. I can't really see, but between the blood squirting in different directions, her gasping and spitting up blood; I guess I cut pretty fucking deep. These are one of those moments that I just feel fucked up, I feel nothing for killing her. It's my first kill, and I don't know if I should feel something or not. I gave her what she wanted. I gave her the relief she wanted. But I feel nothing.

Blood is all over the floor and getting all over me. I push her gently toward the locker in front of me. As I turn her around to face me. The cut was real deep, but I can tell even with her eyes closed she is still alive.

"Shit!" I say out loud. How the fuck do I get in these fucked-up situations? "Fuck!" I get up and put a knee between her legs then grab the top of her head to steady her.

I slice her throat at least two inches deeper. It must be enough because blood doesn't squirt anymore, it just spills out. Her heart has stopped. I felt something like what might be compassion for the first time. I reach down and grab her hand and held it. I can feel tears start to well up in my eyes and I'm fucking pissed. Pissed at her for putting me in this position. Pissed at these fucking people for what they did to her. Pissed at Red. It don't do no good to sit here and be mad but I know what I can do. I can be the animal I have been made to be. Now that I just stared my beast down eye to eye, lets rock.

I go to the door with such wild thoughts in my mind on what I'm going to do, I lift the towel to take a peek out in the hallway. I only raise it a very little in the corner. I see Red out there by his fucking self. The cock sucker who put me in this fucked-up position. I see also that there are people in the room across me. Sadly, they are only paying attention to the women in the room. Hearing her moans of pain, I know rat or not, red gets it real good.

I open the door a crack and whisper, "Hey, Red, I need you a moment."

"What? Your pecker don't work Crazy?!"

Red steps into the room, he sees the blood everywhere and sees the female guard is dead.

"What the fuck you do Crazy? You not leaving this wing now. You can't kill what isn't yours. We had major plans for her."

As Red turns around, I slam the shank into his neck, thankfully it goes all the way in. Blood shoots all over my face. Don't matter because my pants and everything else is already soaked in blood. Hell all I see is red at the moment.

Red tries to grab the knife, pulling it to get it out. I punch him in the side of the head then push him backwards. He trips over Heather's body and lands on his ass. I jump on him real fast to pull the knife out. Before I slam the knife in again, Red croaks, "You motherfucker, I trusted you."

"Why the fuck you bring me back here? You're the mother-fucker! This is for Heather." With that I slam the knife in his throat several more times. Until I run out of breath, as I regain my breath, I realize blood is everywhere. There isn't a spot on me that blood hasn't hit. It's all over the walls, bed, and lockers in this cell. Not the best moment in my life. I've never put myself out there for a rat. Probably never will again, but I just couldn't stand all this. I feel better now that I got Red.

I stand up feeling like a brand-new man. I see a dirty towel in the top bunk. I grab it and pull my shirt off. I don't bother putting on another shirt. I wipe my hair and face as best as I can. "Shit" I say kicking Red in the side. "Stupid ass honky! Bring me back here in your sick ass kinky rape scene calling this a fucking gift. You needed to die, sick ass honky.

Heather's body is all spread out on the floor from where Red tripped over her. I'm not trying to get more blood on me, but I pick her up anyway and put her in the bed. I lay her down on her back and close her eyes with my hand. For some reason, I feel connected to her I don't really want people to see her like this, so I take a sheet off the top bunk, slowly look at it to see if my blood might be on it, or if I was cut at all. After I see I have no cuts, I realize I don't need to check the towel on the cell. I take the sheet again while I slowing tuck heather in. It probably won't matter but it does to me.

I walk back to the door and peak out in the hall. I hear some yelling but I don't see anybody. I open the door and just walk right up the hallway. I make it to the sheet to see Jack, Justin and Heavy. The other six is up by the door where I left them. Jack and Justin are arguing with two people, something about me. The other four guys we brought in with us, all turn to look at me.

"No big deal guys! Here I am right here. Ready to go" I don't even stop walking. Jack, Justin and Heavy must've got the point because they don't ask any questions and just follow me. Heavy is, for the most part, carrying Harley like Harley is a pillow.

"Hey, where all that blood come from?" One of Red's guys asks. Nobody answers, and we keep walking. We make it to the door and as the door opens then somebody yells, "Stop them! That motherfucker killed Red!"

Chapter 15

NUMBERS ONLY COUNT IF YOU HAVE GOT THE STRATEGY TO USE THEM

"Terror made me cruel." —Emily Bronte

As we run down the stairs, I notice there is somewhere between ten and twenty people out in the core. Some are just talking loudly to each other, while a couple of them are fighting. A few of the white boys in D-Upper notice we're being chased and come running to help us. With this many people, I don't feel the need to run. So as I stop to turn around to face them. That's when I realize there's about 30 people chasing us.

Before I can really put this all together; a big black guy pops me dead in the side of my chin. I almost pass out but I will myself to move out of the way when he comes in for a second punch. I swing and hit him in the side of his head; it is like hitting a fucking brick wall. My hand feels like it's broke off this one punch. This fight isn't going to turn out in my favor, unless I change tactics. This motherfucker is too big to fight. Nonetheless, I swing again.

Either I didn't connect or this motherfucker is just too big because I come back in with another punch, he blocks it. He moves faster than I would have believed a guy his size could move. He grabs me around the throat and lifts me off my feet and starts to choke the shit out of me. I'm kicking and screaming and doing everything I can to get free, but nothing seems to faze him. I reach in my back pocket to grab the shank. I swipe it at his face to see him move out of the way, but I still connect and a piece of his ear slices right off. That gets his fucking attention, he drops me to the floor.

I can't get up. I can barely breathe, and it is hell, I nearly pass out again. I'm still trying to catch my breath when he comes toward me again, I see he is getting ready to kick me. Right before he does though, Jack steps in and hits him right in the jaw. I can see Jack's punch did better than mine. The black guy's whole head turns toward the left behind the hit. And still he doesn't go down. The black guy is every bit as big as Jack but somehow this giant is going down. Hell, this black guy may be even bigger then Jack.

Jack is coming in for another punch so the black guy is fully focused on Jack. I stay down so that I don't draw his attention, I have a plan as I creep about four feet. Then, I take my shank and ram it threw the guy's state boot. It goes all the way threw his fucking foot. I pull my shank out and am about to stab him again in the foot but the motherfucker finally falls to the ground.

As soon as he falls, Jack starts football kicking him in the head. I roll over on my back trying to look around me to see if the black guy's group has been beat. About three of them is dead and some ran back to the wing they came from. I'm guessing the rest are just knocked out. The whole core is empty again besides us. I can probably add the Crips to my growing list of enemies. I only can tell the dead ones are dead because blood leaking out in so many spots isn't normal or anyway, a person can live losing that much blood.

I look over at Jack to see this honky is still kicking the shit out of the black guy. At this point, the side of the guy's face is pretty fucked up. It may even be caved in some. I stand up to only find out I'm still a little dizzy. That had to be the hardest hit I've ever taken. I'm surprised, I didn't lose any teeth, or worse.

"Hey Jack. Hey!" I scream at him, but he doesn't stop. After yelling it about three more times he looks over at me with a wild gaze in his eyes. This is one big Crazy fucking honky.

"Yeah, what you want Crazy?"

"Dude is knocked the fuck out. Save your strength for the next dorm, honky," I try to say it real light, shit when a motherfucker has tapped into their inner animal. You don't know what the fuck they'll do.

"Yeah, you right Crazy. Give me that shank you got honky." Jack says this with such calm, I would hate to be his enemy. I hand him my shank, and he rams it in the guy's left eye. All the way down to the hilt, pulls it out then does the same on the right. I let go of a breath I didn't realize I was even holding.

"That's how you do this shit, Crazy. This motherfucker is too big to let him be our enemy. Now we don't got to worry about him no more." Jack wipes the blade off on the guy's T-shirt and hands it back to me. "We need to hurry up. We need to get to the other dorm. We're already behind on time, we should have been over there already." Jack says and starts moving. I take a look at the black guy before I turn to follow. He's dead for sure.

I got about two feet, then Jack stops me." What happen up there Crazy, nobody needs to know. You did what you felt was right little brother, nothing else needs to be said."

With nothing else to say, we head back into D-lower. I wonder if Justin is hurt or not. I see lots of people tying cardboard around their upper bodies then tying thick books to the cardboard.

"What they doing Jack? Why they putting that on?"

"They are getting ready for battle. That is thier prison armor. If they get stabbed in the upper body, most likely the shank won't go through the books," Jack explains. "Also solid punches can't be even really be felt with it on. So that helps their rib cages if hit."

"Hmm, that's pretty smart for real." I say to myself.

I see Justin in the back talking to Bill-Bill, looks like he's okay, so I head back there. I don't see Heavy or Harley nowhere. I pull up on Bill-Bill and Justin. Before I can say anything, Bill-Bill looks at me from head to toe then finally says to me, "Crazy you look like hell. You got blood all over your pants and face. When the rats come in here to break this up you can't have blood on you like that. They'll use it against you for evidence. You are one Crazy fucking honky. I see how you got your nick-name. Jack said you came back to them looking like you dumped a bucket full of red paint all down you. I'm not even going to ask what went down with that.

"Heavy and Harley is in that back cell. You go to the cell next to it and wash up in the sink. Take off all your stuff you got on, boxers, socks, even your boots, then take it all out in the core. You throw it in one of them trash can fires, you'll find some sweat pants, socks, and several pairs of good shoes. Pick stuff that fits you. You only got about five minutes though because we're headed out."

"That's real good looking Bill-Bill. I'll hurry as fast as I can," I say as I head back to the cell he pointed out.

"Don't forget to burn the wash rag you use to clean up with also," Bill-Bill calls after me.

Really, it doesn't take long. There is a mirror in the cell, so I could see the spots of blood I missed. I put all my stuff in a plastic bag I found lying under the sink. When I finish, I put the wash cloth in the bag.

The sweats are brand new. They feel real comfortable and the shoes feel way better than state boots. I grab a T-shirt that I see in the locker. I don't put on boxers, seems a little weird to put on someone else's boxers, so fuck it I'll just free ball. I wonder to myself if the towel I used to wipe my face could be used against me. I doubt it though, none of my blood was on the towel. I remember checking for cuts, so it don't have my blood on it. Hell I lived on that walk, so if they find finger prints, I can just say I kicked it with a guy from that cell.

My chin is swelled up real bad where that black guy hit me. Nobody is in the hallway, they've all moved out to the core. I walk into the core and hear the end of a pep talk Bill-Bill is giving. Bill-Bill is a good leader for real. I can see that people follow him out of respect, not fear but anybody can tell Bill-Bill is dangerous. You don't make it to be a captain in the Aryans without being dangerous.

As I throw the clothes in the trash can and then the state boots, I wonder if the boots will even burn. Everybody else is already headed out the door. I see Justin hanging back and walk up to him.

"Was waiting on you honky! You look better with all that blood off you," Justin says to me. "Do we need to have a talk where all the blood come from honky?"

"Nah, I'm ready to go honky."

"Those fucking sirens are loud as fuck. I don't understand why they don't shut that shit off." They've been fucking blasting them this whole fucking time. I'd bet any person within 20-mile radius is fucking sick of them.

"Yeah, I don't know why they don't either, Justin!" We head across the walkway and down the steps, I can feel the excitement mixed with tension in the air. Everyone is pumped up.

We make it to the next dorm. It's set up just like ours except for all the destruction. Tore up sheets and mats are all over. A few people are on the ground, but I can't tell if they were knocked out or dead. Out in the core, on the wall of the tower is written in blood: *Bloods only in here!* There are white guys dead everywhere. I notice Bill-Bill looked a couple over, heard him mumble, falling brother, your death won't go unnoticed. So some of them are his people. Bloods are looking down at us or even right at us. Though the glass upstairs and down. You can tell they been waiting on Bill-Bill; they knew this crazy-ass honky never gives up.

Already Bill-Bill's group is running around the core and yelling at the top of their lungs. People in the wings are looking out their windows but as Bill-Bill predicted, they are staying in their wings. There isn't really no room here in the core any ways. Not with 400 plus people in there. They are all waiting on Bill-Bill to pick a wing, so they can attack from behind. They know what Bill-Bill does that they don't need to fight for the core, they don't know about the guard.

There are several white guys at the doors, so it appears the Bloods aren't raciest. They just don't like anybody that isn't a part of their group. I haven't seen a lot of whites that are bloods.

I am leaning on the wall for about five minutes when Bill-Bill climbs up on the rail. He yells at the top of his lungs: "Stop! Stop! Stop! NOW!"

Everybody in the core stops running around and picking shit up and throwing it. In a flash, it is so quiet you could hear a pin drop. Bill-Bill doesn't even speak, he just holds up his left hand and twirls it in a circle. As soon as he does this, every door clicks, every door was locked. Every clicking noise, sounds like victory. My entire plan just all clicked together. They shouldn't have made me their enemy.

The Bloods in the wings realize this also. They begin to pound on the glass and then try to kick it out. The Plexiglas is too strong though, they're not busting it out. It feels good to trick your enemy. You can see the cocky fucking look they had on, is all gone now.

Bill-Bill goes and stands in front of A-Lower, looks up at the guard in the tower. The door to A-Lower pops. Bill-Bill is the first to run in, behind him is 400 plus angry white men. I am still out in the core, but I can hear the screams coming from the wing. These are the types of screams that would give the strongest men nightmares. I see Justin and Heavy head into the wing. I see Jack right behind Bill-Bill. They are two big ass honky's that I'd hate to see what it would take to get them to go down. I know it would take a lot, if not their life. In prison you learn to get vibes of people around you. You get the vibe around Jack and Bill-Bill that if you fight them you got to kill them, or they'll kill you.

Chapter 16

BEWARE OF THE MEN YOU TRUST!

"I am tired of talk that comes to nothing." —Chief Joseph

I am standing against the wall listening to the screams coming from inside A-Lower. It sounds like the fucking zombie apocalypse in there, only in this movie, we're the zombies. Sounds of agony and pain, anger and violence all mixed together. I know I'll always remember this, no matter how old I get I will be able to close my eyes and hear these screams.

Justin and Heavy went in the wing with all the rest. I stayed out here for two reasons; the first, it looks like enough people went in on that small wing, but the second reason is the most important one, I found what I was looking for.

I push off from the wall slowly then head up the steps to B-upper. At least 30 people are banging against the glass in the door to the wing. They've carried a metal bunk bed out one of the cells and are ramming it against the window trying to break it. They want to get out here in the core, but for all their trouble, they have only spider webbed a couple of spots. The metal mesh they built in the middle of these Plexiglas windows is just too tough. None of this matters to me.

At the end of the metal bunk bed, helping to pick it up and ram it into the window, is the guy, who is both my enemy and the reason I started all this. He has his shirt off with sweat pouring down his chest. I peck on the window, lightly but enough to get their attention. This is the moment I've been waiting for. Revenge is like a drug.

Gangsta's eyes lock on me with the wildest look I've ever seen, like an animal that knows it's trapped but refuses to accept defeat. The motherfucker that kicked my head into the floor and gave me this fucking scar on my forehead, the guy who is related to the leader of the Bloods. The Motherfucker that thought I was the prey!

Behind me, I still hear the screams but nothing else matters. Everything I worked for, everything I put into play is because this motherfucker not only beat me, but he wasn't going to let it go. I'll remember him for life, every time I look at my scar, so I want him to remember me too.

He puts the bed down, and I see he is the one leading the others in the pod. There is about 80-100 people in this wing, but I can't see into the cells.

"Ren and Stimpy told us what they said. What's your fucking deal cracker?" Gangsta screams through the door. I can hear him through the door, even over all the yells and screams from below.

"You know what my deal is? You're too fucking cocky. I had no idea you're a Blood when me, and Justin ran in on you. You turn around and jump me cool. I could have accepted that, but the problem is you're too caught up on your reputation, and you wasn't going to let it go. Not even after you knocked my head into the ground. You thought because there is so many of your gang here that I couldn't stand up to you. Well, look what that has cost you tonight, motherfucker! Do you hear your brothers down there screaming in pain?" I step back, put my hand up to my ear to act like I am trying to hear, but I am smiling at him.

"Fuck you cracker! You white piece of shit! I should have killed you!" Gangsta says with spit flying out of his mouth and hitting the window. I'm guessing I've got him highly pissed off.

"Well I think that's great, I got you mad, Gangsta. Matter of fact, I find it wonderful. With all your buddies there next to you, let me tell you what's up.

"You gave me these stiches in my fucking forehead. Do you know how painful it is to get sewed up with a fucking sewing needle? It don't matter if you do or not but you better hope you die tonight 'cause, I got a special treat for you, motherfucker. You thought because there was so many of you that I couldn't get to you? Well I out smarted your cocky ass, and I'm going to get my lick back!"

Gangsta turns back to the guys in the wing, but I can still hear him, "Man, fuck this bitch-ass cracker! Let's bust this window out." Gangsta walks back to the back of the bed. Three guys get the left side, and three more get the right and Gangsta picks up the back. After they back up about ten feet, they charge the window, when the metal bunk slams into it. The entire door shakes, but the window holds. They built these windows for this very purpose; to keep convicts on the wing in case of a riot. These idiots either don't get it, or it's desperation. Emotions cloud the truth.

I turn around to look down in the core because I hear a lot of talking and yelling. The Aryans are out in the core again. I would say by the looks of it, they are taking a small break. I walk back down the steps on the hunt for Justin. It surprises me Justin went in, he's normally the voice of reason. For him to volunteer to be a part of all the killing really shocked me.

As I walk past A-Lower, I can see the door is closed and locked. Through the window, there are at least 30 bodies visible, all laid out in the hallway. I can't tell if they're dead or alive. Some are lying in crooked and gruesome ways; those must be dead. There is no way for a person's body to twist or lay like some of them. The yelling and screaming came from these guys when their bones were being broken. And this is only what I can see, the doors to all the cells are open. The tower controls them also, but the guard can only lock them if they're closed. No telling how many more are in the cells. I think a couple of cells in the back are closed, but I can't tell for real.

"Hey Crazy, what you doing just standing there staring off in the wing?!"

I turn around to see Justin with a look of concern.

"I am just checking out your handy work, honky. I was thinking to myself about how I couldn't believe you got caught up in this, or went in there. You're normally so reasonable."

"Ha ha ha, Crazy, I like to get down like any dirty white boy does. I may be a voice of reason, but I'm no coward Crazy!"

I've never seen Justin get mad at me, but he said this to me with so much anger that it's almost like he wants to fight. If he's trying to stage a fall out with me, I don't understand why.

"Look honky, I never said you're a coward. I would never think like that about you. You my number-one honky, Justin. We have been through too much for either of us to be a coward. I just thought that killing somebody is something you was trying to stay away from. You feel me honky?" Justin relaxed after that. I guess he's just hyped up.

"Oh, I see what you sayin'. Man, I thought you were talking down to me. I see now what you saying though. You missed Bill-Bill's pep talk when you was washing up. We're not killing nobody honky, Bill-Bill says that will be too much heat, and we'll all be on lock down forever when they take control over the prison again. So we just setting an example, Crazy. We're just kicking teeth out and breaking bones. You know, putting a good hurt on them, so they'll always remember this day. With all the other killings today. We not trying to add to it. The guards that are dead is going to cost us a lot already."

"Yeah, I get it. I should have been at the pep talk, I guess. Any ways, I'm sorry to come at you like that honky. In the end, all we got is each other to watch our backs."

At this point, Bill-Bill stands up and shouts to get everyone's attention. "Alright everybody listen up! B-Upper is beating the shit out the window. Let's go up there next now and show them what we're all about."

This is my first look at Bill-Bill since he has come out of A-Lower. Somebody cut him badly on the side of his face. From the jaw all the way up to under his left eye. But the way he moves, it looks like it doesn't even hurt. It's leaking blood profusely though.

I still haven't seen Heavy. Don't know where he went. I know his celly stayed behind in the other dorm, still way too high to come with us. I know heavy locked Harley in that back cell.

06

"Let's go! Let's go! Let's go!"

Bill-Bill is standing at the top of the stairs next to B-Upper. He's got about 40 people up on the landing with him, the rest are on the steps and into the core. Bill-Bill turns and looks at the tower, and the door pops. No sooner does it pop; five black guys on the other side try to slam the door into Bill-Bill. I'm guessing they were hoping to throw one of the Aryans over the rail. Probably Bill-Bill cause they know he is the leader. You have to admire their courage. The bed is still close to the door.

Whatever they thought, I'm sure they aren't expecting what happens next. Bill-Bill grabs one of the five that charged through the door and other people grab the rest. While they're holding them, about 60 people are running into the wing. Once they are inside, Bill-Bill takes the one he is holding and throws him over the rail. The other four follow Bill-Bill. I'm headed up the steps, but I pause long enough to make sure none of them are Gangsta.

I am not prepared for what I see though. The sounds from B-Upper fade as I watch the first guy's head bounces off the metal rail at the bottom. The wet thump I hear when he hits pretty much tells me that couldn't have felt good. He got it easy compared to the one that hits head first on the concrete. The next two just land on their sides like sacks of potatoes but the last one tries to land on his feet. The way he lands slams him to his knees and breaks his hips or knees or something. He falls to his side like the other two.

Bill-Bill runs into the wing with all the rest, but I'm not going to be left out this time. I don't want to miss Gangsta so I run up the last steps quickly to get into the wing. It's total chaos in here. There are fights in every spot and I don't see how I'll find anyone in this mess. It looks like a pack of wolves attacking lions.

When I see Justin in front of the first cell, I run over to him to see what's up.

"What you doing over here honky?" I ask.

"That motherfucker is in this cell. He's a fucking coward. He is hiding behind the fucking locker." Justin seems really nervous, but with all this going on, I just let it go.

"Who you talking about Justin?"

"Man you know who I'm talking about! *Gangsta!* Look Crazy, you go up to the door and give the tower the hand signal to pop cell one. Just hold up one finger so the guard can see you. I'll sit right here to open the door when it pops. I'll wait for you before I go in honky. Okay?"

"Okay, I'll be right back." Even as close as I am to the door, I have to dodge two fights to get to it. On the way, I notice a broom in the TV room. That might come in handy. I step into the core and wave at the tower. I don't know what sign to hold up for the TV room, so I just point at it. The rat must've figured it out though, because the TV room door pops. I grab the broom and crack it in half on the floor using my foot to hold one end while pulling up on the handle. I keep the top half and throw the bottom part on the floor.

I run back out onto the landing outside the wing to wave at the tower. When I have his attention again, I hold my hand up and make a fist, then I let one-finger rise as I point at the wing.

When I get back inside, I see Justin open the door this stupid ass honky runs in the cell without me, "Shit!" I yell out loud I run toward the cell as fast as I can.

I dodge fights and jump over a few people lying on the floor. I sprint the last 15 feet to the cell faster than I've ever run before. I don't even bother to look in the window because I'm only thinking about saving my motherfucking ace, but when I get in the room I am beyond shocked! Justin is standing next to Gangsta and he gave his shank to him. They're standing side by side! At first, I'm confused but it don't take but a minute to realize I've been betrayed. Shit is a motherfucker in prison. How many more lessons do I have to go through?

"What the fuck is going on Justin?"

"Shit Crazy, you just wouldn't let it go. I grew up with Gangsta, hell I grew up with his whole family. I was the only white family in the hood, and I survived it all because Gangsta and his crew gave me protection. I never became a Blood but when I came to prison, I became Gangsta's eyes and ears. It's always worked perfect until you fucked it all up."

"What the hell you talking about Justin? You ran in their cell with me! You helped rob them with me, and they beat you up when they ran in on us. You helped me get the info off Ren and Stimpy! Hell Justin you knew we was coming over here to do this plan."

"If you remember, I was in the cell with them alone. I started losing the fight. You came in to finish it. The truth is that Gangsta staged all so I could get closer to the white boys. Gangsta had to do some kind of revenge, or it would not have played out right. They only gave me a sore jaw though. You are so fucking slow you never even questioned why you got stiches. I only got a swelled jaw. As far as the two do boys, I didn't think they were such idiots. Nonetheless, when I left to go take that piss before we go into Ryan's cell, that's when I made sure they knew."

I'm baffled. I don't know what to say to all this or even how to feel. I mean, what do you say when your best friend puts a knife in your back? I know this is prison, but fuck me for even thinking there is some type of loyalty in here some type of code.

The only thing I can think to say is, "Why you two not attacking me yet?"

"I'll tell you why. You're going to help me get Gangsta out of here to safety."

"Shit, Justin they still going to get his people. You know they want him bad. He is the leader and the one that refused to turn over the two brothers to Bill-Bill. Bill-Bill is going to tear this place up looking for them. You two by yourself can't whoop that fucking giant."

"You don't know shit Crazy! They gave Mad Dog and Bulldog protection out of loyalty. I'm the one that kept Gangsta up to date on what you were doing. If you would've just let it go they never would have fucked with us again."

"You think I got a crystal ball in my pocket, Justin? I mean, for real, how the fuck I know that?"

"Shut the fuck up Crazy! We're wasting time, and you're going to help me get his people to safety. You'll help Crazy or I'll kill you myself. I like you Crazy, but me and Gangsta go way back. Don't make me have to choose between you two, or I'm telling you right now you won't like how it turns out."

"Yeah, yeah, I'll fucking help you. You my ace. We'll get past this honky. I got too much love for you." As I weigh this on my scale of life, it goes all the way to the 'no good' area. Fuck now I have to let my monster out again. How many times before he just takes over me?!

"Well let's go then, Crazy!" Justin screams at me, so I turn my back to look out the window, to show them I'm no threat to them.

As I'm looking out the window, I feel them both come up behind me. I close my eyes and take a breath. I've never needed courage more than I do right now. My heart is thumping so loud I'm afraid they'll hear it. This night just seems to get more and more fucked up. So I just let the monster take over and stop fighting him.

"What you see out there Crazy?" I can hear a small tremble in Justin's voice. Justin is scared, either of me or the people in the hallway, I don't know. It don't matter because I'm ready to die today. A man has to stand for what he believes in, and I live by a code. Justin violated that code so only one of us is leaving this cell alive.

As I turn around I drop my hand behind my back to reach for the shank in my pocket. I grip it real hard, as I close my eyes, I bring the shank around and slam it up under Justin's chin with all my strength. I see it go through his mouth, in real slow motion, it seems to go all the way to his brain. I fucking hate him in this moment, looking in his eyes. Why the fuck couldn't he have been straight with me? I either had to kill him or choose to live with him turning me into a bitch. May seem all fucked up to people outside these walls, but I'm in here, making choices on the fly to survive.

No sooner than he drops and hits the floor, Gangsta slams his shank into my side real deep. It feels like hot lava ripping into my side. Kind of ironic that this very shank I'm getting gigged with, I talked Justin into getting it.

"Take that you fucking worthless cracker!" He reaches to try to pull the shank back out.

My best friend dead at my feet, adrenaline pumping, I push Gangsta hard as I can. My hands slam into his chest, and he flies back. Before he can catch his balance, I raise the broom stick handle to slam it down on his head. I hit him so hard it makes him real dizzy. I hit him about five more times until I knock him out. As he drops to the floor, I know I don't want to kill him. I have another plan for him.

I look down at my side and see blood coming out pretty good. I realize I need to hurry up before I pass out too. I push Justin under the bed then I grab Gangsta by his legs. With all my power, I drag him to the door and kick the door open with the back of my foot. The effort sends more lava up my side, and I get a little light headed.

I drag Gangsta as far as I can out into the hall but too many people are lying out here. Most of Bill-Bill's people have left, but not all.

I drop to my knees and tug on Gangsta's pants. I pull them down to his knees. He is lying on his belly. With what's left of my strength, I go back in the cell to get the broom stick I left up against the wall. Then I walk back to Gangsta and I slam the broom stick handle in his ass. I push down on it a few more times to make sure it can't go any deeper. Then I step back to look at my handy work. His click won't ever let this go, they got to cut him out after this. I walk back toward the door, but before I make it off the wing, I hit the floor as the darkness takes me, or maybe my monster has taken over all the way.

Chapter 17

OLD FRIENDS, OLD PRISON AND LEARN AN OLD HUSTLE

"I hear and forget, I see and I remember.
I do and I understand." —Confucius

As I lay in the darkness, I keep thinking to myself that I can't even get no peace and quiet in death. All I hear is somebody yelling at me. I sort of make the words out, but all I get is "I'll smack you!" Jeez, I can't even get away from violence in my time of death, maybe this is hell. It's not like I deserve any better after all.

"Crazy! Crazy! Wake your ass up honky!"

Man that sounds a lot like Heavy. I try to open my eyes, but they feel like a 100 pounds. I keep trying and finally they open a crack after that with a few more attempts they pop open. Everything is so fucking bright, it blinds my eyes and takes me a second to adjust. My body is sore all over, but my side hurts the most.

Sitting in the next bed over is Heavy just lying on his side with a white sheet wrapped around him staring at me pretty hard. When he sees that he has my attention, he leans up on one elbow.

"Hey sleeping beauty, nice to see you wake up." Heavy says with a huge smile on his face and a somewhat joking voice. The whole room looks smallish like an exam room, it is all white, with white sheets and a hospital bed. I guess I'm in the hospital.

I try to talk, but my mouth feels like sand paper. Heavy must have read my thoughts because he hands me a cup of water. I gulp it down really fast. It's not the purest water, but it tastes like heaven at the moment. I sit the paper cup down on the little table next to me. Besides the beds and night stands, the room is empty.

"Ha ha ha, you funny as hell, Crazy! You should have seen the face you made when you drank that. It's the same thing I did when I woke up honky. Man I was so thirsty, drinking that water feels like making parole, don't it?"

"What you...what you...mean when you woke up honky?" I rasp.

"Man honky, you been out of it for a day and half. You lost like half your fucking blood. That fucking shank was so deep in you, when they pulled it out blood came gushing out the wound. I heard them say you had a fever. You were all fucked up honky; you got really lucky for real."

"Yea, I know that's the fucking truth. I thought I'd died. Shit got fucked up in there honky!" As I say this, Justin's face comes back to me, but I shake it off. For now until I learn the lesson behind it all, no need to let it eat at me.

"You don't got to tell me Crazy. I was on A-Lower fighting this one big motherfucker. I got tired of fighting somebody his size, so I pulled my shank out, but Bill-Bill said no killing. I wasn't trying to get Bill-Bill to turn on me, but I also wasn't trying to get my ass kicked either. So I figured I could just give dude a few cuts—nothing serious but enough to slow him down. As soon as

I was getting ready to swing that shank, your fucking dude Justin comes up behind me and hits me in the fucking head with the bottom part of his shank. I turn around to hit him and the big black guy I was fighting pushes me in a cell. Justin and him came in and jumped me honky. Now I know that's your dude Crazy, but I'm telling you that motherfucker is on their side. I'm just trying to keep it 100 all the way."

"Well I don't know how it happen Heavy, but he died in B-Upper, so karma helped you on that one. For real, I know it sucks what he did to you, but I don't even want to talk about him honky. Okay? I'm trying to be 100 also letting you know it's not worth talking about him."

"Yeah that's all good Crazy. It don't matter no ways 'cause like you said karma killed him all the way out. Fake motherfuckers always get what's coming to them."

"Where we at Heavy? This has got to be the most comfortable bed I've laid in ever, and the sheets are new. At least, they feel that way to me," I say running my hands over them. Then I realize I'm not cold or burning up. "Plus the room is just the right temperature."

"We're still at Pink Palace honky. They just got us up in medical. You been out of it for a day and half. They had this place packed but now there is only about 50 of us in here. They built a medical tent on the yard that has about 400 people in it. We're lucky they put all the Bloods out there, they didn't want to mix us. They can sit out there in the hot-ass heat. Some of the people got transferred to other prison hospitals and then there's the ones that had to go to outside hospitals because they were so bad off. These were one-man cells we are in. They put the extra bed and stuff in here to make it a two man cell. "

"How did they break it all up honky? I mean tell me the rest of what you saw." My throat still feels rough.

"Crazy, I saw it all the way until they knocked me out. I already had that head wound, them hitting me in the head again really messed me up bad. Any ways, honky, I finally came awake after they jumped me. When I woke up, I heard a noise that seemed to me it came from the locker, the big stand up locker, so I opened the door. With half the shelves ripped out, squeezed in the bottom half is the big black guy that jumped me. That motherfucker looks up at me and tries to stand up fast, but bangs his head on one of the higher shelves. That stupid fuck lands back on his ass so I punch that black motherfucker so hard at least five teeth get busted out, I don't even stop Crazy. I just lose control and keep hitting him for so long that I only stopped because my wrist and hand were killing me. He had tons of teeth come out. By the time I stopped, he was bleeding from several spots. His ear was also hanging off. Man, I know he was still alive but the side of his face will always remember me. Any ways, I walk out in the hallway to get to the core, I notice just about every other cell that I looked in the locker doors were shut. So I start thinking somebody must have said they checked the rooms, but really they hid somebody in them. I make it to the door and see a lot of people coming out of B-Upper and start waving through the glass. Someone noticed me and got the door popped open.

"After that I find Bill-Bill and tell him what I found. He gets a few more people, so we can go back in A-Lower. Crazy you not going to believe this, but we found six more people, and you wouldn't even believe who they were. Three of them were the Bloods' top ranks, one of them was Mad Dog. His brother wasn't with him though. The other two were Ren and Stimpy, but they were dead way before we got there. But here's the thing, the three top ranking guys and Mad Dog? They were all killed honky!" Heavy drops his voice to a whisper, "At least they were when we got done with 'em. That big black guy was really number seven. The one that jumped me. Turns out he was related to Gangsta somehow so he is no longer here feel me? Also I don't understand why somebody would help hide Ren or stupid ass Stimpy.

"When we got done with A-Lower again, Bill-Bill goes off to attack another wing. I got curious to where you were though so I go up to B-Upper to see if you're up there. I find you in front of the door with a shank in your side. I don't pull the shank out, but I wrap my shirt around it to stop the blood flow. Then we just sat there like that for 40 minutes or so. I remember seeing this black guy several feet away with a broom stick up his ass. I couldn't believe somebody did that. Shit looked like it hurt like hell! The shit we see in here, nobody in the free world would ever believe it.

"I think Bill-Bill got to attack two more wings before hundreds of rats come flying in the front door. I mean hundreds and hundreds of them honky. They had riot gear on, cattle prods, shock shields and they all had army clothes on. These motherfuckers had gas masks on honky. They just run up in there and start throwing canisters of mace. When that shit exploded, the air was filled with mace. Man honky, they had to have thrown 50 of them so by the time they run into the wings everybody is fucked up and can't even breathe worth a shit. But they don't give a fuck honky, about none of that. They just run up in the wings and start shocking people and hitting people with them batons and shields. They also had bean bag shot guns and were firing the shit out of them. I hear most of them rats were National Guard!

"Word is they carried out the guy with the broom stick on a bed, but they left the broom stick up his ass honky. They said medical had to take it out cause when it's pulled out, it could pull splinters out of it and leave splinters all inside. Honky you should've seen the motherfuckers' faces that did see it. I mean, you got dead motherfucking cops all over but people staring at this guy with a broom stick coming out his ass. They had him lying on his side, ass cheeks bare, for the whole world to see. I mean how often a person ever see some shit like that? They got body bags with people in them spread in rows across the ground, but people just looking at him.

"They got a bunch of dorms taped off right now including ours. They got eight guards dead, Crazy. Over in the dorm we lived in, those crazy-ass Crips tried to fight back. Word is that at least three of them got shot with real guns. I didn't even know they could use that type of force. They found two female guards over there. One was dead, and the other was tied up. The one that was still alive, her hair was half burned off, and she'd been raped. Objects were shoved up her ass and pussy, and her face had tons of cuts. From what I hear, her whole body had cuts in fact, and she had burns from where smokes were put out on her. They must've tortured her for hours, honky. If not the whole time this went down. Oh, also they cut her throat when the rats came in, but she still lived.

"The other chick got off easy, they just cut her throat, but she was also raped. They found two tits in one of the fucking Crips pockets! The tits belonged to a dead guard out in the core, and her head was cut off. How stupid is a motherfucker who walks around with cut off tits on them? Not to mention what type of a sick motherfucker does it take to do that? Craziest shit ever honky! Them Crips are some sick motherfuckers. That other chick wasn't tortured at all. She didn't have cuts or burn marks or nothing. She got it better then both the other two females.

"Man Crazy, that Bill-Bill and his lieutenant are two crazy-ass honkies too. Those two had mace shot in their face, and they were both rammed with the shock shields. But those honkies just threw the rats up against the wall. They both had like six rats on them, and they were still fighting hard. This one rat in the back had a pistol and shot Bill-Bill. Honkies went off over that. That guard that shot him got jumped and stabbed seven times. Some of the Aryans almost got that pistol too. In the end, they air lifted the rat and Bill-Bill to an outside hospital. Jack is up here with us in another room. They broke his leg in two places. That honky is a giant Crazy. It took ten rats to take him down, and they broke his leg with the baton. It was the only way they could get him to the ground. Man could you imagine these two honkys as your enemy? I don't know what the bloods were thinking. I'm sure they didn't think all their high ranks almost would be dead and over 85% of the gang either dead or broken bones all over. Bill-Bill is being called a master mind by all his people. He took down a bigger rival with power and mind, that's power Crazy!

"Word is there are 742 convicts with broken bones or head wounds or worse. There's at least 50 dead convicts, not counting the dead rats. Fuck all of them! I heard a rat say there is over one million dollars' worth of damage in all the dorms. Tons of smoke damage. Plus this place made the newspaper, Crazy. They're calling it the worst riot in Kentucky's history! Can't say us country boys can't still throw a party huh?"

"Why they hit you in the head for? I mean shit honky, you wasn't doing nothing but helping me. Motherfucking rats love getting their revenge huh?" I just ignore his comment about a party. I'm starting to see it was my destiny to meet Bill-Bill to learn from him.

"Yeah, well they wanted me to stop helping you, but when they ran into B-Upper, I was already blinded by the mace. When they came in they just slammed that fucking black stick on my head. They didn't say shit honky! I don't know how Bill-Bill and Jack were holding out with that mace on them, and they got it shot right in their fucking faces. It burns like hell. Them two crazy-ass honkies acted like it was water.

"My celly's passed out in the wing over there. That is my ace Crazy. I told his stupid ass to stay in the cell. Harley don't listen to nobody though. Some guys from another wing came over there and raped him real bad honky. I'm going to kill whoever did it. I don't even give a fuck about the time they give me. If I ever figure it out, they're dead motherfuckers. Harley's down the hallway. He won't talk about it, he just lays over there all spaced out and won't talk about anything."

"Yeah, I feel you on that Heavy. I just hope he gives you that same loyalty back." Heavy looks at me kind of strange when I say that last part, and I realize I'm thinking more about Justin and probably shouldn't have said nothin', so I hurry up and add, "I hope he gets better though."

"Let me tell you something, I'm 29 years old, and I've been in since I was 18. I won't get out until I'm 49 years old. I've seen a lot of bad stuff in here in the last 11 years and there is one thing you got to always remember; it doesn't matter what others do or don't do, all that matters at the end of the day is what you do. They have to live with themselves, and you got to live with yourself. If I kill for Harley out of loyalty, but he doesn't for me, then I got to live with the idea that I'm a loyal-ass honky. Harley'll have to live with whatever he decides to do. You remember Crazy, we are the choices we make. What other people do or don't do is on them. There are more fake motherfuckers out there than real-ass honkies. All we can do is be ourselves and don't let the fake motherfuckers change us. Look at Jack, Honky. Bill-Bill's L.T.U and friend, stood by him until they both went down. You can't judge life Crazy, off one bad apple feel me?"

"Yeah, I need to remember all that. That's some real-ass advice. I don't think I've ever thought of it exactly like that, but now you break it down to me, I see exactly what you talking about. I get what you say about Jack and Bill-Bill also. It isn't they Crazy as people think. It's just they are Crazy loyal to each other. So that drives them to go even harder cause they don't want to see one or the other get hurt.

"I didn't at all realize you had prison time like that. You a solid-ass honky though Heavy. How you stay real? I've not been in prison that long at all, but I know this stuff has already made me more violent than I ever was before."

"Shit is what it is. After 11 years of this you become, a person society will for sure hate. By the time I get out I'll be so fucked up, I'll probably kill as many as I can until they catch me and send me back. How do you go from pure hell to just acting normal? You want to survive in here you got to be hard. Switching back? That might be impossible. That's just a fact Crazy, hard objects are most impossible to go back to soft."

"I hope that don't happen. I hope after all that time you can get out there and get you some pussy or ass or whatever is good to you honky."

We pause for a minute. Shit got too deep so I change the subject. "You know what happen to the guard who was in the tower?"

"No one knows he popped any doors. His story is that he tried to lock all the doors for peoples' safety, but some of the doors couldn't be locked because people were in the way. He told the other rats that were questioning him that there was so much chaos that he can't remember any certain person, or detail. He's claiming he was in shock. They probably don't believe him, but there's nothing they can do about it. It's not like there's cameras in the dorms, so they got no way of putting it together. Hell, there's no cameras nowhere at all."

"What about the rat that was in the tower in the dorm we lived in? What's up with him?"

"I hear that rat is telling everything. He's going through all our ID cards and picking people out that raped that rat in the core. Word is he saw the whole murder, but I hear it's a guy, who has life without already so he don't give a fuck. That was some fucked-up shit! He cut that bitch's head off. There's going to be a lot of new charges for a lot of them though. Just so you know Crazy, the rats are just extremely busy right now, but they going to come for us. We'll do years in the hole for their revenge. It's all the game Crazy."

"You talking about the guy, who had a tit in each pocket?" I try to move and pain shoots up my side to my chest. Plus I don't give a shit about the hole. I'm so cold-hearted nothing matters.

"Yeah that's the stupid motherfucker." Heavy stops there and then hesitates. He looks down like he don't want to look me in the eye, "Also, I'm not saying you did nothing'—none of my business anyway—but before I held my shirt on you, I saw Justin in the first cell. His body was kind of half under the bunk and half out. He had a shank that went all the way up inside his mouth.

"Any ways, I took a sheet and wiped off the handle to the blade. Then I wiped down the end of the broom stick that was sticking out dude's ass. Also just so we are clear, yes the dude that had the tits in his pockets is the guy who tore off that bitch's head."

"Well I'm sure whoever did all that is real grateful. I'd say that person owes you a lot honky." I give Heavy a wink. Sometimes Heavy You'll meet somebody like you that follows the code, no matter the cost of pain or any punishment. We agreed to be criminals, and we got a code that some won't follow but some of us live by that code 100%.

"Standing over dude's naked ass had me feeling weird, but that person don't owe me shit honky. I am just being a convict. Besides, whoever did it did me a favor because I was going to fuck Justin up myself first chance I got. Fucking punk-ass dick sucker jump me! My head still hurts where they punched me."

"Yeah, I feel you on that," we lapse back into silence for a minute.

"My fucking side is killing me. These bitch-ass rats won't give a honky a fucking aspirin, huh?"

"No Crazy, we don't get shit right now. We are, for sure, on the rats' shit list."

The next couple days went by pretty smooth, a nurse came in twice and checked my cut. Heavy just slept a lot. When he thinks, nobody is looking, he rubs his fingers under his armpits and then sniffs his fingers. It's pretty nasty up in here, and I guess he is checking to see if he's the one that stinks or not. It's been more than a couple days since we got a shower.

On my third day in medical, a rat comes and gets me and tells me I'm being shipped. Heavy is staying at the Pink Palace. I go through that whole chain and shackles routine then back in a car. When we get to the new prison, it isn't new to me. They brought me to K.S.R., and I hope like hell Megan is still working. I'm so damn glad they sent me here.

It turns out Megan is still working here, but she's on two weeks' vacation. I don't get sent to the yard at all, they put me straight in the hole. I don't have to wear blue this time though, I get to wear red. The ratting-ass sergeant reads me a detention order that says I'm in the hole for the safety and security of inmates and the institution.

They put me on Seg-4; I'm in cell left ten and I get to see out the window to the back of the chow hall. On my second day, I get me a good hot shower and see Pistol walking by. I had thought he was at the Castle. On my forth day, they come take my stiches out, and it still hurt like hell. The scar is wild looking. I see Pistol again later that day and yell through the window at him. When he finally hears me, he looks up at my window. He is on the yard by the chow hall.

"Hey Crazy! Welcome back. Man, you look like you been through hell. You should've have listened to me honky. I got a hustle for you." The wind is blowing so hard I can't make out all of what he says, but I got the word *hustle*, so I scream back to him. It kills my side to yell.

"What you talking about *hustle* honky?"

"I told you before, I got these fags that would love your young ass. Instead of being such a fucking hard ass, you can write them and probably make more than you making with whatever you got going on. Besides, writing letters to faggots ain't gonna kill you like the shit you're into. Besides Crazy, who knows, you might fall in love."

I see Pistol hasn't lost his sense of humor.

Chapter 18

21 IN PRISON!

"That which does not kill us makes us stronger."
—Friedrich Nietzsche

I'm not sure why they built the hole. I'm pretty sure when they built it way back when, the reason was to secure a dangerous convict for a short time till he calmed down. I don't think it was or is made for what they do today; just put a motherfucker in here for years for the smallest of infractions. My guess is Kentucky with many states probably abuse their power and just do whatever, fuck our sanity.

I've been in the hole for two and a half years. It is two years to the board on a ten. My luck is so bad, they messed up on my time and my county jail time was left off my time sheet. So whoever did my time sheet didn't get the nine months in county and the case worker had to fix it. So because of all that, I had to do two years and nine months. All that is to say that I went to see the parole board about 9 ½ months ago. They just gave me a two year flop, I know it was cause the riot but they didn't say. They said it was because I'm in prison for an assault, and now I'm in the hole for assault. The parole board are a bunch of heartless fucks. They want to turn us meaner and colder, then let us loose on the public.

The rat in the tower, from my dorm said he saw me stab a black guy in the foot so they charged me with a write-up for that and the shank. I caught another 6 months while in the hole. It's so fucking crazy in this hole, people cutting themselves and killing themselves. All you have is yourself for company all day, every day. I get restless and do stupid ass slap-rock shit. I clogged my toilet up and just kept pressing the damn button. I flooded half the walk before the rat seen what was up and shut my toilet off. Most times I can talk at least two or three other inmates into doing it with me. That's when it's really fun because when others are doing it with me we will flood that whole walk out. It may sound stupid, but there's nothing else to do. That water everywhere is rec all day.

I mean, you tell me, am I wrong for acting like an animal when I'm being treated like an animal? These rats haven't let me go outside in two and a half years. I'm so fucking pale you would think I'm an albino or some shit. Plus in the wintertime, the snow comes flying through the window. I'll wake up for breakfast and there will be a pile of fucking snow on my floor. It will be so cold in my cell that I can barely eat. I can see my fucking breath!

And all throughout this hole time I never once got sent to the property room. So I never had a chance to shoot my shot at Megan again. I sure have jacked off enough thinking about her though.

Pistol gave me a couple addresses of gay dudes. One of them is Nick and the other is Terry. I've been writing both of them for the entire time I've been in the hole. They both send me 100 dollars a month. I just let it stack up and I don't even buy nothing from the canteen. I knew back in the day when C.J was telling me about this hustle, it was for me. The best thing about this hustle is it don't matter if I get locked up on the yard or not, this hustle comes with me. So the way most hustles go, if you gamble or steal from the kitchen or sell shanks or drugs, when the rats catch you it's over. With this hustle, it don't matter at all, if they ship me or lock me up, my hustle comes with me. That works better for me because I need my hustle to be a safety net.

I look at it like this, Nick and Terry are lonely real bad. For them, I fill that gap and to show their gratitude they send me some money. Nick is like 300 pounds, he hasn't had a person show him love in years. I shower him in words of love every letter and make him feel like a million dollars. Terry is about the same, but instead of being overweight, Terry is in a wheel chair.

I've been saving up for about 20 months and have about $ 3,900 on my account. That's more money than I've ever had in my life. I want to get a car when I get out. I'm not trying to walk everywhere when I get out, so a whip is the first thing on my list. I hope to make parole in the next 14 1/2 months or so.

Nick and Terry aren't the only good news in my life. My dude Eric, the guy they nicknamed Country, he just got here about six months ago. I haven't seen him since R.C.C. and I'm down to a couple weeks in the hole. My dude Country, that never has gotten into trouble has been in several fights. This last fight he got in, he broke three of his fingers, so they sent him over here to set the bones in his fingers the right way. I already know Country, Pistol and I are going to act like a fool.

They kept Heavy at Pink Palace, he wrote to tell me Bill-Bill made it. He said Bill-Bill is too stubborn to die. They put Heavy and Bill-Bill in the hole. I heard they been going off and clocking out a lot, that they got a few years in the hole. They are in the hole at E.K.C.C aka Pink Palace. I would love to be down there with them.

This time in the hole is a motherfucker and to be honest it has done nothing but make me worse than I was. I've had so many evil thoughts over the last couple years. All this time has really done is make me bitter and extremely anti-social. My anger issues are off the chart. I mean you sit in a cell all day. You stare at the wall with no radio, TV or anything to do. You never go outside and don't have a clue what the outside is doing, just years in your head to keep you all sane.

The rat that was in the tower in my dorm made a statement that he saw me go up to A-upper and go behind that sheet that was tied up. They tried to threaten me with outside charges and other stuff. The rats always try to scare you but at the end of the day rats aren't the judge. They can say what they want but I keep it real simple, *I refuse to talk to you*, is all I say. They say I'm still under investigation but to talk to the rats is all the way on the downside of my scale of life. For sure, the downside when it comes to guards that been raped and killed. I don't need either of those charges. In the end of the day only training a cop has, is training to try to scare you, or run his mouth.

I got lucky the rat in the tower didn't say he saw me come out of there with a lot of blood on me. The only thing I can come up with is that the rat wasn't looking at that time since the mother-fucker sure told on everything else he saw.

I'm thinking about getting a kitchen job when I get out. I want to lay low so I can make parole, but prison most of the time won't let you lay low. That don't mean I can't try at least.

The next couple weeks go by smooth, no fights or anything. I sleep a lot and just staying all the way away from people. My trust level is shattered and I'm a mental mess. Most the time, I just hate everybody. It shows in my actions.

Finally, my hole time is over and they let me out. I need all new state clothes and state boots since all I had was the sweat pants, t-shirt and shoes that Bill-Bill gave me. All my other stuff was thrown away or something. At least, they never sent any of it here.

I am looking forward to getting all that because my girl is in the property room. I sit on the bench in the basement and wait to be called in. I know she is in there. Some of the guys on the walk told me she's here today. The rats told me to pack it up early this morning but it didn't matter because I wasn't able to sleep all night anyway. After about an hour she calls me in. I hate that everything in prison is a big-ass wait.

"Well welcome back to K.S.R. Rick, I heard you were here." I don't say nothing but it sure is good to see her. She seems to understand so after pausing a second, she just keeps talking. "I already know you need all new khakis and net bag so I took care of you and got you everything you need. I also got you your sheets, blankets and toilet paper," she has a huge grin on her face. It's hard not to smile back. Megan doesn't look like she has changed at all, it feels like I haven't seen her in forever. I notice she still bites her nails and she still swipes at that piece of hair that falls down her forehead that gets in her eyes.

"Damn girl you hooked a honky up, huh?" It's the first thing out of my mouth in weeks and I say it with my best smile.

"Well I put a fairly new pair of shoes in your bag and I put them on your property list. I also got you a TV." She pauses for a second, but I don't know how to thank her so I just keep smiling. "These were confiscated items from other people so I just put your number on them then got you hooked up."

"Well how sweet of you sexy. I knew you were a woman after my own heart. I haven't seen you in a couple years, but here you are keeping it real." I don't know if she notice or not but I say this in a real flirty way.

"Look Rick, I'm not trying to take you through a loop. I want to keep it truthful with you so I need to tell you first thing that I've been dating a guy for the last year and half. Nevertheless, I need something from you. And before you get upset, I'm not trying to use you, I just feel like I can trust you."

"Shit girl I'm glad you got a man. You too sexy for a person not to grab you up. I'm happy you're happy. Now tell me what you want from me, sexy. You don't have to worry about me thinking you'll use me Megan. You can't use the willing sexy!"

"This is why I like you. You always know what to say. You're a slick talker, but in a good way. As for what I need, well, my boyfriend, his name is Richard, we are both a little in debt. We got a loan on a house but a few things went wrong so we had to ask for more money, and our mortgage payment shot up real high on the house. I need you to sell some things for me, to try to make as much as you can for me. Will you do that Rick?"

I could hear the tremor in her voice. She didn't even look me in the eye the whole time she was talking. It don't matter at all to me though, I know how to calm her down. This is what I am gifted at.

"It's all good Megan, you don't got to be nervous with me. I'm not mad you got a man and I'm not at all mad you need to make some money. Hell, girl, I need to make some money too. It's all good, and I'm your man. Just tell me what the things are then I'll do whatever I can for you sexy!" This gets me a smile from her so I know I am getting her to relax some. "You don't got to worry about nothing Megan. I can handle whatever you need done girl."

"Well, I'm going to start bringing you some real good skunk weed. I'll probably start off with a half-pound because I don't have the money to go bigger but..."

"Hold on a second, I don't mean to interrupt you but I got a few thousand on my books. Tell me what a pound cost and I'll just buy it for us, that we'll keep this simple. After I learn on the yard what things go for, I'll tell you how much I can make for us, okay?"

"Well that works perfect! Richard has a brother that sells it. He can get a pound for dirt cheap from his brother. I'm pretty sure he can get it for $1,200 easy, but anything over that we'll handle." I nod and she continues, "I'll get you an address where you need to send your money to. Then we'll get started. How does all that sound?"

"It sounds wonderful to me Megan. I'm a little sorry you're taken, but this is better. I try never to mix business with pleasure. It don't ever work out right. So let me get my clothes and I'll take off sexy, okay? Don't worry about nothing sweetheart. We'll do good business and I'll keep you safe. But more importantly, I'll get you out of debt."

"Well one last thing, you remember Tammy, or Tom? She still works as my runner but I'm going to request for two runners and I want you to put in a request for property room runner so I can hire you. That way we can talk and you'll have a reason to be down here."

"That sounds perfect to me, but it's best that nobody knows about any of this, not Tammy or none of my friends. Only we will know. It's best that way okay? People will know I have weed, but not where it comes from."

"Yep, that is exactly what I need. I don't need to lose my job over this or go to jail. I just need to make a little extra so being as discreet as possible is what we need." She looks me in the eye and she can see we're on the same page. "You're going to dorm two, cell 10-lower left okay?"

"Alright, all that sounds perfect to me. Who is my celly?"

"It's all single cells here at K.S.R. so you're by yourself. Surprised nobody told you that."

"It's all good then, thanks" As I say this I am putting all my stuff in the net bags she gave me. The TV doesn't fit though so I'll just carry my TV. I'm not worried about telling anyone about her. People don't ever seem to be who they say they are. Justin taught me that lesson.

"Alright Megan I'm out of here. I'll put that request to work in tomorrow. By the time I start work, I'll have all the prices of what it goes for here okay? And now that you mention it, I think somebody did tell me it's all single cells, but I forgot."

"Okay sounds good Rick, I'll have the place where to send the money the first day you start. I may just bring the first pound with me on credit. You'll be sending the money to pay it back. I got to first see if he will give it to me on credit.

"Okay, take care sexy!" I wink at her as I walk out. As soon as I walk out the property room door I see Tammy, Pistol and Country sitting on the bench waiting on me.

"What's up honkies? What you two doing in this basement?" I say with a frown, but I'm just playing with them.

"Shit Crazy you know we would be waiting on you. You know you can't go to the yard with your seg. clothes on. We figured we'd meet you down here. Now go down to the bathroom at the end of the hall and change out." Country says grinning ear to ear.

"What the hell you smiling about honky?"

"I'll tell you why I'm smiling honky! You turned 21 in the hole and we going to *party* today Crazy! So go get changed and let's get our drink on honky!"

Chapter 19

THERE IS NO GOOD IN PRISON, ONLY GOOD MOMENTS FULL OF DRUGS, HOOCH AND FIGHTS!

"Whenever I climb I am followed by a dog called 'Ego'."
—Friedrich Nietzsche

The bathroom is as small as a closet; there is only a toilet in here, no sink. Talk about germs, and I'm not even able to wash my hands. The walls were at one time tan or maybe white, but now they're just filthy. From the stains everywhere, it seems most people just come in here and piss on the walls. Besides, it smells bad in here like piss. I think seriously of changing out in the hallway, not so much because of the smell or even the looks, but because there is nowhere to set anything down. The floor has hair and trash all over it, there is no way anybody has cleaned this in recent memory.

I just hop on one foot at a time, pulling my new pants up the other leg. I then switch while holding old and new clothes under my arms. It wasn't easy but finally I'm able to change out. I open the door and I see everybody is waiting on me.

"Damn Crazy you been in the boom-boom room a long ass time." Pistol says and laughs.

"What you laughing at Pistol and what the hell does 'boom, boom' room mean?!" Really, I'm speaking to all three of them, it doesn't matter to me who answers so I stare at all three of them and wait. I notice Tammy is real touchy feely with Pistol, which surprises me a bit, but I figure it's none of my business.

"Shit Crazy, sometimes I forget how big of a fish you are," Pistol says jokingly.

"Don't tease him Pistol, you know he's young and he's got a short temper," Tammy looks at me like he's waiting for me to go off.

"What you looking at me for, Tammy?"

"I am just thinking when I was young, my mama always called me 'young, dumb, and full-of-cum', now I look at you and see what she was saying."

"What you saying Tammy? You calling me an idiot or dumb or something?" I said as I felt my temperature rise.

All three of them start to laugh together. I let this motherfucker push my buttons and then let him turn it around to show me how he does it. For- real this will sound crazy as hell, but this is the very part of prison I crave. This is con talking to con, if you're not cocky or think you know it all. You can learn something from everybody to educate your con inside you.

"Yeah, yeah you three get your rec. all you want on me. It's all good 'cause, for real, I wasn't even mad. I'm just playing right back at you."

Pistol just looks at me with this stupid ass grin, "Yeah, yeah Crazy, that's your story. Tell it how you want to tell it, I still think we got to you."

I just give Country and Pistol my best smile, then tell them to lead the way. "Not to my dorm either, lead the way to the hooch. Let's get this started," I say, with a lot of excitement. I can't even remember the last time I had fun with friends.

"Shit, you have to go see your dorm officer to get the key to your cell. After that, you have to sign a cell inventory sheet. Just tell the guard the cell is fine and nothing is torn up, that you'll sign the cell inventory, shouldn't take long, crazy, at all."

"Okay then Country that sounds all good, lead the way to my dorm, I guess." I follow them because I don't have a clue where dorm two is.

All three of us head out of the basement. Country carries my TV, and so I carry my net bag. I put my shoes on because the shoes I got at Pink Palace are gone. I don't have a clue where they went, but they're not in my property. It was sure good that Megan hooked me up. Megan is all the way high on my scale of life. As we walk outside, I look over at Pistol.

"You going to keep trying to push my buttons or are you going to tell me what the hell 'boom-boom' room means?"

"I am just giving you a hard time Crazy. The 'boom-boom' room is exactly what it sounds like. Two people go in there, and one of them is getting fucked. So they call it the 'boom-boom' room!"

"Ha ha ha, now I see why you guys were laughing at me, the fucking 'boom-boom' room. You take Tammy in the boom-boom room Pistol?"

"Shit, you not supposed to be all up in my business like that. But since you my honky. I'll tell you like this; are you asking 'cause you want to get drunk and get some or are you just wanting to know?"

"I just want to know what's up honky. I don't give a fuck what you do Pistol. I had not a crumb in my box, and you brought me a hustle. I'm not judging you, player. You my dawg, I just went through some shit at the Palace, but you and country are forever my honkys"

"Well, he's my sissy." Pistol says, then changes the subject. "As long as we're asking questions, me and Country got a question for you. What the hell happen to you at R.C.C.? I was already on the bus and gone, but I heard you got locked up."

"That fucking Tiny ratted on me honky," I reply as I feel the anger bubble up at the memory. "Not only that, he fucking told me he did it all over the hooch I made. He got mad I was taking his hustle."

I see Country give Pistol a funny look, so I ask them what's up. Country stops walking and gives me the most serious look ever, then says in a low voice, "Tiny is here Crazy." I shut my eyes for a moment, it seems in prison when you try to lock your monster up is the very time shit just fly's from everywhere. I live by a code, so again my monster must come out for Tiny. I killed my best friend for my code, I'm not letting Tiny know.

Country can see my mind working on this new piece of information. So he starts talking real fast to me, "Listen Crazy, let's go to your dorm to get your key. Put your stuff up, me and Pistol live in dorm two also. Tammy lives in dorm one, but he'll sneak into dorm two with us. I'll get the hooch and just bring it to your cell. We'll get our drink on some then Pistol and I will go with you to check out Tiny. How does that sound to you, honky?"

"That sounds like a good plan to me. Where does Tiny live? Just so you know now, I'm going to take more than a look at him. I'm going to beat his fucking ass." I have so much anger in me. It truly does amaze me how much me, and my monster have become one.

Country says, "He lives in the bottoms in dorm four."

"What do you mean the bottoms, honky?" I ask.

Pistol answers by laying the place out for me as we start walking again to our dorm. "This place is huge, up here at the top is dorm one, two and three." He draws a semi-circle in the air with his hand and points to each of the spots where a dorm sits on it. "Then they got a loop you can walk around and in the middle of the loop is a grassy area that has volley ball courts. Over here is a baseball field, next to the baseball field is a huge gym. Inside the gym, are four pool tables right to your right when you walk in behind a cage. Then when you walk into the gym to your left is a small square office. Where a guy officer sits and watches people in the gym. A plastic window is like half the wall where they can see out into the gym.

"Don't be fooled by those motherfuckers, they wear pants and regular T-shirts, but they still rats. They'll tell on you the moment they see you doing something. Most these gym workers are bigger rats than the motherfuckers wearing a badge. Hell, let me tell you something, these caseworkers here will help you better than the Palace. The case workers at E.K.C.C are all more rats then a caseworker so they won't do shit for you but act like a cop.

"The gym has a full-size basketball court. In the back are all the free weights, and they got bleachers we can sit on to watch people play basketball. All the way down past the volleyball court is the bottoms. There in a full circle is dorm four, five and six. Next to the gym is another full circle for dorms seven, eight and nine. They built dorm ten years after everything else was here so it got built over behind dorm one. It is a nursing care unit or some shit. It's not been here that long.

"Our dorms are at the top with the chow hall in the middle and dorms seven through nine on the other side. The fucking chow hall is so huge it holds close to 800 people. It's has a wheel chair ramp for the people that can't walk and another exit on the other side for us. It has like five steps you got to walk up to get into the chow hall. There's even a mailbox over there where you drop your mail. You can exit into the chow call on the wheel chair ramp if you want.

"Also, just so you know, dorm two and dorm eight are the oldest dorms here. They redid all the other ones but dorm two and eight got busted out windows just like the hole and no air conditioner or heat. So since it's hot as fuck out here today, look for it to be even hotter in our dorm. Any questions you got Crazy?"

"Nah, not right now, this place sounds like a kiddie place, for sure, after the Pink Palace."

Not to be left out of the conversation, Country answers this time. "Yeah, this place is a hospital, for real. It's laid back here, and lots of these cons are on good pills. You can get anything you want and half of it is passed out at pill call. Just so you know, that's the pill call building over there in front of the chow hall."

From the look, he gives the pill call building, I take it he doesn't think much of pill call, so I ask him what his issue is.

"Shit Crazy, it's like four hundred people that come to it. It takes fucking three hours in the heat to get through it and all I take is ibuprofen." I don't answer back, and for a moment nobody speaks up and we just walk.

For May, it is a bright sunny day. I'm already sweating real badly. As I look around, I realize it's packed out here. Convicts are standing around, smoking or talking. Lots of them are walking too, but with no real destination. Just walking to feel the air move on them, I guess. I see wooden tables everywhere. But every one of them is taken. It will be June in a couple of days. I've been 22 for 15 days, give or take. So I'm ready to have a party.

Just like at Pink Palace, white people all flocked to one area and blacks another. Although, here it feels more relaxed. Not so much tension in the air all the time like at the Pink Palace. I just hope to do more than a couple months on the yard here. Hell, I did only about two months at the fish tank. Then about 60 days in the hole. After that, I did about two and half months on the yard at the Pink Palace, then more hole time. At this point, I've done more hole time than anything. I know that's got to be on the downside on my scale of life.

We make it to the dorm that looks like something from 1920. Dorm two isn't like anything at the Pink Palace. The inside looks old. Right when you walk in, the air feels stale. The place looks dirty, but people keep trying to paint over the filth. There is a guard room within 30 feet of the front door.

Inside the guard room, the rat has a desk. The wall in front of the desk is all brick up to your waist but from your waist up it's all Plexiglas so the rat can look out. Behind the rat's desk is a single door to a second room. This room has mops, brooms, and chemicals to clean with. This room also has Plexiglas from the waist up. It looks into a TV room that the convicts use to watch TV. There are tons of plastic chairs sitting around in the TV room. They are all blue with cut marks, dents, and just looks depressing to be honest. Inside the janitor's closet is a small bathroom for the rats to use.

As I walk the 30 feet to the office, I notice they got ice machines out here in the small core. There's a set of stairs, and I can see there are two wings down stairs. One wing is on my left side, and the other is to my right. The doors to these wings, as well as the walls around them are Plexiglas also. That way the rats can see down the wing. There is a bathroom at the head of each wing, but I can only see half of it through the glass. The whole place gives me the feeling of being in a haunted house. Even the lights in here glow an eerie yellow, like the darkness is trying to beat the light back. It's old, sad, stale and depressing.

When I walk up to the door of the office, I notice a spiral staircase in the corner behind the door going up to the second floor. The officer is a big fat white guy with a mustache like a 1970's porn star. He has crumbs all over his desk and at least three or four *Little Debbie* cakes. When he notices me standing there looking at him. He brushes the crumbs off while he talks with his mouth full.

"Wat you wat inate," he says blowing more crumbs over his desk.

"What the hell you just say to me?"

He swallows hard, then repeats his question, "I said, what you want inmate?" This time, little crumbs are falling out of his dumb-ass mustache. This fat rat isn't going up those steps behind this door. Every rat is thin or super fat.

"Look turnkey, I'm not looking for no issue. I'm not for sure trying to have you ride my ass. So why don't we just leave the name calling out of it, so we can get down to what we need to do. That way I can get out of your face?"

Pistol behind me says, "Yeah turnkey, just let the man get his key and let him sign the cell inventory sheet, and we'll be out your way."

"I don't give a shit what you guys want. I do shit in my time. Now Mr. Smith, you tell your buddies to go somewhere else. This here has got nothing to do with them. When they leave we'll get you took care of."

Country steps up, "It don't matter, Crazy. We'll see you over here on lower left. Don't get too out of control with him, he is a lock up artist. He lies like a motherfucker on write ups."

Pistol puts his two cents in also, "You know that shit is right turnkey, you lied on me two weeks ago. Don't matter though, 'cause court call threw that lying-ass shit out. Lying ass motherfucker."

"Okay, that's enough of you, get out of here now, or I'll call the sergeant and have you guys locked up. And that is no lie, but try your luck if you want." As he spoke, he made sure to look at each of them, so they knew he is taking note who they are.

I don't want my dudes locked up. Particularly when their cell is hot with hooch. To save face I say, "Look honkies, you guys go get some soda pops. It's hot as fuck in here. I'm going to deal with this real fast and I'll see you guys soon okay?" They know I don't mean no damn soda pop, I'm reminding them of the hooch in code. They know what's up.

All three of them kind of mumble a *yes* before heading over to lower right. No sooner did everybody leave, than the officer gets a key out a box that he has in his desk.

"Look Mr. Smith, I like what you said. I won't disrespect you as long as you do the same for me. I get used to people coming in here with smart mouths and over time you get to a point where you say something smart before they do. So you can call me Officer

Greenberg, and I'll call you Mr. Smith okay? I work here five days a week on first shift."

"That sounds perfect to me Officer Greenberg. I'm not trying to have no beef with you 'cause, I don't want you at my door every day fucking with me." I know how the game is played. I'm trying to move smooth right now.

"Okay then we got us an understanding. I need you to sign this cell inventory sheet. I already put on here your windows are busted out. Your table, locker and bunk are in good shape though. Your mat and pillow are new. You have a trash can in your cell, and it's not busted or tore up. If you just agree with me, you can sign at the 'X'. Oh also, I checked the walls, you got some things wrote on the wall. I put it all on here."

I look at the paper and see "light switch" on the list, so I ask, "What does 'light switch' mean?"

"You got a light switch in your cell. I put down that it's not broke or cracked. Now sign where it says 'Inmate Signature.'"

See, I've been through these before. They make us sign these because if a Ro-bo cop is on when I pack up to leave, and say the light switch is broke, he'll pull this sheet out and write me up saying it wasn't broke. That is "destroying state property" by just signing this paper seals my fate. They'll try to give me 45 in the hole, or make me pay for it, or hell, maybe both.

I pause a second then I realize I don't give a fuck, so I lean down and sign the form. Afterwards I push the form back to the rat. Nothing in that cell could cost anything more than about five or six dollars.

"Okay, now you just need to sign this other form saying I gave you your key to your cell that you understand if you lose it, it will cost you $35 to get a new one."

The cost surprises me, "35 fucking dollars? Damn that's a lot for a fucking key. It don't matter though. I'll sign it. Just show me where to sign. Fuck it!"

"Sign right here where it says 'Inmate Signature'." He takes his sausage-like finger and points to where I need to sign. He makes like a sigh kind of sound that lets me know he's calling me stupid for not knowing where to sign.

I sign, then ask "Are we done here now Officer Greenberg?"

He coughs like maybe some of that *Little Debbie* cake didn't get all the way down his throat. He holds out the key and says, "Here take your key, you'll need to find a key chain for it."

I just grab the key and don't say anymore. I walk over to the lower left walk and go straight to the bathroom. The bathroom is on my left as I walk in. There are four sinks and two commodes, they got a stand-up toilet, with a shower all the way in the back. There are no curtains anywhere. A guy sitting on the toilet could see right into the shower area, and it smells terrible in here. Flies are everywhere. There is a trash can in the corner with a swarm of flies buzzing around it.

I walk to the standup toilet, breath in a deep breath when I start to piss, it has been since last night. It's even spookier in here than out on the wing. I don't see anyone around at all. I wash my hands in the sink and head to cell ten. It's towards the middle of the walk. I unlock the cell door and step in. Country was right, it is so humid it is like walking into the bathroom with the shower running on full hot with steam everywhere. Only thing missing is the clean smell. My mat does look fairly new. The room has white walls but lots of the paint has been chipped off, and I can see it was blue and brown in the past. There are also tons of things wrote upon the walls. Peoples' names and when they were here, for the most part. I heard that it is bad luck to write your name on any walls or anything in here. It means you'll come back or some shit.

The locker and table are blue, the locker has several shelves in it. It's kind of weird to be in a single cell after open wings and two-man cells. The only single cells I've been in is in the hole, and they controlled when I came and went. They had the keys, so I couldn't do anything, unless they let me. Now I can come in and out as I please. Country told me the yard shuts down at 9 PM or so but after that we can roam the wings or go to the TV room until 10:30 PM. We get locked down in our wings at that time but we can take a shower anytime we please.

No sooner than I set my stuff down, my door opens with Pistol, Country and Tammy walking in. Pistol is holding a blue plastic chair.

"Here's a chair honky. Every cell is supposed to have one, so it's cool if you want to keep it. If my memories serves me correct, you grabbed me a chair at the tank when our friendship kicked off. "

Country is still carrying my TV, "Take this TV Crazy. I been packing this motherfucker for an hour it seems like. I got you a cable cord also."

"Just lay it on the table Country. Hey, good looking on the chair, Pistol."

Tammy steps in after Country, "I got this hooch here. It's already in drinking containers. You guys ready to get your drink on?"

We all say *Hell Yeah* together. Tammy hands me mine, and I remember a time when I wouldn't take anything, unless I could *pay my way*. Now that I've grown up some, I see how that was childish thinking. At least, *I* feel it was. A person can only trick you if you let them. If someone is your friend or acts like they are, what better way to find out really fast by taking what they offer, then see what happens?

After my second cup of hooch, I'm feeling myself, again. We sit here and cut it up, we catch up with each other and what we all have been up to since the Fish Tank. We're all drinking slow and, for real, having fun. I am feeling good, but I want to go get Tiny before I lose my chance or get too drunk to where I'd get my ass kicked.

"Hey honkies, I'm going to chill on the hooch. I want to head down to the bottoms to get my lick back."

Pistol stands up, "I am for sure coming with you. Tiny is a big motherfucker. We will probably have to jump him. With Country's hand the way it is, he can't help a lot so I'm taking my shank." We all look up at that last part. "Just in case his friends want to jump in."

"What will I do while you're gone baby?" Tammy asks Pistol, real sweet.

"I'll drop you off at your dorm. When I'm done I'll come back and get you."

"Country with your hand so fucked up, I think it's best if you stay out of this," I say, watching to see how he'll react. I don't want Country to feel less of a man.

"Shit Crazy, me and you go all the way back to county. I'm in whatever you in."

Nothing else is said, so the four of us head out. We leave the hooch in my locker. There's still about eight cups left. We drop Tammy off on the way to the bottoms. This place is fucking huge. It's like walking three football felids to get down here. With the sun so bright and all the humidity, it would be an understatement to say it's just miserable to walk this far. I don't envy these guys.

The convicts who live down here got to walk this every day just to mail a letter or go to chow. It is what it is though.

Tiny lives in dorm four. Pistol's friend Teardrop told him where to find Tiny. In fact, Teardrop wants to come with us. I am not too sure about this since I didn't know this dude but in the end Pistol tells Teardrop that he's a grown man and can do what he wants. Teardrop has a joint, and we smoke it on our way to dorm four. Between the hooch and the weed, I'm good.

When we roll up on dorm four. Teardrop is still with us. In the guard's office, there is a female rat. She's reading a novel or something. I ignore her and head to the TV room. There are three people in the TV room, and I ask them, "Do any of you know where Tiny lives? Or what wing?" This dorm is set up like dorm two, it's just newer and way cleaner.

A young black guy says "Yeah, he lives on upper right in cell one."

"Yeah, good looking player" Teardrop says by way of thanks. I say nothing just walk out of the TV room to the stairs. As we climb the steps Pistol says "I hope Tammy is cool. When I leave her by herself, she gets to running her mouth."

"She'll be cool honky," I say although I'm not sure if I believe it. Either way, I don't get anything else out because at the top of the steps, I see Tiny in the bathroom through the glass.

Chapter 20

HUSTLE, MONEY, MONEY, MONEY!

"Be content to act, and leave the talking to others."
—Baltasar Gracian

As I look at the rat through the window, I see he's washing his face. It's really ironic how in prison what you do matters more than it does on the streets. You can be piece of shit or a yap or a rat, but the thing about prison is it's such a small world. Everything you do always comes back to you. That's why many old timers have told me to always keep my word good. Once you lose your word in this world, you can't ever get it back. You could leave prison and come back in five years, you can bet people in here would remember you.

Tiny is still one big black motherfucker. The last big motherfucker I fought almost chocked me out, and even big-ass Jack wasn't able to hurt him much. Tiny isn't big as that guy was, but he still has a lot of muscle, and he is black as the ace of spades. I don't give a fuck about either one of those things about him. What matters is I did time in the hole because of him, so I for sure need my fucking lick back.

Teardrop and Pistol are right behind me, Country is at my right. It's extremely hot in this dorm. The air is so humid it feels like walking through a sauna. I can feel my mouth just dry up. It smells like moldy food mixed with piss.

I don't see any rats on this second landing. There is an office just like downstairs but in this office is just extra mats, pillows, and foot lockers. At least that's all I see in there through the window.

Tiny has soap on his face. He is getting ready to wash the soap off when I run right through his wing door on the right side. You would think I'm a track star doing the 100-yard dash the way I run up on this ass hole. I don't say shit because really what is there to say? *Hey Tiny you ratted on me* or *our pep talk we had in that office that day was blah, blah, blah.* So I sucker punch him dead in the side of his big-ass head. I hit this motherfucker so hard, my fucking knuckle bends in half on my right hand, and I can't tell you how bad this shit hurts. I did pretty well though because I hit this ass hole in the ear, and blood starts coming out. He tries to open his eyes to see who just hit him, but Country takes something out of his pocket and throws it into Tiny's eyes. Tiny starts to scream so loud that I don't know how the rat downstairs doesn't hear it. He doesn't get long to scream because Teardrop grabs a wooden broom then swings it like a baseball bat. Country and I hit the floor as I hear a nightmarish sound. It sounds like a huge chunk of wood that is being bent with so much pressure that it snaps. When I look up, I see the snap was Tiny's jaw, blood and teeth fly everywhere. His jaw looks like it isn't attached to his face any more. It just hangs about six inches down from the rest of his face and the only reason his jaw doesn't hit the floor is the skin on his face is holding it. Clearly, from the way it's hanging, it's broke. This honky is crazy as fuck.

"God-damn Teardrop, watch where you swing that damn thing!"

"Ha ha ha" Teardrop laughs. "Honky, I figured you had good reflexes," he adds matter-of-factly. "I'm just saying Crazy if you want to hurt a motherfucker that big, you got to do it like that you want punch somebody his size." I just stare at him.

Tiny starts to scratch at his eyes, and they look all puffy like they're starting to swell up. I can tell Tiny is trying to scream, but he can't with his jaw broke and he can't see either.

"Now what was that you was saying about my broken fingers Crazy?" Country asks.

"Come on honky, you know I just had your best interest at heart. I would never doubt you Country. What the hell did you throw on him?" As I say this, I'm holding my right hand in my left and hoping the pain will stop. My fingers are killing me.

Country just smiles at me like a cat that stole the milk. Finally, he says, "Crazy, I always have pepper in my pocket. Shit burns like hell but it gets the job done, honky. I have three broken fingers, so I had to find another way to protect myself"

I turn around to see Pistol done got behind Tiny and have the big guy in a headlock. Tiny is trying to swing hay makers, but he's just hitting air. Pistol has Tiny almost to the shower.

Teardrop runs over and takes the end of the broom and jabs Tiny in the gut, then says in a controlled voice in Tiny's ear, "Tiny, you make this easy or hard, but you going to get this broom stick stuck up your ass if you keep trying to hit my dude Pistol."

As Teardrop says this, another convict from the walk steps into the bathroom. I don't even give the guy time to process a thing, I step up in his face and tell him the bathroom is closed.

He looks at me all funny and then looks at Teardrop, "Come on Teardrop you know I'm no rat. You know I won't tell no one what I see or hear."

Country asks, "You know this guy or what?"

"Yeah, I know him, he's cool. What you want Mouse? This better be good though. And don't tell me all you need is the toilet. You know damn well the convict thing to do is to go over to another wing. You shouldn't be up in our business." Teardrop looks Mouse dead in the eyes when he says this and Mouse looks away. Mouse is weak. Predator or prey, Mouse is prey.

Mouse said, "Well I don't need to use nothing in here. I just want to express that I would pay you guys whatever but Tiny is my man."

I just spit on his face.

Mouse squeals, "Why you do that?"

Mouse is probably about five foot tall and weighs maybe 100 pounds soaking wet. He's got solid blond hair and green eyes.

"I spit in your fucking face because you don't even ask why we're doing what we're doing. You just offer to pay this rat's way? Let me tell you something, you can't pay me back for the close to 60 days in hell he put me through sitting in that hot-ass hole. My suggestion to you *Mouse;* is for you to turn around, let me see you walk to your cell, and don't bother us no more."

"Man this really sucks! I always swore to Tiny I would get jumped with him if he got jumped." Mouse whined.

"I'm not a racist person Mouse, but you being a monkey's punk really makes me not respect you at all." Country says. "We're done talking to you. You go now or you get your jaw broke too." Mouse starts crying and sniffling, but he walks away without another word. I watch him as he walks down the hallway and into his cell.

"Look honkies, this motherfucker passed out from the pain. It's count time in 30 minutes. We got to hurry up because we can't be up in here during count or we'll fuck the rats' count up and they'll lock us up for sure. Besides, this rat may tell." Pistol is standing near the door as he says this while looking out the window and making sure no rats are coming.

I love that my word is good, that I can tell Pistol and Country whatever and no matter what, they believe me. They'll ride with me through hell. I never found this type of loyalty in any of the group homes I was in or anywhere else I've been since. The bonds you make with your brothers in prison are deeper than any bond you will ever make. That's what I believe, and that's what I've seen in my short life span so far. Even Justin was loyal in the end. He just had someone who was higher up in his loyalty. I can't blame him for picking a childhood friend over me and his two-month friendship.

"Teardrop, look at my finger and tell me if it's broke or what honky?"

"Shit Crazy, Teardrop is a mountain man. He can barely read let alone play doctor for you. Come over and let me see it." Pistol gestures for me to show him my hand.

As I walk over to Pistol, I take a good look at Tiny. He looks like he's dead, but I could see his chest going up and down. His eyes are swelled shut though. That pepper fucked his eyes up real bad.

"Well I got some good news for you, and then I got some bad news. What you want first honky?"

"Shit Pistol, just tell me the bad news. The way it hurts can't get no worse."

Pistol smiles and says "Well the bad news is that it's going to hurt like hell to fix. But the good news is that it's not broke. It just popped out of the socket."

"Whooweee, honky! That's going to hurt to pop that back," Country says then adds, "Let me do it for you."

"Man, fuck you Country. You way too happy about my finger. You're not touching it!"

Country laughs and says, "I just find it funny. Here you were saying I couldn't come because my hand and boom, now your hand is fucked up. Karma is a bitch, huh?"

I hold my hand out to Pistol. "Pop it back in place for me."

Before I could register what's happening, Pistol grabs my wrist with one hand and with his other hand he grabs my middle finger and pulls hard as hell. I hear a popping sound and enough pain to bring me to my knees. And it's done.

"Motherfucker! That hurt like hell!" and everybody busts out laughing at me.

"Honky, you should have seen your face. That shit should've have been recorded. Your whole face turned red as hell." Country says, still laughing.

"Yeah, yeah, you guys get your rec. on me all you want. Let me finish this, so we can go back to get count over with. While we finish the hooch, you guys can laugh at my pain some more and the face I made."

My finger looked swollen, but it don't matter because I walk over to Tiny and slap him on his face. He wakes up, but he still can't see. I can hear his breathing getting worse.

"Tiny, I know you can hear me but you can't talk. I know you remember me. Remember the pep talk on being married to the game? Well, I just taught you a new rule, never reveal your hand to anybody in life. You should've have kept it to yourself. I got a system called the scale of life, and I would say you making me your enemy is on the down side of the scale.

"So, here's the deal Tiny. You and I can't be on the same yard together so you got to go. I don't care if you check in, or if you stage a fall out with somebody and go to the hole but you got to go. Now nod your head that you understand, or I'll start kicking you and hopefully I'll break something else on you."

Tiny doesn't even try to resist anymore, he's too much of a coward. He got the respect he had because of his size, but beat him up and he just folds.

"Good Tiny. I'm glad we got an understanding because I don't want to hear you ratted on me again."

I say nothing else and walk back out of the wing to head back to the dorm for count time. As I am walking to my dorm a thought hits me, "Hey Country, what happen to our dude J-Bird?"

"I heard they sent him to Green River. That's a laid-back prison for real honky. He left like a week after you went to the hole."

Pistol and Teardrop are walking behind us. I stop and turn around. I look at Teardrop and say, "That was good looking honky. You didn't have to risk yourself or make a new enemy. You stuck your neck out there for me. That is some real shit you just did."

"Ah shit Crazy you don't need to tell me all that. I've known Pistol for ten years, but I would have rode with you any ways 'cause you good people. Look, I live down here in the bottoms in dorm six. I got to go I have some stuff to do and it'll be count time soon."

"Alright honky you take it easy, you know we all live in dorm two if you need us." Country says this so friendly you would think they been friends for ten years.

Pistol and me both say "Take it easy player," and Teardrop turns around and heads down to his dorm. For being this early in the year it's still hot as hell out here. I can even feel my feet sweating. The sun is so bright that it's blinding. I need to come up on some sunglasses. It shouldn't be a problem since I have money and weed coming.

"What's on your mind Crazy? You look like you having some serious thoughts over there."

"Not so serious, I want to get some sunglasses honky. I'm also wondering where I get a job app 'cause I want to file for a job."

"Crazy what you talking about job?" Pistol asks. "If you that pressed out on money honky, I will help you get your hustle on. Hell, we could've robbed Tiny."

"Hmm," I think this over a little then finally state, "Look you two, I got this connect in the front. I gave my word, I wouldn't speak on who it is. I know you both are solid, so it's not about you two. I just gave my word and I don't break my word. The thing is though I have a hustle for all three of us. I can get as much weed as we can sell. How much does a pound go for here?"

"You don't sell it like that Crazy. First, let me ask you this, how much do you think you can get a pound for? You know, from your connect?"

"Shit, I'm told about $1,200 or so."

"Okay here is how we do this. A sugar sack is a single pack of sugar, get three single packs at breakfast time. Two sugar sacks is

100 dollars, and you would probably get 450 sugar sacks out of a pound so you could make 22,500 dollars a pound. You pay 1,200 up front for the pound, give the connect 15,000 and that would leave you 9,300 dollars. To make it right though, me and Country can sell it all for you, and we make like 500 dollars apiece. How does that sound to you Crazy? That's $8,300 profit honky! The sugar packs we get out of the kitchen for almost nothing. They just the little square packs we get for breakfast, but we can buy a whole box of them for nothing really."

I don't answer right away. I just breathe in the fresh air. It's really amazing the things I've taken for granted in my life. Two and half years in the hole changed that. Nothing but pure madness and anger around me all the time. The air in there smells like piss and arm pits—I can't even describe how stale it is—no showers but three times a week. Even with the windows knocked out, you don't ever seem to get fresh air or sunshine. In the darkness like some demon from hell, always hungry and bitter. The depression and loneliness makes even the strongest cut themselves or kill themselves. I've seen guys try to starve themselves for days. Sometimes they get so crazy they even play in their own shit, covering themselves all over or drawing weird symbols on the wall with their shit and blood. No books or movies could even show what it's like. If you ever see a man broke down, beat down to where his mind finally snaps, look into his eyes. The smell alone could knock you to your ass. But the wild look in his eyes will tell the whole story. The prison broke him. He lives in a place in his mind now to protect his sanity.

That's why prison friendships are more like brotherhood. All my brothers have seen this wild look and maybe even been there themselves. They had to find their way back. My brothers have had to find strength from a place they never knew they had. I learned in that two and half years in the hole to respect that. To value that man's word and what he says. That's why Justin hurt me so much. I have nothing but my family in here to walk through the darkness with me. The stuff you go though in here forms a bond like no other. Because of him back stabbing me is why I did it to him.

"I think 750 a piece is a more fair price. You two my honkies and you out here risking prison time, I think that earns you 750 brother."

Country smiles at that and says, "That's what I'm talking about honky!"

I did this for two reasons. As I said, I respect my brothers but because of Justin, I learned to strengthen the con man in me and a well-paid friend is better than an unpaid friend. As long as they're getting paid, I don't have to watch my back (as much). This is what prison has made me. When I look in the mirror, I see a wild man looking back every time. I wish I could fix it but hell, I came in prison already broken, and prison has done nothing but make it worse. I believe in a good solid friendship, but how often does it come? I don't think Pistol or Country is like Justin, but a fool is the only person that doesn't learn from a knife in the back.

Chapter 21

SEEING THE PAROLE BOARD FOR THE SECOND TIME, "NOTHING IS AS IT SEEMS"

"Cunning is but the low mimic of wisdom." —Plato

It has been two months, and I'm still trying to get the job as property room runner. Megan said she didn't realize that to work in the front building you need the captain's approval. The dick sucking captain has a hard on for me because my prison record has so many write ups. The captain wants a more role-model inmate. I say *inmate* because the captain wants a person to kiss his ass and be a yes man. Only an inmate would do that, never a convict. I'm not going to go get his coffee, or I'm I going to talk to him like we're friends. I can be respectful, as long as I get it back.

Megan can't put a word in for me, we think that would draw too much heat to her; that's not what we want. Megan has been working for the department of corrections for over four years, and she has a perfect record. She has never broken a rule except with me, so we want her to keep looking like an angel.

The first dick head the captain hires is this fag named Be-be or at least, that is his nickname. I'm guessing the dumb-ass captain thought hiring another sissy would be best because Tammy worked down there. So the two sissies would get along great. But what he didn't realize is that Tammy is my honky's sissy. I guess the captain don't realize how bad I want this job. Either way, Be-be has got to go. I just found out today that Be-Be is the one that got the job. Nothing is ever easy in prison.

Sometimes patience is all you need for these situations to work themselves out, but sometimes you got to go other ways. Sometimes your con man has to come out, and show its ugly head. When your con side don't work, last opinion is bring the monster back out.

I let 15 days go by before I meet up with Be-be. Not because he's hard to find or catch up to, he's fairly easy to find. I just figured if I pull up on him right when he gets the job that will come across suspicious. Maybe I'm paranoid but this is how I feel it should go. After 15 days I pull up on him on the loop. He already walked around it several times, and I could see the sweat running down his face.

Be-be has got what's called dirty-blond hair. He's about five foot tall and maybe 100 pounds soaking wet. The stupid fuck is confused or something because he talks just like a woman and walks like one too. He has that annoying habit to where, when he talks he use his hands to describe everything. Basically, he's a sorry excuse for a man. This guy is a slap away from being a real woman. He looks to be about 20 years old and good-looking in a feminine way. Where I grew up they would've called Be-be a pretty boy.

Be-be sees me roll up on him, "What you want sweetheart?"

I take a second to answer him because my temper has got worse over the years in prison. When he calls me *sweetheart*, I have to reel the demon back in. Before I fuck up here and smack the shit out of him. I mean, I figured I earned my name, so why can't I be called it?

"Look, Be-be I'm just going to cut to the issue. My dude Pistol is highly jealous of Tammy. He don't like you working around him. So I need…"

Be-be interrupts me, "I don't do the dyke thing baby! So you don't got to worry about me baby!"

"Okay, look Be-be, I'm not your fucking *baby* or your *sweetheart*. You don't interrupt me when I'm talking. You understand me hoe?"

Be-be just looks around real nervous and finally says, "You know my man is Carson right?"

"Check this out Be-be, I just checked in Tiny. He is a lot bigger than your man. You throwing your man's name around like I give a fuck. Now you going to answer my question bitch, or am I going to have to smack you out here on the loop? Plus, let me tell you something, your man came from the tank, to right here. He hasn't earned no name at all, and he has never been in a fight.

"Damn, I don't mean no disrespect. I am only calling you baby and sweetheart because I can't remember your real name. But I know who you are, and I heard you checked in Tiny. I know your face but didn't remember your name. No need to get violent, I know my man hasn't been in a fight. I just meant it as do you know I got a man?"

"Okay Be-be now we're getting somewhere. You acting all tough or thinking you can hide behind your man isn't going to work. First your man isn't anywhere around so if you want your face beat off then say another thing I don't want to hear, and that's what will happen. Got it?"

Be-be looks down where I can see his hands shaking so I now know I own him. Fear is a motherfucker. So I decide to have a little fun so in a cocky tone I tell him "Bitch, call me 'Master', you got that?"

"Yes...yes Master!"

I start laughing at him. This shit is so funny. A couple of words and I can own a person. Fear is like that. A person acts all cocky and tough, but when you break all that down with fear you own them.

"Just so we got a clear start bitch, let me see you do 20 push-ups."

"Yes, Master."

As I watch this idiot, an idea pops into my head. I know it's the demon in me, but I'm always trying to figure out how to take advantage of situations that come across my path. This bitch isn't bad looking and I figure I might be able to sell him and make a little money on the side. There is a part of me that feels bad about all this, but I know no other way.

Be-be finishes "There you go Master! What else you want Master?" He's eager, that's good.

"I want you to come with me. We're going to my dorm to talk about what I need out of you." I start walking, and the bitch doesn't hesitate at all to follow me. I lead him into the dorm and right to my cell.

"Sit Be-be," I say pointing to the chair at the back of the cell. "Good, good Be-be. Now here's what I need. I need you to quit your job and let me sign up. After that, we..."

Be-be jumps up and looks around the cell like he expects someone to pop out the locker or something. "Carson will never let…"

I slap him so hard it jerks his head to the side.

"Oh shit, why you do that? Shit, oh shit that hurt" I draw my hand back to hit him again, and he adds real quickly "MASTER, why Master?"

Be-be sits there holding his face and looking hurt. The left side of his face looks red and I can see my handprint clearly on his face.

"Be-be you going to quit your job. You'll just tell Carson you got fired." Right then, we hear a loud bang from the hallway. "What the hell? Some motherfucker is yelling out there." The voices get closer, "That sounds like my dude Pistol," I say to myself. That is the only reason I even paid any attention at all.

I turn around and see Be-be's face drain of color, then, so low I barely hear him over the noise, "That's Carson out there yelling, Master."

Shit just got real, nothing is ever easy in prison. A simple problem, getting Be-be to quit, just got harder. I walk to the door only to open it a little to see if Pistol is good. I see Pistol and Carson in a heated talk. As soon as Carson sees me, he walks right to my door.

"Where's Be-be at Crazy? I know all about you, and I don't want no issue, but I'm not Tiny. You don't get to bully what's mine. Nothing you can do can check me in, it's not in my blood!"

Pistol is right behind him, looking heated. I put up my hand letting him know to hold on. I close my eyes for a moment. I really just need Be-be to quit his job. I have thousands on the line, plus Megan needs the money too. There is no choice but to allow

my demon out if Carson won't reason with us. I hate this side
of me, but I gotta do what I gotta do. I'm not going to let Megan
down. I'm sure the hell not just going to give this hustle up. The
last person that told me almost the same lines that I can't kill
what is his, and now it is that I can't bully this person. Seems to
be a repeat, but I'm not a bully. These stupid fucks don't know
how big this is.

"Hey, Carson, why the mouth homes? I haven't said nothing to
you. I brought Be-be in here to talk a deal out. I just wanted to pay
him to quit his job because my dude Pistol here wants somebody
he can trust around his sissy Tammy. Now you having a sissy you
can understand that, right? And as you can see, Be-be is sitting there
practically unharmed, just chilling."

Be-be clearly wants to get out of here, "I don't mean to interrupt baby, but I don't got an issue with quitting. It's not worth us
getting into a hassle."

"Man fuck that, I can fight, and I'm good at it..." Carson's voice
is so loud it echoes up and down the hallway. Now he's made this
fight public, and our respect is on the line. Fuck.

Pistol doesn't let him finish what he's going to say. Pistol hits
him so hard in the side of the face Carson falls into me but I push
him really hard. More out of reflex, but I push him so hard he flies
head first into my cell and hits his head so hard on the corner of
the locker that he just falls over. I don't want any of this. I know
Pistol swung because he doesn't want to lose his $750. I hate this
for real. Not to mention Pistol has life, he is not going to take any
disrespect when he lives here.

Be-be shoots straight to Carson's side and starts screaming, "Oh
shit, oh, shit you hurt my baby, oh shit"

I grab a handful of his hair and say, "Shut the fuck up bitch, or you'll get the law down here! We didn't ask for this, your fucking man has a fucking mouth on him. Let's hope his mouth gets better."

"Oh shit," he continues, "Oh shit oh—"

I grab the bitch up picking him up off the floor, then I put him in a choke hold dragging him to the back of the cell. I sit down in the chair with the bitch on the floor in front of me, and I hear him start to gasp for breath.

I whisper into his ear, "I'll kill you in this cell bitch. What did I tell you about you obeying me?" For real, I'm bluffing but between him screaming and Carson disrespecting us we're backed into a corner. Now we got to come down hard on these two or look like pussies ourselves.

I let my grip go a little, so he can talk, but before he speaks, Carson comes around, running his mouth even more to Pistol. "Steel me from the back you fucking coward? God damn bitch! Fuck!" You don't call a convict *bitch*, unless you're ready to die. This fucking Carson has got to be the dumbest fucking honky I've ever met.

Carson starts to get up, but Pistol doesn't let him have the chance. He hits him in the jaw, eye and then dead in the nose with a good three piece. Carson's eyes roll back in his head. Then with a loud thump his head hits the floor. This time he is knocked all the way out. He's just lying there on his side now.

Pistol is old school, he has tats all over him, and he works out every day. He is probably in his 40s, but he believes in keeping himself ready for war at any moment. He can fight better than a real boxer because Pistol grew up in the streets. Street fighting is the dirtiest and hardest fighting there is. Pistol's only rule to fighting is to never lose. So he will use dirty tricks or anything he can.

Be-be drops down next to him again and starts begging, "Please Master, stop this. I'll quit the job or whatever, just let me take care of him. Let me wake him up, and we'll leave! I beg you Master, please!"

My stomach turns looking at him begging like this. It doesn't sound so good anymore, Be-be talking to me this way, calling me "master." A few minutes ago, it was funny, but now that Carson called Pistol a bitch, I know there is no easy way out of this mess so I'm stuck knee-fucking-deep in the middle. Fucking Carson. Why couldn't he keep his fucking trap shut and just fight? He would have gotten a beat down but nothing as bad as what's coming. And I can't walk away at this point, or I'll look weak. Then I can kiss that weed deal good bye. If I'm weak, no one will buy shit, they'll just take it.

All this is running through my head, so it's no surprise when Pistol answers for me, "Nah, bitch this went way too far. Your man here has a mouth. I would guess he hasn't been given an old-school lesson in a long time so you get to watch. When I'm done you can leave bitch! Dumb-ass cracker called me a bitch! When I am done we are going to see who the bitch is!"

Pistol walks over to Carson and pulls Carson khaki state belt out his khaki state pants. When Pistol gets the belt out he grabs both of Carson's arms at the wrist, and he ties his hands up behind his back.

Pistol looks over at me and says, "Crazy, shit is getting ready to get real. If you're not game you can leave and you still my dawg." Pistol is giving me the option but the truth is if I walk out, he'll view me differently. I can't afford that.

"Naw, I'm not going nowhere Pistol. If it's going to get real, I'm ready for whatever honky!"

Pistol nods as he turns back to Carson to flip him over. "You'll need to hold that bitch real hard. Nobody calls me a bitch at all; I'm going to show this motherfucker what's what. You think what happen to Tiny is something, well it wasn't nothing for what Carson gets."

I grip Be-be around the neck a little harder. I feel him trembling everywhere. I'm thinking he should because Pistol is one dangerous-ass convict. He's more than half fucking crazy and may kill dude. I'd hate to get life in prison for a murder charge but this is the roller-coaster ride in prison, and I started this ride. I never thought it would lead to all this. Prey or predator, and now I got to finish the ride and show if I'm the predator or prey. For Pistol to show what he is also.

"Do your thing honky," is all I say. What the hell else could I say at a moment like this?

Be-be is way too scared to speak.

Pistol smacks Carson in the face with a lot of force, "Wake up bitch, wake your punk-ass up!" Once he sees that Carson is conscious, he starts to lay into Carson. He uses Carson like a punching bag, hitting him over and over in the face and ribs and stomach.

Pistol keeps going for what seems like forever. He doesn't take a break until he gets all winded, and you can see sweat running down his face. Pistol's short gray hair is matted to his head. He probably went for a good three minutes just power punching Carson. I know that shit had to hurt. Carson's face looks like hamburger meat, he is already swollen everywhere.

Carson's still conscious all the way but even with his swollen jaw he doesn't know enough to stay quiet. "Ah fuck man, my daddy beat me worse than you. You old bitch, wait until I get my hands untied, and I heal up. I'm coming for your old ass bitch! And Crazy," he says pointing his swollen eyes toward me, "I swear I'm going to stab you bitch! That's my word!" I just stare at him. This fucker is stupid. I mean now fucking dumb can one person be? Why not heal your body then come back for more? Nah, this dumb ass can't shut up for nothing.

Pistol says, "See I was just getting ready to let you go. I figured you had some sense that would see you overstepped here. Maybe you would learn a lesson but noooo. You young fucks come in, and you think you're so fucking tough. The only young real mother-fucker I've made friends with is Crazy here. Then you threaten to stab my fuckin' friend and…"

Carson interrupts "Blah, blah, blah old man! I don't feel pain like normal people you old bitch. I been fighting my whole life. Wait until I heal up bitch but for now, get to swinging or shut your fucking mouth. I got no fear in me old man!"

Carson's eyes are starting to swell shut. It is easy to see his nose is busted up pretty well, and his lip is real fat. I'm surprised he can talk at all. I can see about five knots in his short blond hair from where he was punched. I got to admit they look really red, swollen, with a lot of pain.

Carson is probably about 25 years old, no doubt about 6 feet tall. He is an easy 200 pounds, all muscle whereas Pistol is about 250 pounds. Size shit don't matter anyway, I've been beating up bigger people all my life. I just wish he'd shut up. It makes no sense for him to be taunting Pistol. If he gets killed how will he get any revenge? It seems like any dumb person would figure out quickly to shut up.

I can see Pistol is thinking real hard about the situation. Finally, he comes to a decision, "Okay Carson I see this lesson isn't going to be learned through kicking your ass. You're too stupid to see the situation you're in and too arrogant to see the danger you're in. So let's step this up all the way. You going to feel me when I'm done and stop running that mouth."

Pistol is standing over Carson crouched on the floor. Pistol pulls the belt out his pants and no sooner than he does, Carson half attempts to bull rush Pistol with his head coming up off the ground as fast as he can.

He connects really hard to Pistol, a good solid hit that slams him into the locker behind him. Pistol hits so hard he slides to the ground before Pistol regains to his feet, Carson drops to one knee with renew found strength. He reels his head back to an extremely painful angle, with lightning speed then he head butts Pistol so hard the hit busts Carson's forehead open. He hits Pistol dead smack in the mouth with that big ass forehead of his. Pistol spits a tooth out with a glob of blood. With blood dripping down his mouth onto his shit. I think the problem went bad, so I start to push Be-be to the corner of the cell, so I can jump in.

Pistol sees what I'm getting ready to do and says, "Stop Crazy, I like it this way. Oh I like it like this! A good solid fight! You got no idea what you started little boy. Now I get to show you my gangster side."

No sooner does he get that out then Carson makes it to his feet and aims for Pistol's head with a football kick. Carson's hard-ass black state boot slams into the side of Pistol's face, but even though

I know that hurt like hell, Pistol catches Carson's foot and takes the hit, it doesn't faze him. He grabs Carson's foot to yank trying to slam Carson back onto the ground it works perfect as hell while we watch Carson's head slams into Be-be's side.

Carson won't stop though, "You old bitch, untie my hands, I'll beat your fucking ass." Carson starts to stand up again, and I realize that Pistol might actually kill him. If that happens, I could wind up in here for life as an accessory so if this goes too far. I'm going to have to find a sneaky way to stop him.

"I'm not untying your hands bitch, I play dirty. I don't have an issue with how I win, I just do what I got to do win." Pistol spits some blood out of his mouth onto Carson's leg then Pistol grabs Carson's left leg and yanks Carson towards him.

Carson slams head-first into the floor as Pistol drags Carson over to him. Pistol punches Carson in his left eye, which is already swollen when he hammers on the swollen part. It cracks like a ripe watermelon, blood pouring out. Carson's left eye then pops out of the socket, it lays on the side of his face. The only thing keeping it from falling is muscle and nerve.

I say, "Jesus fucking Christ! I have never seen an eye pop out like that Pistol. Shit that looks creepy as fuck. His eye looks all hollow and nasty! Man who is some wicked looking shit Pistol"

Carson starts to moan loudly it's clear he is in pain now. Be-be starts to cry, then starts begging again, "Please let this end! Please I'll pay whatever but please stop it. Look at my baby's face. Oh god, his eye is laying on the side of his face. Please let's fix it! Let's take him to medical."

Pistol's not moved in the least, "Shut your mouth bitch! Your man took it this far. This lesson isn't over yet. I'm going to show

your man how much of a bitch I am! Get that bitch out the way
Crazy. This motherfucker kicked my tooth out. You think I rode
in the outlaws for 15 fucking years to take 6 fucking murder
charges for them to come to this weak ass hospital prison to get
disrespected by a young fucking pretty boy fag? I'm going to show
you how I lasted 15 years in a ruthless motor cycle gang you bitch."

Pistol drags Carson over to the top of the bed. With Carson's
back up against the bed, his ass checks on the floor. The post that
is one of the four legs that hold the state bed up off the ground.
Pistol takes his belt to the back of Carson's hands. First, he makes
sure the knot is still as tight as when did earlier. Then he takes his
belt in and out of Carson's belt behind him. After that he takes
his belt with perfect ties and he ties it around the leg of the bed
at the front.

After Carson is secure to the bed leg, Pistol takes his khaki shirt
off then grabs Carson's legs to wrap the state shirt around his legs
real tight. Now Carson can't kick or do shit. After that Pistol flops
down on his ass!

"Damn Crazy, this has been fun huh? Who would've thought
all this was going to go down! Shit Crazy!" Pistol says rubbing his
gums with his finger. All for a good hustle honky. The stubborn
fool just couldn't let his pride stop ruling him.

"Pistol, you got to be crazy as fuck! My arms getting tired
just holding this bitch." I let Be-be go at this point and rub my
arm. "Get in the corner. If you move I swear, I'll kill you. Do you
understand that?"

"Yes Master I do," he says, sounding defeated.

Pistol starts laughing like a mad man. "Honky you got one fucked
up personality. You got this fag trained to call you Master huh?"

"Honky I don't got a fucked-up personality. He had to call me something right? I mean you got dude here passed out again. Tied up like a stuffed pig not to mention his eye looks gross so you can't say I'm the fucked up one." Staring at Carson, I wonder out loud, "If I pop this motherfucker's eye what do you think would come out? You think this bitch would say his pain tolerance can handle that, or do you think he'll run his mouth some more?"

"Shit Crazy, I've never seen what an eye looks like when you pop it. Wake him up and ask him how does it feel? See if his Daddy did that to him. I'm pretty sure his daddy hasn't. You pop that fucking eye, I would say it's not going to grow back."

"Shit, you wake him up."

"Good fucking idea Crazy!" Pistol with a quick motion gets up and takes two steps to stand up over top Carson. He takes his hand and grabs a chunk of Carson's skin on his neck, twisting it.

"Wake up bitch! Hello! Anybody home in there? Wake up!" Pistol brings his hand all the way back and with a precise hit. He back hands Carson in the face. Carson's remaining eye pops open with this comes a loud moan of pain.

Pistols says, "Oh you feel this shit now huh? Am I still the *old man*, still your *bitch* Carson?"

"I'm done honkies." He responds through swollen lips. "I get the lesson. I can't take no more." I am praying that Pistol is ready to let it go. I've played my part, but I know taking it this far is wrong.

Be-be stands and starts to walk towards Carson. I slam Be-be real hard back into the corner. "What the fuck you doing bitch? Did I tell you to move?" I only really did this to protect him. Stupid bitch was about to get between Pistol and Carson. If he would have attacked Pistol when he is my responsibility, I'd never hear the end of it. So for several reason Be-be can't get up.

"No Master, but he said he learned his lesson. I figured we could go now." Be-be sounds like a 30-year-old car or something. I can barely understand him with the way his lips are trembling so badly. Plus he seems to gasp for air almost every damn word.

"Bitch, he isn't calling no shots in this cell. Matter fact, get down on the floor right now, crawl your ass to Pistol. You beg, pled or whatever but since Pistol got disrespected, he says when the show is over. You said you love your man, so get your ass over there to Pistol so we can see what your begging game is like. "Maybe if it's good enough we can all get out of here. Without me saying one more word, Be-be bolts to Pistol with no hesitation at all his pride gone, but you can see hope in his eyes. Be-be begged like nothing I've ever seen before. He offers Pistol everything, even his body.

Pistol doesn't say a thing to him it's like he don't even hear him. He turns to me with a smile "Crazy you got to be the craziest fucking honky I know. Why the fuck do you get off on controlling people like that? You one sadistic motherfucker!" Then he finally acknowledges Be-be, "Shut the fuck up. I'm not letting you go yet or your man. Motherfucker disrespected me so bad that the only way I'll get my respect back is to keep this even more interesting. I'm not going to have your man running around telling people he called me a bitch and all those other names he said like I'm nothing. Then word will get around the yard. You can talk shit to Pistol all he will do is beat you up, but he isn't going to do shit else cause he's scared. Your man has a bad mouth, so I got a job for you bitch."

After he is done talking it still takes me a second to comment on what he said. I just ignore his threat to Be-be. "I don't know but it's who I am honky. I've always enjoyed control and running things. Now, let me tell you something, I'm not trying to be a weak motherfucker here, but we should just end this." I'm not good at doing the right thing, so I try to save face here. but this is new territory for me.

"Hmm, that's good thinking for real. I think that's some positive shit. However, I can't let it go yet. My rep is on the line. I can't have Carson running his mouth. I have forever in here honky, to survive is by fear. I don't need this to come back on me so I'll tell you what Be-be; You want this to end?" Be-be just nods. "Fine, then get over here on your knees, put this yaps eye ball in your hand. You know the rest of it bitch. Don't act like you don't, or it will only make me angry at you.

"Oh god, oh god, please don't make me do that. I'm begging you, not that. I can't hurt my man. Oh please not this." Be-be begins to cry again and shake he's head back and forth, moaning "please not that" But he won't look at me or Pistol at all. He just looks at the ground crying and moaning the same shit over again.

I smack Be-be real hard again but this time Be-be swings back and hits me in the chin. Fuck! I don't blame him after what he's been through, but I am trying to end this. This only makes it harder. I only hit him to do him a favor before Pistol got ahold of him. I know he don't see it that way no I'll need to hurt him, *Shit*!

Pistol starts to laugh "Yeah Crazy who is the Master now?!"

I grab Be-be by the hair violently then quickly push him to the ground, "Your weak-ass punch didn't do shit bitch but I got something for you. You going to like it fag!"

I drag Be-be to the bed, jerk his head back, and then I slam his head on the metal of the bunk. It hits so hard the bed shakes a little, but I have to do it again. I feel like an ass hole but I can't let him get away with that punch. Or maybe I don't want him to get away with it. This whole thing is making me mad as hell. My body feels like a damn heater turned up to 80 degrees. I starting to lose control of my temper. I can tell by how hot I feel. That can only mean one thing.

Be-be seems to realize the position he put me in. He knows he just fucked up really bad. He gets all the way on the ground to beg some more, "Oh god, I'm sorry Master, I'm sorry Master! I'll do whatever you ask. Please no more!" The whole fucking gasping for air and his fucking stupid ass trembling now just threw fire on top my fire. If this Idiot wasn't such a coward, he could have stood up to his man and quite his job no matter what. He wants to be so passive that it has now gotten everything twisted. It's all his fucking fault.

"Reach over and pop his fucking eye. Then this can be over."

"Oh god..." BOOM, I slam his head again not letting him finish his sentence. This time his forehead splits open. Lots of blood starts streaming down. His whole face is covered in blood. I feel his body get tense. At the same time, his neck and ears seem to turn a bright-red color. Now we're getting somewhere here.

Pistol doesn't give Be-be time to think this over at all. He reaches down and sticks his fucking finger inside the cut on Be-be's forehead and starts to dig into it. This moment is the first flash I have that makes me realize how my violence has been wrong. That it hurts people in more than one way. It took Pistol beyond cruelty to make me realize I've been a terrible person in my life and why

Pistol does it. He will never get out but I also now feel this is an excuse to hide behind. He's a trapped animal, so he has learned to act like one but looking weak seems to be a fear of his. Either cause he's getting old, he's afraid to be alone, and doesn't want people picking on him or something.

Be-be screams and swats at Pistol's hand. He digs deeper, and I can see by the look in his eyes that a demon has taken over. This is a side that won't stop at "enough." A side I don't ever want to see turned on me because I'd have to kill him. At this point, these two are on their own. I realize there is nothing I can do to stop him.

Pistol digs in deeper and Be-be tries to fight back, but he is too dizzy and weak at this point. I look around wishing there was something I could do but there isn't short of taking on Pistol myself. I can't bring myself to do that. These motherfuckers brought this on themselves. Even though I feel I've learned a great deal of lessons here about myself. I still feel empowered by loyalty so in my confusion I just tap my foot and hope all this is done soon.

"Pop his fucking eye bitch or I pop yours! I don't give a fuck you love him, do as I say!" Pistol has stopped digging in his cut but Be-be sees the look in his eye and realizes that there's no other choice so, with no more hesitation, Be-be leans over to grab Carson's eye laying on his face. I realize Carson is out of his knocked-out stage. Fully awake just staring at Be-be with no words. It's like he knows or feels their love is so great that Be-be would lose his own eye before he hurts him. I've never had that feeling of love, and it makes me jealous that Carson has it.

"Don't do this baby. Stay strong! Oh shit, don't make me go blind. Don't do it baby! I love you! I can't lose my fucking eye. You'll ruin me baby!" I for the first time am so jealous of what they have. I find joy in the fact that Carson's trust in Be-be is breaking down fast.

Pistol smacks Be-be again, "Pop it bitch! Last time I tell you!"

"God damn Pistol, you got one wicked fucking side!"

"Snap out of this trance you in honky. Hell he isn't hearing me."

Be-be cries, "I love you so much Carson, I'm sorry." Then he squeezes, and Carson's eye pops like a balloon. All I can think at first, is what a fucking coward to hurt the person you love.

Dark black liquid oozes out and runs down the side of Carson's face. Carson starts to scream but Pistol opens my locker to get a sock, so he can cram it in Carson's mouth. I let Be-be go to watch as he falls to the floor with limbs like jelly, then he just folds into a fetal position and begins to suck his thumb. I feel like shit but I mask it. That's what teaches you the best. I just hope it's finally over.

Pistol still half in his rage starts to talk to me, "Well look at that shit! That shit looks nasty as hell Crazy. Look how thick and dark that shit is that popped out of his eye. Jesus, that's nasty! Let's finish this up and throw them out in the hall. If they rat, they rat but don't worry, it will be our word against theirs."

"What do you mean finish this up honky? We done aren't we?" I try not to sound annoyed but what the fuck could be next? I have an instant thought that I should just pop Pistol in the face, but I dismiss it quickly cause this is my dawg.

"Honky, we almost done but we done took it this far we might as well take it further to make sure this bitch never comes back at us." With no more words, Pistol starts to pull his zipper down and unbuttons his pants. He unties Carson from the bed.

When I realize what's about to happen, I try to come up with a way to stop it, "Shit honky, I don't want to see your dick!"

"Well Crazy, look the other way! I don't want you to look at my dick either."

I get up and sit back in the chair, Be-be hasn't even moved. He just sits like he's in a fucking trance, sucking on his thumb in a fetal position. I see him rocking back and forth every now and then but other than that, not even his fucking eyes have blinked.

Pistol picks Carson up by the stomach just tosses him on the bed. He unties Carson's legs and then rips Carson's state boots off one at a time. Carson is trying to kick but there is no strength to it. I believe he is in too much pain. He wants to fight it, but he can't, hell who wouldn't want to fight this?!

Pistol unsnaps Carson's pants, then with a hand on each leg at the ankle; Pistol yanks really hard, and Carson 's pants comes off. He pulls them all the way down his legs until Carson is butt ass naked from the waist down. With that, Pistol throws boxers and pants on the floor. Carson's hands are still tied, behind him.

Carson is laying there with a kaki t shirt on, when it hits me that I get in the most fucked up positions. I look over at Carson, and the hate in his face is unreal, he has the wildest look ever in that one eye. He's a fucking horror show with blood and gore all over his face and neck. It looks fucking nasty as hell to see his eye socket black as an ace of spades, all hollowed out. The smashed eye ball just dangling is just like something out of a fucking horror movie.

Pistol whispers in Carson's ear, "Time to see who the bitch is Carson. All we wanted was for Be-be to quit his job. All this 'cause you wanted to be a tough guy." Then he flips him over.

A man who knows when all pride is about to be taken looks like a trapped animal getting ready to die. I look down at Be-be but he doesn't move. Looking at Carson sends chills down my back with how much hate he is letting off. So I just start at the locker.

Pistol just mounts him and slams his dick inside of Carson without any lubrication. Carson almost chokes on the sock, and I see a tear run down his cheek. Even with that tear you can still feel the hate in the air that he is letting off. While slamming in and out of him extremely hard Pistol tells Carson over and over "take this dick bitch."

I try to look everywhere but at them. That's easy to do but the sound of skin slapping on skin is loud in the cell, and Carson is screaming through the sock. I can't believe that little conversation on the yard turned into all this. I can't stand I'm a part of it.

After several more minutes, I hear Pistol moan with release like that was the best ever. Soon as he does he stands up and pulls his pants up. Letting off the vibe that he is the shit. It makes me even more realize the wild terrible animal I have let myself fade to.

I just try to laugh it off, cause that's what life has taught me, but to do this to a man is the most horrible thing. Carson pushed Pistol too far. You don't push lifers unless you're ready to go there. I wonder why the world would let such a vile place like these be made. Why not just put us down like the animals we've become?

Without really looking over, I say, "Damn honky, you would think you in a rodeo over there. You got to be done with those sounds you making."

Pistol laughs at me, "I'm not in no rodeo over here. I'm just making an example. I'm all for our team Crazy. You can't let this motherfucker talk like that or if you do it could be us in this bed. This is the life we were given Crazy. I just try to stay on the top of the food chain. Now, help me throw him out in the hall way." Pistol finishes zipping back up. Remember Crazy, you are just young, I see what you try to hide from me, but understand this, I love you like a son, and I didn't make prison these violent lion dens. I'm just the guy down in the den that has learned to beat a lion is to outsmart it, not strength.

"Shit Pistol, you just going to throw him out butt ass naked?"

Pistol seems to think about that then says, "Yeah, we will throw him and his clothes out there. He's bleeding out the ass where I ripped him. Let's get him out of here before he bleeds on your bed anymore."

We throw Carson out in the hallway. I also throw my bed sheet out. Carson is just lying there with the look of a dead man. No guards are around so it's all good. We drag Be-be out also, he's locked in a trance, sucking on his thumb. Carson took all that in order to finally shut up. Now he just lays straight as a board, with a glossy dazed look in his eye that gives you the feeling you get when you go to a haunted house.

I clean my cell up so there is no proof then Pistol, and I go outside and wait to see what happens. There are no video cameras in the hallways so the only way they can get us is if they rat.

It takes about an hour before we see medical and tons of guards running into the dorm. In the end, the internal affairs questions me because they were found laying out in front of my cell. I tell the main IA, Richard, that I don't have a clue what happened because I was outside all day.

Internal Affairs are the people that are supposed to bust guards, and they do all the major investigations on the yard. They're the top rats in other words. They would rat on their own mother if they saw her doing something wrong. The government has these guys brain washed to the point that they have no issue with being a piece of shit. They'll lie to you or anything else they can, to set up a con. They're all pieces of shit.

Nothing ever comes of any of it so Carson or Be-be didn't rat. We are now In December with a month, and a week passed right by. I finally do get the job. They gave the job to one other guy before me, but we got him to quit pretty easy. After Tiny checked in, and this Carson deal, we are the predators. The captain got tired of dealing with hiring new people so finally he gave me a shot at the job. I've been working with Megan for now two weeks. It feels good being around a female every day.

The word is Be-be killed himself with a razor. He cut his wrists, then went to bed to bleed out. That will haunt me all my life. I know I'm responsible for his death. Shit should never have gone down like that.

Carson is still in the outside hospital from what I hear. I'm guessing he don't want a second go, so I figure he'll stay in line, or maybe he's just waiting to get his lick back. There's always tomorrow in prison. Worst case, we'll just take his other eye, and he'll be no more threat.

Country seems like he's mad he didn't get to be a part of it. Country used to be the voice of reason. The guy who didn't want to fight unless he's in the right. But I can tell prison is ruining my best friend. On his 20-year sentence, he'll have to do six flat to see the board. They'll no doubt flop him. He'll probably do ten flat or close to it, so I can only imagine the animal he'll be then. I'm sure even his mother won't know him anymore. I just hope he can find his way back someday. Some way to snap back when he gets out.

The next eight or close to eight months go by smooth. It took six months to get this hustle up and started. I needed a legit post office to send Megan her money, but I also need to send my money there. If my money came to me, it would set off a hundred red flags. And it took Megan's boyfriend a long time to make the deal for the pound of weed. In the end, his brother agreed to sell us one pound a month for $1,200. If we wanted more than that, we needed to pay higher than the regular price. Megan, and I both agreed one pound a month is all we need. No need to get greedy.

In the last three months, we pushed $45,000 to Megan, but it was a lot harder than we thought. Lots of people wanted single joints and there is a hell of a lot of joints in a pound. Even so, that wasn't the hardest thing to work out. Most could only pay by canteen, buy us a TV or fans, coolers, cd players, or cd's, but cash was hard to come by.

Pistol, Country and I are eating top-of-the-line food. I have everything in my cell you can own in here. I even got real sheets and real blankets, none of that state shit. Not to mention I got a nice pair of Oakley's sunglasses that I love.

After paying to buy the pound, we were still able to pump 4,000 dollars more into my account. I've never felt so rich in my life. I figure, even if I don't make it on the board, I can live off this money the rest of my bit. I stopped writing my fags. I just didn't feel like keeping up with it and don't need the money. They stopped writing also.

No more issue went down though and for the first time, things are looking up for me, and I really feel like a king. In addition to the $4,000 on my books, I've got $14,000 at Megan's place. Megan done bought a house with her boyfriend and got out of debt. So everybody is happy, and it is all low risk. Internal Affairs doesn't even seem suspicious. At least, I don't think so, but nobody really knows what IA is doing in their office. I felt pretty proud of myself. It took only four months to make that $14,000 of mine. It varies at what I pull a month, but it's all good.

Megan uses a real long thermos, the kind you put coffee in and where you can pop the top off and use it as a cup. She crams that full of weed then puts it in her lunch bag. They never check it. She puts coffee in her lunch bag too so if somebody did pick it up and gets confused on why it's so light she can say she is going to make coffee at her desk. At least that's the plan, but so far we haven't had an issue.

Pistol and Country took a little while to learn a pattern. Eventually, they learned who can be trusted with credit and who needs to pay right up front. They found eight high rollers that bought most of it for a deal. Those eight paid the money going to the post office, they are the only ones that knew the post office number. At the post office, Megan's boyfriends' brother picks it up, then it is spit up. Easy for the first time in a long time.

Hell, all I do is go to work. I grab that thermos off the desk when Megan is in the back. I do this to protect her because if somebody caught me, I would say I'm stealing it so they would lock me up in the hole and give it back to her. After I get it, I take it down to that dirty-ass bathroom, the one they call the "boom boom" room, at the end of the hallway, and empty the weed out in a bag. The thermos hides the smell, this weed is real good skunk weed, and the smell helps us sell it faster. After I put it in a black trash bag, I put the bag in the corner of the bathroom and take the thermos back to the desk. I send Tammy out to the yard to tell Pistol it's ready, then Pistol picks up the weed about an hour after that.

It's a good system that has worked real well, all of us know our job and understand if we're caught, we take the hit and do our hole time, then regroup after. None of that has gone down though.

Even Pistol's old ass is looking refreshed after six months of us grinding. He took the state boots and threw them away, now he has fresh white Nikes on. Plus he has bought a gold chain that matches the gold sunglasses he bought. He's looking all gangsta now.

At the 14-month mark, I see the parole board, and now I've got four years and nine months in. I wouldn't have had to do that much if the rats didn't fuck up on my jail time but fuck it, I'm 23, but I just turned it a couple of months ago. The shit I've seen, had to hear has all made me a man faster than 30 years on the streets would have. The animal in me has been woke up but the board doesn't see that, the board tells me, "We grant you parole Mr. Smith!" And my first thought is that I hope I can turn off what I've become in here. I got to find a way back to normal. I'm more scared shitless going out then I was coming in. I feel paranoid and shaky as hell.

By the time I got parole, I have $24,000 but not a hole to crawl in and how do you walk out of here to just shut down the person you had to be to survive? I'm confused as a bear that thinks it is a beaver.

They tell me I'm going to a halfway house. A halfway house is another prison for real. I got to go find a job and work my way to an apartment. It's just another step in my journey.

Megan is really happy for me, but Country and Pistol didn't really say anything. That is just prison code. Never show weakness and all that *bye, I'll miss you*, and all that is too much emotion. Sharks eat the weak and they got to continue to swim with sharks, so we just settle for *Alright my dawg it's been real, you keep it real out there, don't forget a honky.*"

As I pack my stuff, the guard tells me I got a letter. I'm guessing it's the parole board because I've never got mail except for my fags, and they stopped writing months ago. Maybe this is some cruel joke, and they're telling me they took it back, but I look at the envelope anyway. It is post marked Paducach, KY and I'm going to Lexington, so I don't have a clue who this is. Return address says *Jackie Melon*, I don't know her, either so I just open it. Besides, Jackie Melon sounds like a fake name. I've never in my life heard somebody's last name being 'melon' then you put that with a female. Shit, bet she has heard a thousand tit jokes cause her last name.

Hello Rick, AKA Crazy

I have thought of you every day for years. I dream of taking my revenge. At first, I wasn't sure I was going to write you this letter, but I want you to look over your shoulder everyday knowing that knife is coming for you. I loved my brother with everything in me, he was my best friend, and you took my best friend from me. You'll pay for Mad Dog and for his life. You probably forgot about me, but I'll never forget about you. I know you made parole. I know what halfway house you're going to. Wait till you meet my other brother, Pit Bull. You and me are far from over, and you don't got a clue what Pit Bull looks like but he knows you!

Sincerely, Bulldog

I lay the letter down, "Shit!" Just when I thought, this was over.

—The End, Part 1—

Turn the page for a sneak preview of *Freedom to the Monster,*
Part 2 of the Con Man Series by J. W. Bennett.

COMING OUT SOON

facebook.com/ConManSeriesJ.W.Bennett

twitter.com/jwbennett0513

INTRODUCTION

It took one more month for the paperwork to come through. The halfway house is called the Dismiss Charities. After all the years in prison, this is like stepping out of a nightmare. Everybody around me is smiling and they all just seem so care free. I'm so fucking paranoid around them all. I refuse to take anything that people offer. Plus the nicer the person is makes me extremely rude to them. I just feel like people are trying to trick me. I'm waiting for the hammer to drop.

After all the murders and rapes I've seen in prison, it's really hard to not be nervous around all of these guys. My biggest issue is that I want to do right, but I'm confused at where to start. Can I tell people I've been to prison or not mention it? All sorts of questions at where to start, but I got not a single person to ask.

When I was in prison, we had to live by a certain code, had to live by certain rules. I can't seem to adapt how I act now to how they want me to act. Having been a total of four years and nine months in Prison will probably take me years to get over then get me back to this shit out here. The staff here acts like I'm supposed to turn it off like a light switch. So if you talk to them about your issue, they red flag you and stare at you like you're going to blow any moment. So I'm stuck in my fucking head, lost, hurt, confused and my paranoia off the chart. I got only myself to learn how to retrain myself.

I've been here about a week. The prison had a transfer officer at Kentucky State Reformatory bring me here. People in prison couldn't show weakness, but these guys around me show weakness all the time. I don't know how to take that. But it makes me mad they can act normal, but I can't for some reason.

My best friend that I met in the county jail and went to prison with, Country—his real name is Eric, but they nicknamed him Country in prison—I've not heard from him, but then again, we didn't plan to write each other. I wish he was out here so we could do this together.

Country has a 20-year sentence with many more years before he can get out. I'm sure he don't want to hear about street stuff, not inside prison. He robbed a bank.

Our other friend Pistol he's got life and at least when I left prison they both got not only each other to kick it with, but we all had a killer hustle. We all had plenty of money to eat good. They saved four or five thousand dollars apiece. So as long as they budget good I won't need to send my honkies no money, at least not right now. I left both of them at Kentucky State Reformatory.

The hustle was pretty cool. I had this female guard who brought in weed. Megan is an angel to the other guards so no one suspected shit. She had worked there for years and never even broke a rule. When she brought the deal to me to sell weed, I realized it was the perfect set up. Megan brought in a pound of weed a month and me, Country and Pistol sold it. None of us got busted ever. We had a great set up in prison, we sold that weed for Megan for years. Megan got a house and out of debt and she never even got on the other guards' radar. Pistol and country are my dawg's, but I never told them about Megan or who I got it from. I gave my word to Megan I wouldn't let anybody know.

I made 24,000 dollars on my end. I had all my money sent to a post office box that Megan's boyfriend's brother set up. He went there to pick up the cash and put it in the bank. I couldn't get the money sent to me, if that much money was sent to me I would have had every guard in the prison on me. It took a lot of trust to be honest, but if you're in prison, you don't have much of a choice. You just got to hope you're not getting fucked, or going to get fucked.

When I got here from the prison, I was a little anxious but Megan was true to her word. Her boyfriend's brother brought me the envelope full of the cash, $24,000 is going to get me a fresh start. All this was in my last few years in prison. My first couple years were a lot harder. The last couple were not a walk in the park, but compared to my first couple years it was heaven.

They assigned me a caseworker when I got here. Really all we said to each other is our names, and he gave me a hand book of the rules. His name is Mr. Davis. I would bet he is every bit of 60 years old. You get the feeling when you're in the room with him that he has been here for a very long time, and he's sick of it. I don't know why he don't just quit but really don't care because I don't care if he wants to talk to me or not. I find it disrespectful as hell, I got to go talk to him, and his old ass makes a 100 reason to leave the room to go do something. Just leaves me waiting on him every time. Then when he is in the room, the guy won't even look at me at all so fuck him.

On my fifth day here I get to leave for the first time. They want me to go out and find a job. Walking up and down the sidewalks, I felt everybody watching me. I don't have a clue what job to get. I don't know how to fill out a job form, so even more confusion. I don't have a clue what job to get. I don't know how to fill out a job form, so even more confusion.

Before I left prison, I got a letter from an enemy of mine named Bulldog. I met Bulldog at a prison in eastern Kentucky called the Pink Palace. Actually, I never met Bulldog but he and his brother Mad dog were there. All this was before Megan, back at the start of my prison time.

Mad Dog and Bulldog were Pecker woods to the Aryan Brothers, the big prison gang for white guys. They were getting weed from the Bloods but lying to their brothers about where it came from. They told their gang they were getting it from the guards since the Bloods are a mostly black gang and the Aryans wouldn't take the weed if they knew where it come from.

None of that was any of my business, but I messed up when me and my celly Justin robbed these two black guys. Turns out the black guys were Bloods. The black guys came back six deep and busted me up pretty good. I robbed them because I was trying to get my foot into a hustle and taking stuff was it, or a foot to just have some food to eat at night.

I made enemies of the Bloods, or thought I did. But it turned out Justin, my celly and supposedly my friend, he and two of the Bloods were friends. They set the whole robbery up. They wanted to be robbed and rob us back to make it look like Justin had a beef with the Bloods, but really Justin was their eyes and ears. They hoped this plot would get Justin closer to the white gangs. The only issue was I didn't know so I kept thinking the Bloods would come back to get me and Justin again.

I figured the best defense was a good offense, so I conned these two due boys to tell me about Mad Dog's and Bulldog's hustle. The Aryans don't take kindly to being tricked and they don't like blacks so tricking them into selling for the Bloods was a huge insult.

To get my enemies off me, I gave the information to the Aryans. I figured the Aryans would go after the Bloods and the Bloods would be so busy defending themselves. They wouldn't have any time for looking for a couple of white boys. Besides, this got the Aryans to protect us without having to join their gang. Even though I never met Mad Dog or Bulldog, what I did exposed them. When the Bloods found out the word was out, they started a riot. In the end, Justin got killed and the Aryans found Mad dog and killed him.

Mad Dog and Bulldog were actual brothers. This shit got so messed up in prison. All I wanted was to get my enemies off me but in the end, I made even more enemies. Bulldog blames me for his brother's death, and Bulldog sent me a letter letting me know his other brother Pit Bull (weird-ass family for real) is out here and knows what I look like. I don't got a fucking clue what Pit Bull looks like. So here I walk around with $24,000 in my fucking sock and a psycho that could be any-fucking-where, that wants to fucking kill me. And they wonder why I can't "adjust."

Chapter one

ALEXIS BELL

The tongue like a sharp knife…
Kills without drawing blood." —Buddha

My name is Alexis Bell, but friends have called me Lil Bird since the fifth grade. Not that I had all that many friends. I just turned 19 years old and to be honest I feel way older. I am 5' 5" tall with long black hair, and I weigh 130 pounds. I need to lose at least 15 pounds before I'll feel good about myself. They nicknamed me Lil Bird 'cause I love to whistle everywhere I got. People said I sound like a bird, but I don't see why they put the Lil' on the nickname.

I've never felt like I fit in. I don't even dress like everyone else. Everybody around me has dressed wigger style—that sort of hip hop look with high heels tight jeans for girls, basketball shoes, and shorts or saggy pants for guys and tom boys. I myself love my tie-dye and comfortable clothes. I'm more hippy than hip hop. All the woman around me want to wear tight low-on-hip jeans but not me. So even at first glance, you can see I don't belong. I'm like that kids' game "which of these things is not like the other," well, it don't take much to figure it out when I'm standing there.

I went to school here in Lexington, Kentucky and my mother Donna Snipe is the best mother ever. My father I've never met and at my age now, I couldn't care less about him. My mother raised me, and I have one other sister who is 15. Her name is Katie, hands down she is my best friend. She knows I have a hard time getting along with people, and she is always on my side. In some ways, it's like she's the older sister. The three of us, Mom, Katie and me, are close as family gets I suppose. Mom kept our dads last name. She won't speak on it but she had me and Katie's last name changed back to her family name.

My mother caught a felony charge back when she was younger. Felony charges don't end when you leave prison, they follow you your whole life. I've never understood why, after you've *paid your debt* to society, you have to keep right on paying. Anyway, because of that, she has an extremely hard time finding jobs, so we grew up poor. Clothes were handed down from Mom, to me and then to Katie. Poor Katie wore them until they fell apart. We had a two-bedroom apartment and me, and my sister shared the same room all the way up until a year ago when I moved out and got my own place.

It always felt like we had enough though, I love shopping at the thrift stores and at Goodwill. I find cute hippy shirts and skirts. Katie dresses a lot like me. She has a tougher skin and lets what kids say just roll off her back. She really just doesn't care what others think.

I'm not tough like Katie, so I smoke a lot of weed. I don't really get high but it relaxes me and smoking weed makes me feel normal.

After I smoke, I can cope with things around me. Maybe it's a cop out but for now I'm okay with that.

I got me a job at Burger King when I was 16 years old. It took me two years of saving, but I finally got my own place. It's just a simple one-bedroom apartment right on the outskirts of the hood. Don't matter though, I've grown up in broke down neighborhoods my whole life, but at least I'm on my own. I feel so proud of my little apartment. The joy I feel for doing things on my own makes me burst with pride.

The living room is real nice, there is a small dining room next to the kitchen and a small hallway that has a bathroom at the end of it. My bedroom is off to the left. The carpet is new in the whole place, the walls are also freshly painted. Best of all, no bugs anywhere!

I collected hand me down furniture from thrift stores, yard sales and other such places. I got some nice sofas from the thrift store. My bed I got at a yard sale for five dollars and it's a nice queen size. I'm always amazed at what nice stuff people just throw away or sell for nothing at all because they just up and get the thought they want to buy new stuff. The old stuff don't even have a rip or stain or anything. They just ready for something new and want to waste money.

Katie is the only company I get but really that's fine with me. I work six days a week, I'm normally trying to do ten hour shifts. I hate dating, at least I hate dating the men around me. Maybe a good fuck every now and then but on dates I just feel awkward with the whole set up. I have never felt a connection at all with nobody I've ever dated. So I mostly just stay home except when I'm working. I'm cool at how things are going for the moment. I'm only 19 so I got a ton of years to put things together.

I walk to work and back every day. I also walk the two blocks to get Katie whenever she wants to come over. She won't never walk to my apartment alone, it's only two blocks but she is scared of the halfway house they got right up the street from me. It's full of criminals and she is afraid one of them will hurt her I suppose. For a girl with such a tough skin, she is such a scaredy-cat.

My mother also works six days a week. She works at a company that sells household goods. Her felony assault really hurt her in life. She won't never tell us the story but I know it had something to do with our father. That's why she won't change her last name.

Today is Sunday and I'm off work. I'm going to walk down to Mama's place here in a little while and get Katie. We love to play music, just dance for hours together. I'm a better dancer then Katie. It just all comes natural to me and I just follow the beat. Katie tries to follow me but it don't flow for her. It really don't matter who is better. We have a blast just being together; we can let ourselves go with nobody to judge us or put us down.

The only problem with my place is that my neighbor next door is a creep. He is probably in his late thirties and thinks he is god's gift or something. One moment he is beating on my wall yelling for me and Katie to hold it down—we're not even loud but he's just being an asshole—the next he tries to hit on Katie. I think his name is Jesse but really I don't even pay no attention.

As I lock up the apartment to go outside so I can go collect my sister, I notice the creep is out here in the hallway. I got my hair typed up in a ponytail because it's probably about 90 degrees out here. The sun is out and it's so bright I even wore my big girly sunglasses. I don't normally wear sunglasses but today it's just one of them really humid miserable days.

Jesse sees me and starts talking real fast, "Hey Alexis, what you doing girl? Your hair looks nice pulled back like that!"

I've never told him they call me lil' Bird because he's not a friend. He is probably about 5' 9", you can tell he eats too much junk food and drinks too much beer because he has a gut and his face has bad acme scars. Also, he puts grease in his hair to hold it back, people stopped doing that 40 years ago. This guy doesn't realize how stupid he looks though, he wears mismatched clothes and thinks he's just cool as hell. With all the hair he's got on him, he reminds me of a spider monkey.

"I got my hair pulled back because it's too hot out here and my black hair holds heat, I didn't pull it back to look cute Jesse." I say this with enough edge in my voice to let him know I find him annoying.

"Damn girl, you always give me such a hard time. I just be trying to get along sweetheart."

I don't bother answering, I just walk out the buildings hallway so I can walk around the apartment building to head to get Katie.

As I walk down the back side of the building, I notice a guy in the shadows, and I hesitate to keep going. He is between the apartment buildings, and it's a narrow path. I need to get to the other side, I could take the long way and go around and whole front of the building. But as I'm considering what to do, he looks up at me.

"It's OK, I'm no threat to you; I just need your help little lady."

I think about this for a minute and take a good look at him. As my eyes adjust, I can see he is about 22 or so, that he has a deep scar on his forehead. He's slender but looks to be in good shape. Actually, now that I look at him, he's really very handsome. Even so, I'm not letting down my guard. I can see he is holding his side with his left hand and despite his smile, he has a vibe of being dangerous. Just by the way he stands like he is ready for action. Furthermore, he is sneaky about it, but he is always looking around like he's looking for danger.

"I don't understand what I can do for you. What do you want? I have got to get to work," I say, trying to sound brave.

"You live around here?"

"Yeah, I live right around the corner, why?" I almost slap my hand over my mouth 'cause I can't believe I just said that to a complete stranger.

"Not to be too forward but can you take me to your apartment little lady?" as he asks this he pulls his hand away, and I can see blood has soaked his shirt where his hand was. "I got stabbed real good and somebody is looking for me. I got away but who knows if he saw where I went. I can fight pretty good but this guy is fucking huge, and I've lost too much blood. I need to get sewn back up."

"Sew you back up, what? I don't even know your name? Plus, surely you don't think I'm going to sew you up 'cause you would have to be crazy to say that."

"Actually, that's right. They call me Crazy, what's your name?"

www.ingramcontent.com/pod-product-compliance
Lightning Source LLC
Chambersburg PA
CBHW030002290326
41934CB00005B/200